JOHN F

Languages of
CLASS
Struggle

COMMUNICATION AND MASS MOBILISATION
IN BRITAIN AND IRELAND 1842-1972

PRAXIS PRESS

JOHN FOSTER

Languages of
CLASS
Struggle

COMMUNICATION AND MASS MOBILISATION
IN BRITAIN AND IRELAND 1842-1972

Print edition: 978-1-899155-19-4
Digital edition: 978-1-899155-24-8

Published by Praxis Press 2024
Email: praxispress@me.com
Website: www.redletterspp.com

Praxis Press
c/o 26 Alder Road
Glasgow, G43 2UU
Scotland, Great Britain

CONTENTS

Preface

This account of five short episodes in the history of the working-class movement of Britain and Ireland has been undertaken for three reasons:

- To restore to general knowledge five occasions when working people have collectively challenged the power of the capitalist State and, in doing so, in one way or another, changed the course of history

- To examine how this was done: how the arguments for action were won and how working people gained the collective confidence to do it

- In one case in particular, the general strike of 1842, to demonstrate the importance of this episode for the development of Marx's own ideas about working class mobilisation and revolutionary challenges to state power.

Each chapter will seek to employ Marx's ideas, as originally developed between 1844-1847, to help explain why such challenges are so infrequent, what obstacles stand in their way, but also why such mass revolutionary mobilisations are themselves essential, as Marx put it, to found society anew. In doing so, the focus will be particularly on the role of language, of how arguments are used to mobilise for change but also the nature of the social barriers that stand in the way.

The first chapter is more general. It looks at Marx's understanding of revolutionary mobilisation, and the obstacles to it, as taken forward and developed by Soviet theorists of language in the aftermath of the Soviet revolution. Readers may want to look at the case studies first – as the initial presentation of the theoretical arguments remains, in the first instance, somewhat abstract.

Nonetheless, theory remain central to what is being argued here. Its object is to recover and re-emphasise a central aspect of the arguments advanced by Marx and later Lenin. This is that social 'structures' under capitalism, though apparently of enduring permanence – locking people into various conformities with the capitalist order – are not themselves of an ultimately determining character. Rather, in face of historical change, it is how people respond to capitalism's own contradictions, economic and political, that can, once focussed and organised, be used to challenge these apparently permanent structures and the generalised understandings that sustain them. Such moments have been relatively rare. But it is these moments of crisis and the contradictions they reflect, not the apparently stable structures of social alignment, that are critical for our understanding of social change.

In all five of our case studies we hope to show that it was what people said in these moments of crisis, how arguments were won (and lost) and the resulting challenges to ruling class power that determined long-term shifts in politico-economic assumption, distributions of wealth and authority and the resulting social structures.

In putting together these studies I am indebted to many others but in particular to Dr Eric Rahim, Professor Charles Woolfson, Professor Chik Collins, Dr Jonathan White, Gavin Brewis, Dr Fearghal Mac Bhloscaidh and, not least, Dr Renee Prendergast.

THIS PAGE LEFT INTENTIONALLY BLANK

Introduction

For the production on a mass scale of communist
consciousness, and for the success of the cause itself, the
alteration of people on a mass scale is necessary, an alteration
that can only take place in a practical moment, a revolution:
this revolution is necessary not only because the ruling class
cannot be overthrown in any other way but also because
the class overthrowing it can only in a revolution succeed
in ridding itself of the muck of ages and be fitted to found
society anew.
Marx and Engels, *The German Ideology*, 1846.[1]

It is only after this, and only in the actual process of an acute
class struggle, that the masses of the toilers and exploited can
be educated, trained and organised around the proletariat
under whose influence and guidance, they can get rid of the
selfishness, disunity, vices and weaknesses engendered by
private property; only then will they be converted into a free
union of free workers.
Lenin, *Theses on Basic Tasks*, Second Congress of the
Communist International, 1920.[2]

These statements on the nature and origins of mass class consciousness,
though they might initially appear somewhat exaggerated, cannot
easily be dismissed as the products of naïve enthusiasm. Marx had
been directly involved in the revolutionary movement in Germany in 1842
and, more critically, had in August 1844 also acquired – through Engels – a
fairly detailed knowledge of the acute industrial struggles that took place
in Britain earlier in the 1840s. He had, as a result, visited Manchester in
1845 to further develop this understanding in the only country in which
proletarianised workers then constituted the majority of the population.
Engels himself was in Lancashire only a few months after the events of 1842
and engaged in detailed discussions with those who took part. Lenin, in turn,
had been actively involved in a long series of revolutionary mobilisations in

Russia since the 1905 uprisings and it was in 1905 that he made somewhat parallel comments about revolutions being 'festivals of the oppressed and exploited.

> Revolutions are festivals of the oppressed. At no other time
> are the mass of the people able to come forward so actively as
> the creators of a new social order.[3]

Taken together the quotations focus on two aspects of such mobilisations in remarkably similar terms. These are, first, the relative suddenness with which changes are seen to occur in working class attitudes. 'A practical moment'. 'The actual course of acute class struggles'. And, second, the potential magnitude and scope of the impact. 'Liberation from egoism, sectionalism...'. 'Ridding itself of the muck of ages'.

1 Transformations of consciousness

This introduction seeks to explore why these key figures in the development of historical materialism came to lay such stress on the rapidity of these transformations, on their revolutionary context and their consequent importance for structural changes in society. It does so as an introduction to the practical case studies of a number of working class mobilisations in Britain and Ireland over the past two centuries.

The approach adopted is Marxist but somewhat different to that of the structuralist Marxism that has tended to dominate debate on class and classes over past decades.[4] It seeks instead to grasp a key part of the nature of class and class struggle as argued by both Marx and Lenin. This is the capacity for sudden change, one that can transform the way people identify themselves and thereby also wider social structures. But at the same time there is the need to be aware that such intense mass mobilisations are in most cases short-lived. They will have material and wider political consequences. Concessions will be made. But, unless a replacement of capitalist state power is achieved, new identities will crystallise – in terms, as Lenin put it, of the 'sectionalism' that splinters class unity, 'the vices and weaknesses' engendered by private property.

This approach also focuses on another apparently transitory phenomenon. This is language, on what is said, on how those arguing for a direct or indirect challenge to the rights of capital (and ultimately its state power) can – in certain material and political circumstance – break through these sectional identities to create wider working class unity.

The starting point for such analysis is what is said in the local day to day battles to mobilise support for challenges to capitalist authority: between what its advocates say and how others oppose them – that is, on debates that determine action. Second, this approach stresses the need to place these debates in their historical context: to reconstruct the wider balance of class forces, of what those in authority said, and, alongside this, to identify key moments of change, particularly alterations in material conditions – as well as internal divisions and conflict among those upholding the existing order. It is this constantly changing 'living stage' that, it is argued, provides the wider context for understanding the many localised debates in workplaces and communities that collectively determine class mobilisation and movement.

Third, this approach seeks to understand in their real-life embodiment two underlying social processes which condition these responses and which Marx described as those of 'alienation' and 'estrangement' (later writers often using the term 'reification').[5]

Marx first used these terms in his early writings, in 1844 and 1845, and further developed them later. He used the term 'alienation' to describe the process in any class society by which the ownership and control of what is produced by the subordinate class, whether as slaves, serfs or wage workers, is 'alienated' from them and appropriated by the ruling class.[6]

Marx saw this process as a fundamental characteristic of class societies and one which challenged the essentially collective 'species nature' of human beings as developed during humanity's much longer period of physical and mental evolution. This loss of control over productive identity was (and is), also experienced directly by each successive generation, a consequence of the collective way in which each individual child, each future producer/worker, is from birth nurtured and educated in terms of mutual reciprocity – but then exploited. This process, analysed particularly by Engels, involves the development of a child's creative abilities within an inherently mutual and supportive relationship and ultimately results in their full development as personalities through the assimilation of 'instrumental' and then 'abstract' or conceptual language, the full use of words as tools.[7] Yet in any class society what is then produced on the basis of those skills is 'alienated' – becoming the property of those who control the surplus. And in capitalist society that alienation was particularly profound. As wage workers, individuals sell their labour power before production. In doing so control over how their labour is used, whether for the creation of material products or the provision of services, for weapons of war or socially useful commodities, passes immediately into the hands of others. This is what Marx meant by alienation.

'Estrangement' or 'reification' was the corresponding process by which those who sold their labour power in these circumstances tended, in response, to identify their position in society not through what they did in terms of productive work but in terms of their wage, of what it bought and how this defined their position in society. As Marx put it, 'domination of the thing over the person, money as the sensuous, even objective extension of this alienation'.[8] Reification therefore meant social fulfilment through the ownership of things, through consumption – and, within capitalism, differential earning power largely defining social stratification.

Engels, discussing social structures in England in the 1880s, described English workers' 'deeply ingrained sense of middle-class respectability. The division of society into innumerable, incontestably recognised gradations, each having its own pride but also its innate respect for its "betters" and "superiors".'

He then comments, with reference to the Paris Commune 18 years before: 'you have only to compare them to the French to see what the benefits of a revolution are'.

However, this specific historical example itself reflects the material potential for change. Engels was writing in early 1889. He goes on to outline how such change might occur: how shifts in politico-economic circumstances in working class London now held the possibility of rapid transformation. It is an assessment based on the close involvement of himself and Eleanor Marx in the re-emergence of the trade union organisation among London's unskilled labouring workforce, the first for two generations. What were these material circumstances? A decade of deteriorating economic conditions, of growing unemployment and mass impoverishment, particularly in London followed by an unexpected and fast tightening of the unskilled labour market towards the end of 1888 in the London docks, gas works, transport and other basic services, itself the result of wider shifts in the trade cycle.[9] Combined with active political discussion and organisation, such material changes held the potential for new working class unity that transcended existing 'reified identities'.

By May 1890, following one of the biggest May Day demonstrations in Europe, Engels was able to write, though with some qualifications:

> the English proletariat, which for fully forty years had trailed behind the big Liberal Party … awakened at last. Its long slumber … is finally broken. The grandchildren of the old Chartists are stepping into the line of battle …[10]

In his letters and articles covering these two years he focussed closely on the importance of how interventions were made, of how real socialists and false ones posed their arguments and the critical role of a new cadre of trade union organisers, including Tom Mann and Eleanor Marx, who understood the need to combine organisation with political explanation and frame it in terms that could be readily understood. These interventions finally enabled a new unity bringing workers from different grades and occupations together organisationally and to some extent politically across divisions of trade, skill, national origin, gender and the otherwise 'reified' identities that had previously prevented any form of wider 'class' organisation and identity.

Thirty years before, when writing *Capital*, Marx had made a parallel analysis – though of development in a reverse direction during and following Chartism's collapse. He described the process by which Britain's rulers had intervened to divide and co-opt what had previously been a relatively cohesive mass movement and, for them, a politically very dangerous one. Here, again, Marx stresses the interplay of language, of day-to-day demands, counter-demands, apparent concessions, changes in material conditions and ultimately social subdivision – focused in this case on the cost of subsistence, the repeal of the Corn Laws, and the length of the working day:

> However much the individual manufacturer might give rein
> to his old lust for gain, the spokesmen and political leaders of
> the manufacturing class ordered a change of front and speech
> towards the workpeople. They had entered upon the contest
> for the repeal of the Corn Laws and needed the workers to
> help them to victory. They promised therefore not only the
> double sized loaf of bread but the enactment of the Ten Hours
> Bill in the free-trade millennium …[11]

Later, in the same volume of *Capital*, Marx also examines the relative exposure of each 'stratum' within the working class to poverty in the subsequent period after the disintegration of any united movement. He notes that during the economic crisis of 1867 even the well paid 'aristocracy of the working class', skilled workers in shipbuilding, was in some areas reduced to destitution.[12]

Marx's comments on the 'change of front and speech' in the mid-1840s should also remind us of how Marx wrote history in his works of contemporary analysis, *The Eighteenth Brumaire of Louis Napoleon* and *The Civil War in France*. In both he provided a framework which anchored each social stratum, within both the bourgeoisie and the working population, to specific material interests, ones that also framed their immediate self-perceptions and perspectives. Yet the great bulk of each work is taken up with what was said on a day-to-day basis: how spokespersons from different social positions sought to hold together alliances – or break up those they opposed. Marx then interprets their often abstruse and high-flown language on the basis of what it really meant in material class terms. Marx's account of this day-to-day clash of rhetoric focussed on how it opened up, or sought to close down, opportunities for wider working class unity and mobilisation.

As we have seen, sectional identities within the working class were, for Marx and Engels, not fixed and immobile. They had indeed real political force. But they had no necessary permanence. They derived from the weight of capitalist exploitation, its apparent inevitability, from identities defined by consumption and social standing, from 'reification'. However, capitalism's own politico-economic contradictions, its transformations and crises, also meant that these identities were ultimately transitory – because capitalism itself would on occasion threaten particular levels of consumption and the identities they sustained. At these points the benefits of class unity, if deemed credible, could pose an alternative. How far it did would depend on people actively developing these arguments and the degree to which the supporters of a challenge to the existing order secured victory, or suffered defeat, in attempting to mobilise support, in actual or virtual debate.

That would seem to be why Marx's great historical works were written as they were. They focus on what was being said, the victories and defeats within a contest of different class positions – and also how the language of these political contests interacted with emerging class identities within what were constantly changing material circumstances.[13] It is also why, in the quotations that began this section, Marx, Engels and Lenin stressed two things. The first was the potential for relatively sudden revolutionary mobilisations when material conditions threatened existing sectional identities. However, such changes can occur only when this potential was explained effectively and understood in a mass way, when arguments were won. The second was the necessity, if society was to be founded anew, for such 'revolutionary' mass mobilisation to be secured, taken forward and understandings of these new, 'non-alienated' social relationships given specific form. The understandings of these new, 'non-alienated' social relationships had to be given active material form. Otherwise, it would not be possible to overcome existing sectional, 'reified', identities. These would continue and in doing so would obstruct – in any new non-capitalist society – the development a non-alienated relationship between all those who produced and their conscious, collective fulfilment of social needs.

2 Language, alienation and rapid social change

> The ruling class strives to impart a supra-class, eternal character to the ideological sign, to extinguish the struggle between social value judgements which occurs within it, to make it uni-accentual. This inner dialectic quality of the sign comes out fully in the open only in times of social crises or revolutionary changes.
> Valentin Voloshinov 1930.[14]

The years following the Russian revolution saw Soviet theorists of language and society developing a new materialist understanding of this relationship between language and social change. Vygotsky was later joined in Moscow by Alexander Luria and Alexei Leontiev. A parallel group emerged in Leningrad: Valentin Voloshinov[Volosinov], Mikhail Bakhtin and later

Pavel Medvedev. Their work was rooted in that of Marx and Engels, as discussed above, particularly in Engels's 'The Part Played by Labour in the transformation from Ape to Man'.[15] It was an approach developed in conscious contrast to the dominant non-Marxist 'Western' structuralist analysis of language led by Saussure (which stressed the structure of the language system in isolation from its social use and context). It also distanced itself from Freud's individual-centred focus on the dynamics of personality.[16] Its stress was on the use of language in society. The new Soviet school continued through subsequent decades – principally under the guidance of Vygotsky's pupils, Luria and Leontiev, developing applications in remedial and educational psychology both in Russia and internationally. It strongly influenced, among others, the work of Ilyenkov on dialectics, Porshnev on the understanding of historical change and, in its earlier period, Eisenstein's use of montage in film: the rapid conjunctions of clashing social imagery.[17]

A key characteristic of this approach, as Voloshinov put it in the quotation above, is its focus on the social dynamics of language in a class society: the 'struggle between social value judgements which occur within it' and how they are only fully liberated and exposed in times of revolutionary change. It is an approach that further implements Marx's own historical analysis of the processes of social transformation – encompassing in particular the role of language in the 'reification' of social relations as well as its converse role in moments of revolutionary challenge.

The general assumptions of this approach may be summarised as follows:

First, that all language is inherently dialogic; that any statement assumes, and is based upon, dialogue, on reference to other statements. Either directly or implicitly it will refer to other positions and assume a certain knowledge among those addressed. Examples might be speakers with different political or class positions addressing a mass meeting – or a speaker addressing a mass meeting recently exposed to a written statement or broadcast putting a contradictory position. Any speaker will 'talk through', answer or assume knowledge of previous statements.

We will see this, for instance, in our case study of class mobilisation on the Clyde in 1971-72. In a key mass meeting that determined whether the occupation of the shipyards would continue, the shop stewards exposed the 'sensible compromise' advanced by both the government and right-wing trade union leaders. To accept any closures would, they argued, cripple workers' ability to defend wages and conditions in all yards. And they did so with a blunt humour that was particular to the yards – as deployed, among others, by Billy Connolly. Had that argument not been won, the mobilisation on the Clyde, and its key interactions with class mobilisations elsewhere in Britain in 1971, would have been at an end.

Second, this approach assumes that those listening, in this case the thousands of workers at a mass meeting, will bring with them particular understandings of words as 'meanings'. These understandings will both reflect those of society at large in a somewhat diffuse, unformed and general way and at the same time be more specifically moulded by immediate social contacts, understandings that are 'dug into' people's bonds with associates in work and outside. And, as Leontiev put it, it is these socially-embedded meanings that will predispose choice.

> meanings – representations, concepts, ideas – do not passively
> wait for a person's choice but energetically dig themselves
> into their connections with people forming the circle of his
> real contacts. If the individual in given life circumstances
> is forced to make a choice, then that choice is not between
> meanings but between colliding social positions that are
> expressed and recognised through these meanings...[18]

Third, following Voloshinov in particular, it assumes that the process of understanding what is said, that of associating words with meanings, is an active and continuing one. It involves listeners in a constant search to find context, of aligning the immediate usage with previous knowledge and future vision. Hence, in the real life circumstances of debate over contested meanings and in the struggle to determine social 'choice', the objective of speakers will be to transform context – or conversely to prohibit such transformations. Voloshinov describes this as the dialectic of "theme" and meaning – where theme refers to the way speakers will seek to construct contexts that modify meanings, and particularly to use emotive contexts to "tear away at" and decompose established meanings. This is what Eisenstein sought to do in film through the visually clashing images of montage.[19]

It is also what the stewards were able to do in 1971 – to use humour specific to the time and place – to interrogate the public 'meaning' of the government and expose a deeper and more sinister class significance.

Fourth, this assumes that moments of fundamental challenge and change, in which workers confront issues of exploitation and oppression, will be relatively rare because of the sheer weight and apparent permanence of the existing order – buttressed by the disseminated strength of its ideology. At the same time, these rare moments of challenge will be critical in changing established meanings and, if they themselves become socially-embedded in actual new relationships, also sustaining longer-term changes in social consciousness. To quote the opening excerpt from Voloshinov more fully:

> The ruling class strives to impart a supra-class, eternal
> character to the ideological sign, to extinguish the struggle
> between social value judgements which occurs within it, to
> make it uni-accentual. This inner dialectic quality of the sign
> comes out fully in the open only in times of social crises or
> revolutionary changes. In the ordinary conditions of life, the

contradiction embedded in every ideological sign cannot emerge fully because the ideological sign in an established, dominant ideology is always somewhat reactionary and tries as it were to stabilise the preceding factor in the dialectical flux of the social generation process.[20]

Voloshinov adds: "theme is always socially accentuated" as a result of "an intersecting of differently oriented social interests within one and the same sign community, i.e. by the class struggle ... This social multi-accentuality of the ideological sign is a very crucial aspect ... It is thanks to the intersecting of accents that a sign maintains its vitality and capacity for further development." It also means that in any process of class mobilisation, as in 1971, those making the arguments for such mobilisation have themselves to be part of that 'sign community', embedded within it, and to know and understand how this 'multi-accentuality' can be taken forward.

We have already mentioned, very briefly and schematically, how Marx wrote history. In explaining, for instance, the disintegration of working-class unity in France between 1848 and 1851, his focus was always on the clash of language in debate, of how, 'theme' was used to transform 'meaning' within rapidly changing material contexts.

In Britain it is principally Charles Woolfson and later Chik Collins who have sought to apply and develop this approach in the course of industrial and community struggles. In 1976-77 Woolfson published his initial sketches in *Working Papers in Contemporary Cultural Studies* and in *Marxism Today*.[21] His *The Labour Theory of Culture* published in 1982 sought to apply, in particular, Engels's analysis of the social development of language and then to do so in a series of successor studies.[22] He did so to analyse the high point of working-class mobilisation in Britain in the 1970s – when workers occupied Clydeside's shipyards for a 15-month period in 1971-72. In the 1990s Collins further developed the same methodology to analyse the reverse process: how governments sought, through detailed local interventions, to transform the same working-class communities on Clydeside that had sustained the earlier challenges. To do so Collins analysed the contest of languages which erupted when the Scottish Office sought to subvert and close down, through a series of 'community regeneration' interventions, earlier socially and politically critical perspectives in specific local communities.[23]

In doing so, Collins applies and develops Voloshinov's comments on the "inner dialectic quality of the sign" and how this is fully revealed only in moments of social crisis. Importantly, he uses this to qualify and critique the term "emancipatory language" as developed by Michael Husbek in a North American context. Collins argues that the power to transform does not reside in language itself. The key focus is not of "language-in-context but primarily with the context of the language".[24] Its emancipatory potential is only realised within an active relationship with existing 'embedded meanings' (those within people's immediate circle of contacts), their material embodiment (the degree to which these might be under challenge) and the ability of those using such language to transform contexts not just by passive illustration but by being able to present new social relationships and alliances that change meanings.

The conclusion drawn by both Woolfson and Collins is that this socially-embedded character of language, its inherently dialogic nature, means that any specific analysis must be concrete, historically positioned and materially referenced – as Marx himself sought to demonstrate.[25]

One further element needs to be added to this analysis. It concerns 'historical positioning' and is one to which we will return in more detail after the case studies.

It relates to the 'circle of contacts' that frame people's immediate 'meanings' – as, for instance, with those that resulted from Engels's 'innumerable gradations'. They act, as Porshnev noted in regard to language, to filter and protect, to limit communication and invidious comparison as well as to signal similarity.[26] But because these identities are, in this case and most others, 'reified' and rooted in particular levels of consumption and conferred 'rights', they are also dependent on a specific balance of class forces. Those which Engels described as existing in the 1880s had crystallised after a period of acute class struggle in the 1840s. They did so around new and different material levels of consumption and also a new and different distribution of occupational and civil rights to those that subsisted before. Similarly, these identities will also reflect the historically changing requirements for the effective reproduction of labour power in terms of different levels of skill and knowledge. They therefore demand concrete analysis – hence the case studies to which we will turn next.[27]

3 Languages of social transformation

These attempts at reconstructing the social context of language are drawn from Britain and, in one case from Ireland, over the last two centuries.

The first attempts a direct contrast between processes of working class mobilisation on Clydeside in 1919 and, half a century later, in 1971-72. The 1919 general strike originated on Clydeside in the weeks immediately after the end of the first world war. It was led by the workplace-based shop stewards movement that emerged during the four years of wartime full employment. It sought to encompass all grades of worker – including recently unionised women workers. Its declared aim was to win a drastically shortened working week in order to combat the rapid return of unemployment and to ensure the employment of mainly female workers laid off from the munitions factories and the (to a large extent unskilled) workers returning from the army. It secured the support of the Scottish Trades Union Congress and spread within its first week across almost all of industrial Scotland. It continued for a further two weeks despite the military occupation of Clydeside and linked with parallel strikes in Belfast, South Wales and London. The government viewed these developments as a major threat and announced, two days before the official end of the Scottish strike, major concessions on council house provision, health care and education – which the prime minister, Lloyd George, described as 'insurance against Bolshevism'.

This mobilisation provides a direct comparison to that of 1971-72, also centred on Clydeside, when 8,000 shipyard workers took possession of the yards on the upper Clyde for a 15-month period. This triggered two one-day general strikes in Scotland, a series of parallel workplace occupations across Britain and interfaced with, and deepened, the mobilisations in support of the victorious miners strike in January-February 1972 and the release of the dockers imprisoned for defiance of the Industrial Relations Act in August 1972. Again it ended with a major reversal of government policy, described as Edward Heath's U-Turn, in March-April 1972.

The comparison of language is based for 1919 mainly on the daily bulletin issued by the strike committee and the contemporary press. For 1971-72 it is drawn from recordings of mass meetings and those of the strike committee alongside the daily press and television broadcasts.

The conclusion is that, maybe surprisingly, the political depth of debate was, in terms of discussing socialism and a different social order, stronger in 1971-72 than it was in 1919. In 1919 the strike's socialist leaders were very careful to avoid using the term 'socialism' – particularly to maintain support among the older generation of workers – while the strike's opponents, the employers, their press and the government, used it frequently in order to undermine support. In 1971-72, although used with some care and circumspection, the call for another social order and the collective ownership of capital was by no means absent.

This historical comparison is supplemented by two interrelated case studies.

The first relates to the parallel 1919 strike in Belfast. Evidence is mainly based on the *Strike Bulletin,* a fuller and more ambitious one than that on Clydeside as well as reportage in the Belfast press. The strike's principal interest lies in the degree to which its strike leaders directly confronted and managed an additional and deeply entrenched division of identity ostensibly based on religious affiliation. Their success in doing so was at least partly because the strikers themselves were won to the realisation that cross-sectarian unity was itself a condition for any success and hence in preventing a return to pre-war conditions. In the months after the strike Belfast's socialist trade unionists built on this new awareness to secure a major advance for their candidates in the subsequent municipal election – an electoral challenge that caused the Unionist elite to shift strategy and tactics in ways that had much more fundamental consequences for the future.

The second case study examines events 18 months later at British level in August 1920 when the TUC threatened a general strike to halt further British military intervention against Soviet Russia. Up to 300 Councils of Action were set up at local level across Britain in part drawing on the experiences of 1919. Again, the government speedily reversed course – in face of what appears to have been, in terms of both its language and government assessments, a challenge that, on this occasion, did raise more fundamental issues of social system change.

A final study is made of the general strike of summer 1842, an episode of class engagement that, as we have noted, was of formative importance for Marx and Engels and in which the contest of language and leadership was particularly complex. We examine both the evidence for class mobilisation as well as the subsequent major shifts in government policy that enabled the destruction of a previous, rather special, solidaristic working-class culture and the subsequent crystallisation of a new, highly segmented one.

4 Common themes and issues

In the concluding chapter an attempt will be made to comment on common issues that arise from these case studies.

The first is the importance assumed in each of these instances by 'local' class mobilisation: that is, the visible local reconfiguration of communities to reflect class unity at the same time as a conscious, class opposition to the oppressing class. These manifestations include the Committees of Public Safety in 1842, the District Committees of 1919 on both Clydeside and in Belfast, the Councils of Action in 1920 (and again, but only partially, during the 1926 general Strike) and the importance attached to local community support committees and trades councils in 1971-72. Working people could see and feel the bonds of class comradeship and do so in terms of relevant collective activity that, to some degree or other, challenged state power.

The second common theme is a corollary of this. It is the importance not just of local working class self-awareness but also its cohesion nationally, at the level that more directly challenges state power and hence the significance accorded to communication and coordination at this level among those challenging the existing order. Hence the conscious need to capture control of issues that could unify working people nationally as a class in conscious opposition to government and the power of the state apparatus. This is apparent in each one of the case studies. So are attempts to stop any such national level mobilisation.

This, in turn, is linked to a third issue: the immediacy of language. The episodes we examine all depended on winning arguments, at mass meetings, in workplaces, and doing so at key moments of potential change more or less simultaneously. There is therefore again the issue of timing and coordination across many workplaces and many localities. The necessary arguments had to be won more or less simultaneously if a movement was to succeed. How is this secured? What were the appropriate organisational forms?

The fourth issue concerns the recrystallisation of 'reified' identities. In some form or other this occurred after each of these episodes (and even though there was some continued momentum of class mobilisation between 1919 and 1920 quite sophisticated attempts were made to limit it). Such 'reified' structures of identity were not (and could not be) the 'old' ones simply reconfigured. Nor, once established, were they (or could they be) static or without their own internal contradictions and dynamics. We will attempt some brief general assessments on the basis of these case studies.

Finally, we come back to our quotations from Marx, Engels and Lenin. We highlighted at the outset the apparently overblown rhetoric – the working class 'ridding itself of the muck of ages', its 'liberation from egoism, sectionalism' 'only possible in the course of acute class struggles', 'only in a revolution'. We will therefore conclude with a brief assessment of this apparently common conviction in terms of what Marx, Engels and Lenin saw as essentially revolutionary about it. This stress on the necessarily 'revolutionary' transfer of state power from one class to another was not so much about its forceful aspect (Marx and Engels saw armed 'coups' by small elite groups as useless in securing social change for working people) but in its 'transformative' aspect. It was about how to create a new ruling class on the mass scale necessary to achieve social system transformation, for workers to be able to rule.

As we proceed we should again remember that it was largely as a result of the revolutionary challenge by workers in Britain in 1842, and Marx's knowledge of it through Engels, that moulded their joint understanding of social system transformation, of the power and character of class struggle, an understanding which was first expressed in mature form in their writings between 1844 and 1847. Marx's meeting with Engels in Paris in August 1844, after Engels's 21 months stay in Salford, was of key formative importance for the development of their mature work – as Eric Rahim has recently reminded us.[28]

We will move next to the first of our case studies, on how working-class mobilisation prevented the closure of shipbuilding on the Upper Clyde in 1971-72 – an example chosen because the evidence on how language was used is particularly plentiful.

NOTES

1   K. Marx and F. Engels, 'The German Ideology', *Collected Works*, Vol.
     5 (Moscow, 1976) p.53.

2   'Theses on Fundamental Tasks of The Second Congress of the
     Communist International', Lenin, *Collected Works*, 4th English
     Edition, Progress Publishers, Moscow, 1965, Volume 31, pages 184-
     201

3   'Two Tactics of Social Democracy in the Democratic Revolution'
     (1905) Chapter 13, Lenin *Collected Works* , 4th English edition,
     Progress Publishers, Moscow, 1965, Vol 9, p.113.

4   This includes the Althusserian school that prioritises the
     identification of social formations within a wider schema of
     production modes and also the post-Weberian school of Meiksins-
     Wood that focuses on positioning within 'class' boundaries. This
     is not to say that either school is without merit but to argue that
     neither encompass an essential part of Marx's legacy.

5   Introductions to the use of these terms are provided by David
     McLellan, Marx's *Grundrisse* (Macmillan 1971), Bertell Ollman,
     Alienation: Marx's conception of man in capitalist society (first edition
     1971; second edition providing a critique of Althusser and the
     analytical philosophers (Cambridge 1976); Allen Wood, *Alienation*
     (Routledge 1981) and Terrell Carver, 'Marx's Concept of Alienation',
     in Marcelo Musto (ed), Karl Marx's *Grundrisse* (Routledge 2008)
     where he defends the presence of these concepts in *Grundrisse* and in
     Capital (vol. I, chapter XXIII) as well as Musto's *The Last Years of Karl
     Marx* (Stanford 2020).

6   K. Marx, 'Comments on James Mill' (1844), Marx Engels,
     Collected Works Volume 3 (Moscow 1975) pp.220-221: 'labour
     to earn a living [within capitalism] involves 1) estrangement
     and fortuitous connection between labour and the subject who
     labours 2) estrangement and fortuitous connection between
     labour and the object of labour … estrangement represented by
     money …the domination of the thing over the person, money as
     the sensuous, even objective extension of this alienation…'. This
     analysis is developed in more detail in 'The Economic and Political
     Manuscripts of 1844', *Collected Works* IV (Moscow 1975) pp. 273
     ff. where Marx talks, particularly on p. 279, of 'private property is
     thus the product, the result, the necessary consequence, of alienated
     labour, of estranged life, of the estranged man'.

7   Igor Andreyev, Engels's *'The Part Played by Labour in the Transition
     from Ape to Man'* (Progress, Moscow 1985). Engels's MS as written
     in 1876 and first published in 1895 in *Neue Zeit*. Andreyev's
     Introduction brings this out particularly clearly and links its later

development to the work of Vygotsky and Leontiev.

8   Marx, 'Economic and Philosophical Manuscripts', *Collected Works*, Vol 3, p. 221.

9   Eric Hobsbawm, 'Economic fluctuations and some social movements since 1800'. *Economic History Review* 5.1 (1952): 1-25.

10 Engels, 'May 4 in London', *Arbeiter-Zeitung*, No 21. Vienna 23 May 1890: CW, vol. 27 (Moscow 1990) pp. 21-26.

11 *Capital* I, CW vol 35 (Moscow 1996) p.286.

12 *Capital* I, CW vol 25, p. 660.

13 Foster, John. "On Marx's method and the study of history: concepts and dialectics in history." *Theory & Struggle*, vol. 116 (2015): 53-59.

14 V. Volosinov [Voloshinov], *Marxism and the Philosophy of Language* (Seminar Press 1973; Leningrad, 1930); Igor Andreyev, *Engels's 'The Part Played by Labour in the Transition from Ape to Man'* (Progress, Moscow 1985), p. 21.

15 See particularly, Igor Andreyev, above. Engels's MS was written in 1876 and first published in 1895 in *Neue Zeit*.

16 V. Volosinov [Voloshinov], *Freudianism: a critique* (translation: Academic Press, New York 1976)

17 These sources, and references to them, are discussed and sourced in the postscript.

18 A. N. Leontiev, *Activity, Consciousness and Personality,* (Prentice Hall New York, 1978) p.94.

19 Jacques Aumont, *Montage Eisenstein* (London, 1987) pp.191-2.

20 Volosinov [Voloshinov], *Marxism and Language*, p. 21

21 C. Woolfson, *Working Papers in Contemporary Cultural Studies* No.9 (Birmingham 1976); *Marxism Today*, Vol.21, 8, 1977.

22 C. Woolfson, *The Labour Theory of Culture* (London 1982).

23 C. Collins, *Language, Ideology and Social Consciousness: developing a social and cultural approach* (Andover, 1999).

24 C. Collins, "The pragmatics of emancipation: a critical review of the work of Michael Huspek", *Journal of Pragmatics*, 1996, Vol. 26, pp. 791-817, p. 812 (see also C. Collins, 'Language and Discourse' in *Theory and Struggle*, Volume 116, 2015).

25 The recent development of Collins' work has been largely in partnership with Peter Jones: P. Jones and C. Collins, 'Activity Theory meets History', *Theory and Struggle*, Volume 117, 2016; 'Some Strange Version of Marxism: the Luria-Chomsky exchange', *Theory and Struggle*, Volume 119, 2018; P Jones, C. Collins and M. McCrory, 'Transforming Theory for a Transforming World', *Theory and Struggle*, Vol.121, 2020. In these articles they have sought to defend the revolutionary essence of Vygotsky's work against the rival approach of Norman Fairclough's Critical Discourse Analysis that gives the linguistic narrative of the ruling class a controlling role. Subsequently, in 2018, Jones and Collins critique the way that Activity Theory, originally based on Leontiev, has been increasingly developed as a depoliticised educational tool. More recently Anna Stetsenko, who was partly instrumental in transferring knowledge of Vygotsky and Leontiev's work to the West, sought to reassert its revolutionary character: 'Making Vygotsky and AT dangerous again: reclaiming the tools of the past for today's struggles: radicalising Vygotsky via Marx' in Λ Levant and others, *Handbook on Activity Theory* (New York Columbia Press 2023)

26   Boris Porshnev, *Social Psychology and History* (Moscow, Progress 1970). This work was strongly influenced by the Vygotsky school (Igor Andreyev, as cited) and bears some resemblance, in terms of its characterisation of language reification within capitalism, to Lucien Seve's *Marxisme et theorie de la personalite* (Editions Sociales, Paris 1972). There are also similarities to some work of the Frankfurt School in the 1930s – specifically Kurt Lewin on 'in and out groups' and that of his pupil Leon Festinger on cognitive dissonance: Kurt Lewin, *Resolving Social Conflict* (University of Michigan 1948); Leon Festinger, *A Theory of Cognitive Dissonance* (Tavistock, London 1959).

27   One attempt to do this in a historical setting was the measurement of 'social distance' through frequency of inter-occupational marriage and housing proximity between different working-class occupations in three contrasting industrial towns in the 1840s with high and low levels of class mobilisation: J. Foster, 'Nineteenth Century Towns: a class dimension' in *Nineteenth Century Towns*, ed J. Dyos (Leicester University Press 1967).

28   Eric Rahim, *A Promethean Vision: the formation of Karl Marx's worldview* (Praxis Press, 2020).

1

Clydeside and Britain 1971-72

'And, if this social order cannot provide it, let us have another'

We begin with this episode because of the richness of evidence. It provides a relatively full record of discussion and debate among workers within Clydeside's shipyards, within broader communities in Scotland and also, and no less critically, within the Conservative government. We can therefore detail, almost on a day-to-day basis, colliding social positions and do so over a relatively long time period – from summer 1971 to autumn 1972.

The main players

First the Conservatives. Pre-1970 the party's leadership was itself split – divisions only partly patched over in its pre-election 'Selsdon Manifesto' of January 1970. These divisions principally reflected different strategic priorities within British big business as it faced the escalating crisis of commodity price inflation and the breakdown of international dollar-sterling dominance from the late 1960s onwards.

There were two main conflicting constituencies. One was large-scale regional capital and the other, more dominant, corporate capital represented by the City of London and Britain's still considerable array of international companies.

Large-scale regional capital provided the local bedrock of Conservative support and felt itself penalised by the previous Labour government's policies which principally reflected the interests of large-scale corporate capital within the City of London.

As implemented on Clydeside and other 'development areas' these policies supported industrial modernisation through the attraction of growth industries from elsewhere. Such 'regional' policies had been implemented through 1960s to distribute investment more evenly across Britain – at least partly to reduce wage pressures in the south and midlands. To this end regional policy subsidised the wage bills of multinational plants moving into the regions to the detriment, it was claimed, in terms of wage pressures, on pre-existing regional employers. These regional industrialists, largely owners of heavy industry, engineering and shipbuilding industries, wanted a withdrawal of such state intervention. Their grievances were given ideological expression by the Conservative Party's leading free market neo-liberal Keith Joseph.

Joseph's proto-monetarist perspectives required a return to more traditional Conservative values: the ending of state aid for industry, trimming the welfare state and allowing unemployment to rise significantly above post-war levels. Joseph's detailed agenda was informed by pre-election consultations with regional business leaders. Those for shipbuilding had been conducted by Nicholas Ridley, a member of the Tyneside shipbuilding and armaments dynasty, who eventually became the junior minister for the shipbuilding industry in 1970.

The other major Conservative faction was led by the party leader, Edward Heath. This represented the City of London merchant banks and the multinational companies they controlled. Its spokespersons favoured, as previously under Labour, a continuation of industrial modernisation but now, in particular, sought better access to European markets through membership of the Common Market. This group wanted to maintain, but improve, the Labour government's tripartite structures for wage negotiations between government, employers and the Trade Union Congress in order to hold back what it described as wage inflation.

These tripartite wage structures had broken down spectacularly in 1969 when the proceeding Labour government under Harold Wilson attempted to impose new laws to penalise 'unofficial' strikers and tame the mass shop stewards movement that had been developing over the previous decade. Led largely from the Left the shop stewards movement was now challenging the previously dominant right-wing leaderships in the major unions. In face of mass demonstrations and partial general strikes organised by the Liaison Committee for the Defence of Trade Unions, the Wilson government scrapped its legislation. Heath proposed a new approach. This was to strengthen 'responsible' trade union leadership through a system of trade union registration and make trade union leaderships themselves legally responsible for disciplining unofficial strikers.

In face of the conflicting factions in his own party, Health brokered, before the election, the Selsdon agreement to harmonise the two competing positions. Its main emphasis was on continuing industrial modernisation to facilitate membership of the European Community and plans for trade union reform – but it also proposed to end regional subsidies to incoming industry, to abandon 'lame duck' firms in public ownership and more generally to limit public expenditure.

Labour movement

Within the trade union movement equally conflicting perspectives existed. At British level, particularly within the TUC, leadership was exercised by right-wing Labour loyalists. While they were ready to challenge the government whenever it sought to infringe existing rights, they were only willing to do so within the law. At shop floor level, on the other hand, change was occurring. The move to workplace-based productivity bargaining, especially by the major international firms, had increasingly shifted the balance of power away from trade union officers to shop stewards. In general the resulting unofficial action had remained largely sectional and economistic in character up until the earlier 1960s. At this point, however, new 'regional' policies were adopted, first by the Conservatives then by Labour. This was, as noted earlier, to take advantage of the higher unemployment and lower wages in the North and West and to divert new corporate investment there. The shop-steward response was the establishment of all-Britain combine committees to prevent managements exploiting wage differentials between plants in the south and the new ones in the north and west. The creation of such combine committees generally resulted in a more strategic and Left-led approach focussed on combatting attempts by the combines to divide workers and exploit these regional wage differentials. Working class unity was increasingly and explicitly prioritised.

By the mid-1960s most large workplaces, particularly in cars, engineering, aircraft and parts of shipbuilding, had Left and quite often Communist conveners. By 1968 the new mood was reflected in the election of left-wingers to the leadership of the country's two major unions: Jack Jones winning the election to replace the retiring Left-winger Frank Cousins in the transport workers and Hugh Scanlon in the engineers. In other unions, however, right-wing leaderships remained entrenched – particularly, as far as shipbuilding was concerned, in the Boilermakers, organising skilled metal workers, and the General and Municipal Workers Union organising unskilled and semi-skilled grades.[1]

In Scotland the leftward move was somewhat more pronounced. There were left-wing conveners in most major industrial workplaces across the central industrial belt from Greenock to Dundee, the Left was dominant in both the Transport Workers and the Engineers and the Communist Mick McGahey was president of the biggest single union, the Scottish Miners. This influence was reflected in the General Council of the Scottish Trades Union Congress where Communist Jimmy Milne became Deputy General Secretary in 1966 and General Secretary in 1975. At the same time, the shift in attitudes was at this point largely confined to the active cadres of the trade union movement and not to the membership itself. Politically workers in Scotland were no more Left than England. The Conservatives had won a majority of Scottish votes in the 1955 elections and still in 1970 held solidly working-class seats in Glasgow. Ethnic divisions between Catholics and Protestants remained important. Most Catholic workers voted Labour; a significant minority of Protestants voted Conservative. Very few voted further left except in one or two pockets of remaining Communist influence – in the mining areas of Fife (where there had been a Communist MP up to 1950) and Clydebank where there was a group of five Communist councillors.[2] But this was not typical. Most workers on Clydeside would have been described as, and described themselves as, non-political.

Conservatives come to power

The Conservatives came to power in summer 1970 and quickly began to implement their new programme. Regional wage subsidies were withdrawn, support for public sector firms limited and the Industrial Relations Bill tabled. By early 1971 unemployment was beginning to rise near the million mark for the first time since the 1940s. In Scotland job losses were proportionately greater and closures particularly marked among smaller industrial firms and suppliers. In terms of our earlier analysis an attack was beginning on existing patterns of consumption and employment rights.

Initially, however, unemployment blunted the edge of workplace militancy. The Clydeside shipbuilding shop stewards committees had been to the fore in mobilising unofficial regional strikes in 1969 against Labour's *In Place of Strife* and again in January and March 1971 against the Conservative's Industrial Relations Bill. But by the early summer 1971 wider support for further action was ebbing.[3] By then also it was clear to the stewards that shipbuilding on the Upper Clyde was itself at risk.

Upper Clyde Shipbuilders had been created by the Labour Government in 1968 as a semi-state firm out of the five pre-existing privately-owned but failing shipyards.[4] The new firm was encumbered with the debts of previous owners and by the compensation payments involved in buying them out.

The yards had been long starved of investment and it was understood that an element of government subsidy would be required for some time. One yard, Govan Fairfield, had also been made, in 1966, the basis of the 'Fairfield experiment', notionally involving some measure of worker participation. Sponsored by the right-wing Labour minister George Brown, local businessmen aligned to the powerful lobby of US multinational plants (the West of Scotland had the biggest concentration of US investment in Europe at the time) took over the yard with government backing and sought to transform industrial relations by introducing new US-style management practices, particularly productivity bargaining.[5] The result, partly though effective shop stewards' intervention, had been a significant escalation of wage rates that spread across the Clyde and caused great resentment among the remaining privately-owned yards. It was these employers (including the biggest shipbuilder on the Lower Clyde) who briefed Ridley in early 1970 that the new Upper Clyde Shipbuilders was a 'cancer eating into the whole industrial life of the Clyde'. Ridley's confidential report recommended that a "government butcher" be put in to "cut up UCS and sell (cheaply) to the Lower Clyde".

On 12 June 1971 UCS applied to the government for further credits. On 14 June these were refused, an 'expert' panel appointed to report and a provisional liquidator appointed. The subsequent 15-month campaign by the workers can be divided into five periods.

The first started on 13 June with the announcement by the stewards that they would not accept the closure of any yard and would 'work-in' if such a proposal was adopted – that is, take physical control of the yards and continue working. The second started on 30 July when the government endorsed the experts' call for a two yard private company with new shift patterns and lower pay. It was at this point that the stewards instituted the work-in and did so with at least the tacit support of the liquidator. The creditors, to whom he was responsible, stood – as local supply firms – to lose substantial sums, as well as their major customer, if the UCS consortium went under.

This period, from the end of July and through August, saw the government involving national trade union officials in unsuccessful attempts to broker a 'sensible compromise' to 'save' a minority of jobs.

The third phase began at the end of August when John Davies, the Secretary of State for Trade and Industry, took direct charge of negotiations and attempts were made to break the work-in financially by paying off large numbers of workers. The failure of this pressure, and the impact of much wider solidarity action directed against the government's agenda for industrial relations reform, initiated the fourth stage from the beginning of October. In this the government conceded the inclusion of the third yard in order to put the national trade union leaders back in control of negotiations but still sought to impose detrimental working practices and lower wages.

This fourth stage was the most testing for the control exercised by the stewards – but unity was maintained largely because of the government's insistence on detrimental working conditions. Finally in February 1972 the government conceded in principle that it would finance a "four yard solution", and did so at far greater cost than what was required to finance the four yards in June 1971. More generally, Heath significantly changed course and reintroduced a more active industrial policy and restored regional subsidies

The final phase concluded in September 1972. During this phase the stewards maintained the work-in until the legal basis for the continuation of all four yards was finally agreed. It was during this stage that Sir William Lithgow, who controlled the yards on the Lower Clyde and had earlier been appointed a government industrial adviser, wrote privately to the prime minister recalling their discussions "a year ago" and complaining that "private enterprise in shipbuilding is now even further undermined". By conceding the continued presence of merchant shipbuilding on the upper Clyde the government had "put a premium not on achievement but on militancy" and that he himself was now obliged to oppose wage demands that would cost him "£1 million a year".[6]

For the government this turn of events was politically very damaging. It was also unexpected. Cabinet discussions in May and June 1971 show no awareness that there was likely to be such a scale of opposition. Heath's fateful 'U-turn' required a massive re-engineering of government policies across Britain and a reflation of the economy that amplified the inflationary pressures then dominating the world economy – followed by the election of a Labour government at least formally committed, in terms of its election programme, to an irreversible shift of wealth and power in favour of working people.

Within the Conservative Party, in turn, it saw, within three years, the seizure of political control by those committed to a 'neo-liberal' experiment in political control that was, internationally, of much wider significance.

The Work-In: the stewards use a new term

What, then, were the key material and ideological factors which persuaded workers on the Clyde, in June 1971, to make this stand – rejecting the two yard plan, uniting against the government and in doing so redeveloping a movement of resistance against the Tories across Britain.

Our first case study of language focuses on the term "work-in". Winning the argument for physically taking over the yards was achieved in two stages. The first was at a meeting of 200 shop stewards on 13 June at which the concept was initially agreed. The second was at a mass meeting of the 8,000 workforce on 30 July that secured the agreement to put the "work-in" into operation. This meeting took place after the publication of the expert report that recommended retention of the Govan and Linthouse yards – but not the two yards on the other side of the river at Scotstoun and Clydebank. Workers at the former two yards now knew that their own jobs were safe. There was a strong potential for division.

The way the term 'work-in' was introduced shows that the leading stewards were acutely aware of the constraints imposed on them both by the wider ideological debate promoted by the government, of public sector incompetence and waste, and also by the entrenched assumptions of the workforce. Externally they had to develop a tactic that gathered wider regional support, hemmed in the national officials and challenged the anti-union discourse of the time: that of irresponsible, strike-happy stewards who threatened technological progress and the country's economic survival. Internally, they had to keep all four yards united, prepare for a long struggle and be able to assure those workers who would soon be laid off that ways would be found to continue to pay wages and provide work.

The term 'work-in' was carefully crafted. It was new – so it could initially be filled with whatever meaning the stewards chose to give it. The work-in was not, it was stressed, an occupation. Nor was it a sit-in or a strike. It was, as described by the leading stewards, an assertion of the right to work in face of external 'wreckers'. It was to demonstrate that workers could run an enterprise far more efficiently than the old owners who were not fit to 'run a bingo hall'. As a tactic it exploited the legal technicalities of the situation. The liquidator represented the 2,000 creditor firms, in sum seven per cent of all Scottish companies, which stood to lose very considerable amounts as a result of what could be construed as politically-motivated intervention by the government. In these circumstances the liquidator had a responsibility to maximise income while existing orders were completed – although also to lay off workers as this happened. The existing management also remained in place. The stewards' objective, and one ultimately achieved, was to get the management and the majority of the creditors to declare support for the workers against the government.

On the face of it such a "work-in" was a difficult proposal to sell to the workforce. Their instinct would have been to strike – or, if things went the other way, to settle for their sectional interests of saving their own yard. Instead they were told they had to continue to obey the management, to work, indeed to work harder and more efficiently, and in addition pay for it through a levy on wages to support workers who were laid off. The first meeting with 200 stewards in June was described as "stormy" but ended with the idea being agreed. The mass meeting in July, on which implementation depended, began uncertainly.

Woolfson describes the intervention by Jimmy Reid, as Chair of the Joint Shop Stewards Committee. Reid, Woolfson writes,:

> moves quickly back and forth between galvanising anger
> not at management but at the 'faceless men' in Whitehall

(outside Scotland) and invoking an all-encompassing solidarity that outflanks sectionalism. If the Scotstoun men are made redundant, 'we will all march together' back into the yard. He defines the work-in as not being a strike – but does so in a context that stresses the power of the workers. They have 'taken over the yards'. Nothing will come or go without 'their permission'. He seizes on the core of sectional identities, 'rights' within a specified order, and generalises it in quite a new way: 'the right to work'. In doing so Reid mixes in a series of powerful 'universal' word meanings: dignity, responsible, disciplined. He uses them to frame and introduce the critical relationship that will continue between the workers and management.[7]

The call for the immediate adoption of the work-in was successful. But it was only so because it had already been used to mobilise a powerful alliance. This formally declared its support the following day on 14 June. A meeting of 800 stewards representing workplaces across central Scotland backed it on 18 June. This all-Scotland meeting of stewards also agreed to a levy and called for a half-day stoppage and demonstration on 23 June – 80,000 attended this demonstration. A week before the publication of the government's 'expert report' on 30 July, a meeting of creditors denounced the government's action as politically motivated. The same week the STUC convened on behalf of the stewards a meeting including the Scottish Executive of the Labour Party and the leaders of the Confederation of Shipbuilding and Engineering Unions (CSEU) leaders to discuss support for the work-in the context of the regional economic crisis affecting the Scottish economy. The Confederation leadership on whom the government had been relying for a compromise deal, particularly the right-wing leader of the Boilermakers Union, Danny McGarvey, was temporarily immobilised.

In analysing the language used, Woolfson makes an important point. Nowhere, in addressing the mass meeting on 30 July or in the earlier meetings with stewards, did Reid or Airlie ever refer to "struggle", "alliance" or "monopoly capitalism" or even "working class". Just a mention of the term "class" in a mass meeting at this stage would immediately have given rise to claims that they were introducing "politics" – and opened themselves to accusations, which the government and media were only able to start using at a later stage, that they were manipulating the situation for their own political ends.

Yet both Reid and Airlie were leading Communists. At meetings of the communist party executive committee and party congresses they discussed strategy in terms of strengthening working-class consciousness, building an anti-monopoly alliance, winning over smaller local firms and suppliers against the big monopoly firms controlled from the City of London, doing so particularly by using the national dimension at Scottish and Welsh level, highlighting uneven regional development and winning the support of all those professional and scientific strata relying on the development of the productive economy. None of this 'strategic' language was ever allowed to surface at mass meetings. Nevertheless it was this framework of analysis that was essential both for the development of strategy and for the scaffolding of meaning on which the leaders' popular interventions depended.

It was in this sense "emancipatory language", as Huspek has called it, because it targeted an exploitative social system and identified its key contradictions.[8] It was therefore quite different to the language of social-democratic partnership used by right-wing trade-union leaders and developed through the three decades of tripartite administration of a Keynesian managed economy. The instinct of the then leaders of the TUC and the Confederation of Shipbuilding and Engineering Unions would be to offer concessions to get concessions and accept analyses about streamlining the economy and minimising irresponsible action on the ground. There would have been no comprehension of the need to change the balance of class forces and to build alliances. Had such perspectives been more effectively projected at yard level at this stage, the acceptance of some yard closures would have fatally divided the workforce. The wider alliances already secured by the stewards meant that the Confederation leadership, despite its prior discussions with the government, felt unable to put forward any compromise proposal short of the four yards.[9]

Stewards block right-wing offensive of September 1971

Our second case study is provided by Collins. It focuses on the period in September 1971 when the government and the right-wing Confederation leaders were finally able to project such 'moderate' arguments.

August had seen the effective failure of government attempts to float its two-yard vehicle Govan Shipbuilders Ltd. On 3 August the Secretary of State, John Davies, visited Glasgow to win support for the government's "compromise" solution and also to appease local business by offering the prospect of a Scottish development agency. His visit was overshadowed by press reports of the workers' 'take-over' of the yards on 30-31 July and the refusal of admittance to anyone, including Davies and his new management team, who did not support the work-in. Thereafter the momentum of the stewards' campaign moved ahead. There was an all-British shop stewards meeting of support on 10 August at which there was the first tentative uses of the term "working class" and "solidarity". On 11 August there was a conference of Scottish local authorities to discuss the crisis. This saw a split in the 24 strong Conservative-Progressive group on Glasgow City Council – with the 12 Progressive councillors, whose main political base was in Protestant working-class areas, declaring support for the work-in.

On 12 August Glasgow Chamber of Commerce attacked the government's economic policies. On 16 August there was a special emergency recall of the STUC Congress which pledged full support, set up its own public enquiry and initiated steps for the convening of a Scottish Assembly to represent all sections of Scottish life, a development of major long-term significance. On 18 August there was a further one-day strike supported by 200,000 workers and a 100,000 demonstration in Glasgow attended by leaders of the Labour Party and the TUC. On 23 August the pro-Conservative *Glasgow Herald* described the shop stewards as winning the propaganda battle right down the line.

From the end of August, however, the struggle became much more difficult. While the government-appointed liquidator was legally responsible to the creditors, he was dependent on the government for working credit. Ships on the stocks were in some cases nearing completion. Ships already ordered but not begun would require more funds. This gave the government a key economic lever. Projected weekly redundancies went up from dozens to hundreds. At the same time Davies opened very public negotiations with McGarvey and Vic Feather, the TUC general secretary, to discuss a wider regional development deal that would allow flexibility on the number of jobs to be preserved in the yards.

Sections of the press began to question the viability of the work-in and suggest that the inflexibility of the stewards was risking the loss of all jobs. Attitudes in the yards began to soften. Against this the stewards retained the bargaining assets they had already secured: the STUC public inquiry which opened on 4 September and heard supportive evidence from the managing director of UCS and the previous owners of the Scotstoun yard. They also benefited from action by the creditors who on 5 September launched a legal challenge against the liquidator and by proxy against the government for unnecessarily enforcing liquidation. Finally, they revealed their possession of the Ridley Report. Photostat copies were published the day after creditors launched their legal action. The government was unable to deny their authenticity. The document, talking about a 'government butcher', was distributed at the TUC September Congress and in a 100,000 copy broadsheet throughout the trade union movement.

This was the background to the 24 September mass meeting at which the stewards sought to rally the workforce for an uncompromising adherence to the Four Yards demand.

The numbers of workers receiving their redundancy notices had been increasing steadily and included those at the two 'saved yards'. Danny McGarvey and Vic Feather, TUC Secretary, were continuing negotiations. The language of both the government and the 'Confed' was now couched in carefully social-democratic terms: realism, flexibility, making the best of a difficult situation. Press coverage of their discussions was beginning to eclipse that of the stewards. On 22 September the Conservative *Glasgow Herald* wrote: "the full-time trade union officials now have a duty to take over from the shop stewards and work with management to ensure that the maximum number of jobs is saved". The same day the Labour-inclined *Daily Record* ran its front page story as "Speak Up Brother Dan".

In analysing the debate on 24 September Collins draws on the same methodology as Woolfson. He seeks to identify the way the leading stewards sought to use their knowledge of "socially embedded meanings", of the understandings of workers in the yards, to destabilise and expose the language of the government and their trade union allies. In the earlier case study we saw that dialectic in operation. The unknown term "work-in" was populated with meanings drawn from the tight sectional worlds of boilermakers, fitters and caulkers: control over the job becomes power over the workplace, group loyalty is generalised across all yards, sectional rights become the right to work. On this occasion the stewards had a far more difficult task. The government was now itself using the social-democratic language of reasonableness and flexibility and was doing so through the mouths of the Confederation. It was no longer a class government attacking Clydeside. It was presenting a joint 'solution' for employment on Clydeside – and it was the inflexibility of the stewards that was blocking it. Up to half those present at the meeting might have felt they had a personal economic motivation to go for McGarvey's offer.

The stewards had three potential bargaining strengths. One was an appeal to solidarity and wider working class loyalty. Attitudes had changed over the previous three months in response to the massive levels of financial support from workers across Britain which had sustained the work-in – a solidarity expressed in human terms by the scale of the demonstrations. But the stewards were uncertain as to how far this reorientation had gone. Secondly, they could draw on the Ridley Report itself, released less than three weeks before, to expose the class motivation of the attack. Thirdly, they could exploit one aspect of McGarvey's deal which the government had insisted on: that the two rescued yards adopt new shift patterns and payment procedures which would, on the insistence of remaining private owners, bring them back into line with the yards on the Lower Clyde.

The stewards realised that they would have to rely on all three. Jimmy Airlie in introducing Reid read verbatim from that morning's *Glasgow Herald*: "the future of merchant shipbuilding depends on the workers agreeing to new commitments on hours and wages". McGarvey, the traditional champion of boilermakers' sectional privileges, had given these rights away. Reid said:

> We are being criticised as we're inflexible and the Press are
> saying that this is the best way forward. We are of the opinion
> that it is not any alternative. They are saying that half a loaf
> is better than nothing. It is not even half a loaf and in order to
> get that part of a loaf you've got to grovel and crawl; that is

not an alternative for any men and women.

Reid continued:

> they have pushed through their policy to butcher our
> industry and don't let any leader writer talk to us about
> reasonableness and inflexibility. The unreasonableness and
> the inflexibility is that of the Government. For our part we'll
> go and see Davies, Heath, anybody ... on the basis ... that we'll
> discuss any proposals ...that deals with the four yards and
> gives guarantees to the labour force in these yards. [We'll] talk
> to anybody ... but all the time they come back to the butchery
> of our industry. And I want to say here and now, don't let
> there be division in our ranks, I'll tell you this much, and I'm
> speaking personally here, if the Government succeeded in
> the butchery of our industry I'd rather be on the dole than
> be amongst the two and a half thousand that would be left
> to grovel, accept wages reductions and all sorts of other
> things, and I'm telling you it would be a short term solution
> because their objective would take place in a year or so, and
> it would be the end of our industry in the Clyde, and it's
> like a murderer who wants to murder us, we've found out,
> we've defended ourselves against the murder and people say
> 'please negotiate with the murderer, you might stop him from
> piercing your heart, but he can cut off your legs and arms
> and there's a sensible compromise'. And when you're lying
> bleeding they will tell you in a year or two, wi' you minus
> the legs, why aren't you standing on your own two feet ?
> And, brothers, our proposals therefore spring from a sense
> of responsibility to ourselves and to our families and our
> community and in the last resort to the British working class.
> It's impossible for us to accept this ... we are not capitulating
> to the butchery ... There will be no cooperation, and this is
> what we're putting to you with this board, no cooperation,
> that we close the ranks as a united labour force and tell them
> that they are not on ..,

Collins highlights two things: the thematic building up of an evaluative context or 'theme' to transform meaning and at the same time the use of one language to speak through another. Reid repeatedly links the words "co-operation" and "butcher". As he does so, the bland mask of John Davies is peeled away to reveal Nicholas Ridley: the language of class control is made to speak through and annihilate the language of social democracy. At the same time McGarvey is implicitly exposed as an accomplice in a "sensible compromise" that directly attacks the rights of his own members, the hard-fought differential in terms of wages and conditions over the Lower Clyde. This then frames Reid's successful appeal to identity – one that moves upwards from "ourselves", "our families", "our community" to responsibility "... in the last resort to the British working class".

The government retreats

Had the vote at the mass meeting gone in favour of McGarvey, the work-in would have been over, recrimination would have broken out and the whole alliance of forces built up to sustain it would have crumbled. On the other hand, the ultimate victory of the stewards, and the implicit repudiation of McGarvey, reinforced the wider alliance, including the now very considerable section of Clydeside business aligned with the creditor firms and Glasgow Chamber of Commerce. This was a particular blow to Davies. Over these weeks in September he had struggled to give local legitimacy to what the stewards described as his "quisling" company. Despite assembling an array of West of Scotland business leaders at a special dinner, he could find no one willing to go on the board. It was under these combined pressures that the government gave way. In its first major capitulation it started negotiating a "Three Yard" solution.

Now that government papers have been opened we know something more about the background. On 30 September the Cabinet Secretary Burke Trend published an evaluation of the government's first year in office, "Report on Government Strategy" based on materials from Lord Rothschild's Central Policy Review Staff. [10] The report highlighted the threats emerging to the keystone of the government's overall strategy: its attempt to reform industrial relations.

> **IV Industrial relations**
> Situation in 1970
> Labour's failure to reform trade unions
> The increasing power within the trade union movement of
> left-wing militancy – often operating at shop-floor level and
> in defiance of trade union executives
> A high and rising level of industrial stoppages
> Underlying two general problems:
> a deep-seated mutual antagonism between the two sides
> a labour-management balance of power which has shifted
> decisively in the former's favour over the years

Trend then goes on to evaluate progress. The Industrial Relations Act had been passed. Nevertheless "extreme militancy has become more rather than less evident than it was fifteen months ago" and as a cause Trend highlights, among other disputes, the "UCS situation". The immediate challenge was "how to lower the current inflamed temper of debate about industrial relations" and overcome the impression that government had shown "lack of concern over the plight of individual groups of workers". This was now impeding the most central plank of the government's programme.

Burke clearly saw the "UCS situation" as having changed the overall balance. Its example had galvanised workers in other threatened workplaces to follow suit – with over 100 workplace occupations occurring over the following twelve months.[11] Across much of Scotland and parts of England support committees had been set up that united trades councils, workplaces and community organisations in a way not seen for a generation. The work-in had also forced something of a transformation of attitudes to unofficial (and now illegal) stoppages. Leaders of the official trade union movement and the Labour Party had to march alongside stewards and strikers in the UCS demonstrations of July and August 1971 and visibly give support to actions that were technically illegal. In turn this seems to have had some impact on the September 1971 TUC, with the UCS stewards invited as honoured guests, and its decision to refuse compliance with the Industrial Relations Act and to expel unions that did register.

Davies himself was dismayed by what he described on 21 September as the stewards' ability to "secure a monopoly of publicity in the press and on TV" and to "pre-empt the government's efforts to put the true facts".[12] Throughout the dispute he maintained close contacts with McGarvey and was constantly urging him to take the initiative: "can you do anything to get negotiations going as we both intended?".[13] Joint high profile public events were organised specifically to "keep the stewards out of the limelight" (as it was put in the confidential note of a meeting between Davies and McGarvey on 7 December).[14] Yet none of this was enough. A crucial material obstacle throughout was the need, as part of any settlement, to enforce the reductions in wages and conditions that would satisfy what were described in departmental jargon as "the government's supporters", more specifically Sir Eric Yarrow and Sir James Lithgow, owners of the two remaining big private yards on the Clyde.[15] That requirement sank the two yard deal. Later it probably tipped the balance against the three yard deal. Always in the background was the political constraint represented by the industrial barons who were the godfathers of the Conservative Party in Scotland, Lithgow, Yarrow and Lord Clydesmuir, representing steel. The prime minister's private secretary wrote on 25 January 1972 expressing the prime minister's concern at the lack of progress of negotiations on wages and conditions. The prime minister considers "the commitment from the unions still not adequate and that maximum pressure should be exerted while the government still has some bargaining power".[16] It was probably this insistence, representing a direct material attack on the wages and conditions of workers in the Upper Clyde yards, which as much as anything ensured the stewards' victory.

'The word is the most sensitive index of social changes'

To this extent the language of these debates, anchored in the changing perceptions of the workers in the yards, does enable us to pinpoint key moments of change and some of the material factors involved. As Volosinov puts it, "countless ideological threads running through all areas of social intercourse register effects in the word.. the word is the most sensitive index of social changes, and, what is more, of changes still in the process of growth, still without definitive shape and not as yet accommodated into already regularised and fully defined ideological systems. The word has the capacity to register all the transitory, delicate, momentary phases of social change".[17]

In July the stewards' victory depended on their ability to relate the tight sectional loyalties of workers in the yards, their distrust of the old owners and the combativeness of the shipyard tradition to support new wider alliances, already real and demonstrated, that allowed the fight for jobs to take on a more universal meaning – one which also sustained unity across the yards and across trades. In September, against a tougher test, this re-ordering of meanings was taken a stage further. The newly adopted social democratic rhetoric of compromise and flexibility was nullified by the stewards' ability to combine the figurative butchery mentioned in the Ridley report with the material butchery of wages and conditions and the potential loss of any future bargaining power. In its place they were able to advance a far more confident affirmation of a different type of class politics, one in which the workforce had wider responsibilities to the "British working class" to defend basic rights.

Here it is important to stress the interlinkage of particular struggles across Britain and, in this period, their mutually reinforcing effect. Over the first two months of the work-in massive amounts of money flowed into the shop stewards fighting fund from across Britain – collections that had to be organised in detail by other workplaces and from local (mainly trades council-based) support committees. This, and the two one-day support strikes, gave active material substance to the term 'working class unity'. The visible context of the dispute changed – moving beyond the tight sectional worlds of trade groups and particular yards to this lifeline of wider solidarity.

The action on the Clyde also triggered action elsewhere. Local support committees often became the basis for new local challenges to workplace closures across industrial Britain: the dozens of other occupations over the following 12 months. Stewards from the Clyde travelled across the country to sustain solidarity.

There was also the symbolism of the mass demonstrations. Trade union leaders, including right-wingers, felt obliged to march at the front – arm in arm with Left-wing and Communist shop stewards engaged in technically illegal industrial action and occupation. And so, by the time of the second August demonstration, did leaders of the Labour Party in Scotland. At the mass rally on Glasgow Green, attended by an estimated 100,000, they had to speak on a platform agreed by the shop stewards Coordinating Committee that included, most unusually, the Scottish leader of the Communist Party, Alex Murray. The stewards took this step with some hesitation. It could have been used by the right-wing to claim 'manipulation'. Murray's prepared script was carefully limited to immediate material issues. But on the day, in light of the tone of the meeting, he felt able to depart from it.

'And if this system cannot provide it (full employment and decent wages), let us have another' – which received the biggest ovation of the day.

This mood was carried forward to the conference of the Trade Union Congress 10 days later that was to decide its position on the Industrial Relations Act attended by the stewards as honoured guests. The original position of the General Council had been to permit limited cooperation with the Act. This was overturned. The Act should be defied. No union should register – a decision then strengthened to the expulsion of any union complying. This was the context for Heath's remark three weeks later, in discussing Burke Trend's report, that the government had been seen to be hard-hearted rather than hard-headed – and then side-lining, and subsequently sacking, Nicholas Ridley and demoting the other minister most involved, Sir John Eden.

Critical throughout was the 'interlinkage' of disputes, of political developments played out on the 'living stage' at British level. It was this that provided the overall context for what, locally, could be said by the workers' leaders – and how it could be said.

Interlinkages that frame the UCS struggle.

January-February 1972 saw the first major miners' strike for a generation. It was ultimately won by the deployment of mass pickets, most critically the thousands of Birmingham car-workers who turned out, technically illegally, to shut down the Saltley Gate coke depot. In Scotland it had been the miners who provided much of the human and financial support for UCS. This was now reciprocated. The strike itself directly coincided with the convening of a 'Scottish Assembly' by the STUC which had been agreed at the STUC's emergency conference in July to highlight the crisis of economic development in Scotland and in doing so to mobilise support for the UCS workers. The Assembly represented all Scottish trade unions and the shop stewards committees from across Scotland – but was also backed by local authorities representing over 90 percent of Scotland's population. by Chambers of Commerce representing smaller businesses and by political parties – eventually even the chair of the Conservative Party felt obliged to attend.

By then Scotland's centre of political gravity had moved strongly towards the Left – and, more to the point, towards labour in struggle. The Assembly's ultimate call was for a Scottish parliament. This, said the STUC general secretary, had to be a 'workers parliament'.

Six month's later came the climax of the battle against the Industrial Relations Act with the arrests of the London dockers and general strike action across Britain – initiated by the unofficial Liaison Committee for the Defence of Trade Unions but then officially backed, for the first time since 1926, by the TUC. Again the interlinkage of struggles, including the UCS, is evidenced. So also is the interlinkage of personnel: the degree to which., largely as a result of the creation of a national shop stewards movement over the previous decade, workplace conveners across Britain knew each other. On the Saturday, following the arrests of the dockers, London printworkers had been holding a solidarity rally in London to raise funds for one of the most celebrated of the worker occupations, Briant Colour, a work-in directly modelled on and supported by the UCS. A UCS speaker was in attendance. The chair of the Liaison Committee, Kevin Halpin, seized the opportunity to call, successfully, for the print workers to halt the printing of the Fleet Street Sunday papers – providing the springboard on Sunday for an appeal to rail workers at Waterloo to stop the trains on Monday. The stoppage of both newspapers and trains then precipitated the TUC into action. Virtually simultaneously, it brought the release of the dockers.[18]

However, in this case as well, as at UCS, every decision to strike had to be argued for in each individual workplace – and argued for in a way that linked and matched local circumstance to national events, arguments generally won but sometimes lost.

Conclusion: 'a change of front and speech'?

How, then, finally, should we assess the significance of what happened in and around the Upper Clyde Shipbuilders work-in over these 15 months in terms of the long-term sequence of developments in class identities and attitudes. The work-in was only one part of a wider movement, though a very significant one, and also one that had a decisive influence on government policy.

Its material trigger was a perceived attack on existing rights and material standards and therefore potentially on identities. It derived from splits within capital and the way the interests of dominant 'modernising' corporate capital had clashed with those of large-scale regional capital – resulting in an explicit attack on rights to full employment and the wages and conditions secured over the previous decades. But it could only have been taken forward through the actions of an anti-capitalist Left that knew the rules of the game.

The work-in itself then impacted on, as we have seen, a series of other mobilisations against government policy across Britain. In combination these raised the much wider issue of working-class strategy nationally – particularly in terms of how to respond to the Industrial Relations Act, a move that took the trade union movement beyond the cautious constitutionalism of the TUC and explicitly invoked class solidarity and mobilisation for the first time since the 1920s. Within the Labour Party all talk of legal intervention against strikers ended. As we noted, within twelve months, by summer 1973, a new manifesto had been produced explicitly talking about an 'irreversible and fundamental shift of wealth and power in favour of working people'.

In Scotland there were possibly more profound political and cultural consequences. The hitherto dominant position of the Conservative Party within the 'Unionist' working-class community crumbled very quickly – its wealthy patrons exposed as enemies of the people and its subaltern ranks divided. As communities mobilised to collect cash and win political support, local influentials had to take sides. In Clydebank the Area Committee of Church of Scotland clergy descended into rancourous conflict as members were faced with calls to assist cash collections and the use of church halls. Similar divisions emerged within the Orange Order. In the yards managers and the privileged technical grades backed the work-in. So did local shopkeepers. Cultural expression was transformed. Theatre groups, novelists, artists worked to a new working-class agenda. And the Scottish National Party, after a meteoric rise in 1974 as the Conservative vote collapsed, then itself saw its own vote collapse in 1979 when it backed the Conservatives in voting against the nationalisation of shipbuilding.

How far, then, was there a shift of front and voice as Marx talked about in the 1840s ? Heath's Conservatives found any effective response difficult. It was attempted – but frustrated by its own Scottish supporters. With Labour the initial changes, though fundamental, were only temporarily. The irreversible shift was soon teamed up with a 'Social Contract' under which there was to be voluntary wage restraint.[19] This drew the support of Jack Jones and key union leaders and also some of the rank and file Left. But in so doing it split the wider movement. The LCDTU remained committed to free collective bargaining and continued to resist what turned out to be, by 1977-78, a very significant reduction in real wages. Inside the Labour Party this split opened the way for the right-wing to intervene and, in late 1975, oust Wilson and install a pliant timeserver as prime minister.

For corporate capital the 1974-75 'change of face' represented one last attempt to stabilise a corporatist style of state management. With support from some sections of the CBI, there was further nationalisation (shipbuilding and aerospace and partly oil), a significant limitation of the powers of management in the workplace over health and safety but matched with 'voluntary' wage restraint. And this, as noted before, won a degree of ideological support within the trade union movement – dividing the Left and enabling the right again to take the offensive.

In parallel, a quite different 'change of face and voice' was emerging within the Conservative Party in the course of a bitter five year long internal battle fought out between 1974 and 1979. For the ruling class this new

Thatcherite line, in detail largely developed by Nicholas Ridley, was much more far reaching -but also potentially very risky. It sought to close down entire industries, to use the pound as a petro-currency to export capital and establish the City of London as a global financial centre – and then, for the near-time future, to redevelop a new generation of 'sunrise industries', modelled on those of the then feted Japanese economic miracle, that were, in terms of production units, small scale, far more proof against union penetration and exploited international outsourcing.[20]

As part of this initiative there was also a quite explicit attempt to redevelop and exploit 'reified' consumerist identities. As early as 1974 a Conservative research department report called for the sale and privatisation of council housing – which 'on Clydeside' gave the working class a monolithic character reminiscent of 'iron curtain countries'.[21] The required legislation was one of the Conservative government's first major initiatives in autumn 1979 – enabling tenants to buy homes at discounted prices.[22] The sale of publicly owned utilities was also conducted on terms which appeared to be those of a people's capitalism and individual profit. At the same, and in parallel, the government moved quickly to scapegoat 'scroungers' and 'immigrants' as exploiting the public sector to the detriment of 'hard-working families'.

This then returns us to our overall theme – of alienation, reification and the 'mercurial' character of class consciousness: powerful enough at key moments to destroy governments (and sometimes more) but also vulnerable, as Marx himself noted, to the ability of a ruling class to respond. However, this is only if the agents of the ruling class understand the rules of the game, know how to exploit newly emerging tensions and do so in language, however meretricious, that engage with the fear, insecurity and the search for identity that is inherent in the alienated world of capitalism.

The early 1970s therefore remind us of the special characteristics of working class mobilisation, that it is a process that depends on detailed, local argument, on winning debates, sometimes virtual, but manly in practice, direct. As Leontiev stressed, it is the words and meanings that 'dig themselves into their connections with people forming the circle of real contacts' that have to be transformed by the dialectic of theme and meaning – and they have to be transformed by those who understand those meanings directly, are themselves identified with them, but also understand the wider contradictions of capitalism itself.

NOTES

1   This process is followed in greater detail in J. Foster, *History of Unite* Volume 4 1960-1974, chapters 2 and 3 (Liverpool 2023).

2   The politico-economic background is outlined in the first three chapters of J. Foster and C. Woolfson, *The Politics of the UCS Work-In: Class Alliances and the Right to Work* (London, 1986). Jim Phillips provided a more recent appraisal: Phillips, *The Industrial Politics of Devolution: Scotland in the 1960s and 70s* (Manchester, 2008).

3   After strong turnouts in Scotland in March 1971, the strike action proposed by the Liaison Committee for the Defence of Trade Unions for 1 May 1971 had to be abandoned: Alan Troup, "The Defence of Trade Union Rights 1969-1974" in *Essays in the Social and Labour History of Renfrewshire*, ed. Tony Clarke, Renfrewshire Council, 1999 and A. Troup. 'The Mobilisation of Political Protest Strikes 1969-1984', PhD Dissertation, CNAA, 1987.

4   Originally this included five shipyards, Govan, Scotstoun, Linthouse, Clydebank and Yarrows. In February 1971 the Heath government removed Yarrows, primarily a naval yard, and returned it to its original owner, Sir Eric Yarrow.

5   McKinley, A and Knox, W, "Working for the Yankee Dollar: US Inward Investment and Scottish Labour, 1945-1970", *Historical Studies in Industrial Relations*, 7, 1999, 1-26.

6   National Archives, London (NA) FV 36/79 (Department of Trade and Industry) Sir William Lithgow to the Prime Minister 7 March 1972. Sir Eric Yarrow, owner of the admiralty yard on Upper Clyde, sent a similarly angry letter.

7   Woolfson, "Capacity for Class Struggle", p. 309

8   C Collins, "The Pragmatics of Emancipation: A Critical Review of the Work of Michael Huspek"', *Journal of Pragmatics*, Volume 25, Issue 6, June 1996, pages 791-817.

9   Briefing to Prime Minister 13 September 1971: NA PREM 15/612 makes this very clear.

10   NA CAB 129/59 Review of Government Strategy 30 September 1971.

11   The best source here is Albert Mills, 'Worker Occupations 1971-1975', Durham University PhD thesis, 1982.

12   NA CAB 128/49 Summary of Conclusions 21 September 1971.

13   NA FV 36/79 f.21 Letter draft dated 23 December.

14   NA FV 36/79 f. 18 Note of meeting with CSEU 7 December 1971.

15   NA FV 36/79 f 26 Note meeting Secretary of State and Lord Strathalmond 12 January 1972 and CAB 134/3487 Paper 6 23 February 1972.

16   NA FV 36/79 f.49 Peter Gregor (Downing Street) to Eric Wright DTI 28 January 1972.

17   Volosinov, *Marxism and Language*,. p 19. Collins explores these issues further in his critique of Fairclough: "Discourse in Cultural-Historical Perspective: Critical Discourse Analysis, CHAT and the Study of Social Change', in B. Van Oers et al eds, *The Transformation of Learning*, (Cambridge 2009) pp. 242-272.

18   J. Foster, *History of Unite* Vol 4 1960-1974, (Liverpool 2022) p.144.

19   Richard Leonard, 'Labour's 1973 programme', *Theory and Struggle*, vol. 124, 2023, pp. 61-65.

20   Nicholas Ridley, Final Report of the Nationalised Industry Policy Group, July 1977, Margaret Thatcher Foundation, https://www.margaretthatcher.org/document/110795.

21   B. Patten, 'The Eclipse of the Private Landlord', Conservative Political Centre 1974, p.4.

22   Housing Act 1980.

THIS PAGE LEFT INTENTIONALLY BLANK

2

Clydeside and Britain 1919

> Society is really built up of conventions. Habits are formed
> which become as strong as iron bands. Well, the war has
> broken through the crust ... in large parts of Europe there is...
> revolution.
> Conservative leader Bonar Law speaking in Glasgow in
> December 1918

In some ways the struggles of 1919 were, very similar to those of 1971; in others quite different. In 1919 also the government saw itself as reliant on the official trade union leadership and the language of social democracy. Then also the challenge came from a shop stewards movement which derived much of its power from wider alliances within the working class. And then also the experience of building these wider alliances, and challenging state institutions, seems to have been associated with the development of a new kind of mass class identity. Moreover, in 1919 as in 1971, the longer term consequences were highly detrimental for the wider implementation of government strategy. On the other hand, the 1919 strike failed to win its immediate objective, its alliances were very different from those in 1971 and it was far less successful in securing leverage over the institutions of Scottish society.

The constraints facing the governing Lloyd George coalition at the end of the war were considerable but not, it seemed, insurmountable. As a populist Liberal, Lloyd George's takeover as prime minster in 1916 had been with the support of both the Conservative Party and the Parliamentary Labour Party. His skills as a politician, and his identity with the Liberal insurance reforms of 1911, were seen as essential for increasing war production and maintaining popular support in face of increasing hardship and military conscription. Lloyd George immediately strengthened the agreements with trade union leaders made in 1915 which had guaranteed the post-war restoration of working practices in return for a ban on strikes and cooperation with management in labour dilution. Now Lloyd George gave the leader of the Labour Party, Arthur Henderson, a seat in the War Cabinet and created a Ministry of Labour with another Labour MP, the previous general secretary of the engineers, George Barnes, as Minister. Trade union leaders, often Labour MPs and often also junior ministers in the government, played an increasingly active role in putting over the government's case in face of growing levels of unofficial militancy. Although, at the end of the war in November 1918, most but not all of the Labour ministers left the Coalition and re-established Labour as an independent party, this generation of Labour and trade union leaders maintained much of their earlier constitutionalist and 'British' rhetoric. Their vision of the future depended on working within existing powers structures.[1]

At the end of the war Lloyd George's own position as leader of what was now a mainly Conservative Coalition depended on his populist appeal and his ability as victorious war leader to handle a politically uncertain situation. Trade union membership had tripled during the war and extended to many previously excluded semi and unskilled workers including, particularly, the younger generation of women who had been conscripted into armaments production. In face of rising levels of industrial militancy in 1917 the government had established a Ministry of Reconstruction to put forward plans for a post-war transformation of housing provision, health and employment. The Coalition also committed itself to a "widely extended suffrage", though still short of full democracy.

At the same time the Coalition represented the interests of British capital and more specifically the nexus of banking and industrial capital that had up till 1914 controlled much of the world's financial markets. During 1918 discussion intensified on how to restore this position. The Treasury, the Bank of England and the City of London wanted the earliest possible return to gold payments, if possible on 1914 levels of dollar-sterling exchange. This was seen to involve squeezing wartime inflation out of the system, re-establishing internationally competitive wage rates in export industries and, as a tool for achieving this, a gradual though not socially destabilising increase in levels of unemployment. In early summer 1918 the Treasury told the Minister for Reconstruction not to plan for any increase in expenditure at the end of the war.[2]

However, events in Russia in 1917 and then in Germany in November 1918 caused concern and there was uncertainty about how far wartime militancy would continue. Government advisers such as Geoffrey Dawson, editor of *The Times*, urged Lloyd George to hold an election as soon as possible after the end of the war so that he could claim an electoral mandate in face of any political challenge. This Lloyd George did with some success. In the general election of December 1918, the Coalition won 531 seats. The non-Coalition Liberals were decimated and retained only 26 seats. Labour won 61. With these results it appeared that the Coalition would be in position to pursue the economic objectives set by the City of London for a speedy return to the gold standard and a recovery of its global position as lender of last resort.

The new government had particularly strong links with Clydeside. The leader of the Conservative Party, Arthur Bonar Law, was a Glasgow MP and a partner in a Glasgow steel broking firm. Previously Chancellor of the Exchequer, he now held the position of the Leader of the House of Commons and was effectively deputy prime minister. Another Glasgow MP in the Cabinet was the Scottish lawyer Sir Robert Horne, the new Minister of Labour. The Glasgow industrialist Sir William Weir had been Air Minister in the wartime administration and remained influential in government circles as did Sir James Lithgow who had been Controller of Shipbuilding. Another key figure among Conservative MPs was Sir Allan Smith MP, a Glasgow based lawyer who headed the Engineering Employers Association and was later instrumental in establishing the Federation of British Industry.

In December 1918 Bonar Law gave his political assessment of the current challenges in the somewhat sheltered environment of a meeting in Glasgow for Conservative women electors in the Christian Institute:

> I am told that there is a very large Bolshevik element in this which I may almost say is my native city...I am not afraid of it. There is a danger. Society is really built up of conventions. Habits are formed which become as strong as iron bands. Well, the war has broken through the crust in many cases. The result in large parts of Europe – I am not sure it is not going to extend to the whole of Germany – there is...revolution. In a sense there is no country where this danger would be greater than in this country because in European countries there were always the men who were employed on the land who were what was called a conservative element. We had only a small proportion of such men. But we also had something else. . Our people had the knowledge, by our past history, that whatever they could justly claim they would get by constitutional methods.. The only danger of anything approaching revolution in this country was if the conditions of life became intolerable.[3]

Bonar Law went on to praise the patriotic role of labour in the Coalition, which included his fellow Coalition candidate in Glasgow Gorbals, George Barnes. He projected the Coalition as a government "free from party views" and ended by attacking the Asquith Liberals:

> The one danger was that they should have a government that took the view that they should have no spending for social reform and anything else until the war debt had been wiped out. That would be absolutely fatal.

In line with this perspective of constitutional amelioration, Sir Allan Smith, as head of the Engineering Employers Association, negotiated in December 1918 a significant reduction in working hours with the Federation of Shipbuilding and Engineering Unions as part of the process of restoring pre-war practices. Hours were to come down from 54 to 47 – with some changes in shift patterns and the elimination of some meal breaks. This was seen as a key first move in shifting negotiations back to an industrial footing and out of state control and in doing so reinforcing the status of union leaderships. The Federation balloted its membership on this in December and claimed a majority across Britain – although on Clydeside and in Belfast the votes were reported as negative.[4] Another move to reduce state involvement was the closure of the state-run munitions factories, mainly employing young women but also some injured ex-servicemen. The government's Chief Labour Adviser, Scottish lawyer Sir Thomas Munro, urged extreme caution both on this and on army demobilisation. He wrote on 1 December that there was "deep resentment" among workers at "the too rapid discharge" from war factories and "the inadequacy of out of work benefit":

> the risk that exists and cannot be overlooked is that a dangerous situation may occur at any moment if large numbers of workers are thrown out of employment during the next few weeks. I am especially apprehensive of the attitude of discharged soldiers and sailors who are banded together in an organisation which is insistent on its demands and somewhat aggressive.[5]

It was at least partly for such reasons that the policy adopted in December for army demobilisation was for a gradual release of servicemen and the retention of significant numbers for occupation duties in Germany and Central Europe and also for service with the British armies then operating in support of Tsarist forces in Northern Russia and Siberia.

The big problem on the labour front, as seen by both the Ministry of Munitions and by local employers, was the loss of authority by the trade union leaderships. Ministry of Munitions staff on Clydeside reported a total disregard by shop stewards of their officials during the closing months of the war – a comment borne out by the case papers of the Clyde Shipbuilding Employers.[6] Sir William Weir returned in December 1918 to take over general management of his engineering works in Glasgow. His letters show acute concern at the virtually complete loss of both management and official union influence at workshop level.[7] This disregard of union leaders was linked to the wartime experience of workers on the shop floor that governments always responded to direct industrial action. Faced with disruptions to war production, the government had generally intervened over the heads of employers to enforce settlements. In January 1919 the Conservative *Glasgow Herald* editorialised on the need to break with this wartime practice in the new circumstances. During the war when "directly challenged, the government on several occasions was compelled to adopt concessions in order that the larger interests of the nation might be safeguarded. The government are not now under the necessity to intervene". The editorial was referring specifically to the movement then emerging "among workers" to repudiate the 47 hour deal, to demand 40 hours and to "dragoon their own unions into taking action".[8]

This movement, which emerged in the course of December 1918 and January 1919, culminated in the general strike of 27 January. It had a number of different sources.

The most central one was undoubtedly the grouping of shop stewards in the Clyde Workers Committee which brought together representative of the main engineering and shipbuilding works across the Clyde. In 1915-16 this had initiated the strikes on rent levels and on equal pay for 'dilutees' and in 1917-18 the even bigger strike wave for wage increases in line with wartime inflation.[9] Politically the leading figures belonged to three separate organisations, the British Socialist Party (BSP), the Socialist Labour Party (SLP) and the Independent Labour Party (ILP) – though by 1918 these divisions were of minimal significance, all were supporters of the Russian Revolution. Members of the BSP and ILP were also affiliated to the Labour Party. As well as William Gallacher (BSP), Tom Bell and Arthur McManus (SLP), the group included the ILP members David Kirkwood, Emmanuel Shinwell and Neil McLean. McLean was the only Glasgow Labour MP to be elected in 1918, representing the shipyard constituency of Govan. He headed the British Hands off Russia campaign and in January joined the Joint Strike Committee. The Scottish BSP leader John Maclean, arrested in February 1918 for sedition, remained in prison till December 1918. On 1 May 1918 the Clyde Workers Committee, in association with Glasgow Trades and Labour Council, had organised a one-day strike to demand the withdrawal of British troops from Russia, the release of Maclean and a negotiated peace. The 90,000 strong May Day demonstration, though illegal, was too big for the authorities to disperse.[10]

By 1918 Glasgow Trades Council had assumed a central leadership role for the trade union movement on Clydeside. Delegates were elected by local trades union branches and it had a regular attendance of over 200.[11] Its chair was an official of the sailors union, Emmanuel Shinwell, who played the main organising role in the strike until his arrest on 1 February. Another key organisation was the Glasgow District Committee of the engineering union, ASE. Its full-time secretary, Harry Hopkins, was also a member of the Joint Strike Committee and similarly arrested on 10 February.

At Scottish level the main pro-strike organisation was the Scottish Trade Union Congress. This had been formed in 1897 when trades councils, generally socialist inclined, were excluded from the British TUC.[12] The STUC had affiliations from Scottish unions, a number of British unions and from trades councils. Its constitution, unlike the British TUC, committed it to the social ownership of the means of production. The STUC Parliamentary Committee, which included representation from all three constituencies, assumed an increasingly active role during the war in negotiations with the government. In July 1918 it agreed to accept a place on the government's Labour Resettlement Committee. In September 1918 it protested to the government at its intervention in Russia as a "challenge to democracy and socialism" (the use of the term democracy is significant: it represented a challenge to a government that still refused full democracy in Britain). In November and December delegations were sent to London to lobby against any speedy discharge of workers from the munitions factories. In November the Parliamentary Committee was sufficiently concerned at the terms of the discussions in the government's Labour Resettlement Committee to convene a conference of all affiliates for 28 December on the Industrial Crisis. Its proposals included compulsory unemployment insurance and a "reduction of hours by legislative enactment to a maximum of 40 hours per week" with the object of "reabsorbing the sailors and soldiers into civil life and giving greater leisure to the working classes". The conference broadly endorsed this proposal – although the leaders of some British affiliated unions protested that it cut across their negotiated agreement for 47 hours and some members of the Clyde Workers Committee argued that 30 hours would be necessary to prevent the return of large scale unemployment.[13]

Over the New Year the employment situation dramatically changed as the government reversed its policy on demobilisation. Mutinies had occurred at the channel ports. Soldiers in the camps around London commandeered lorries and marched down Whitehall demanding demobilisation and a 44 hour week. There was widespread refusal to embark for Russia. In Scotland there were disturbances among the troops stationed at Stirling and in the Forth garrison.[14] On 6 January chief of imperial general staff Sir Henry Wilson noted in his diary that army discipline had collapsed and that there would be "no army at all in a very short time".[15] An emergency meeting of the Cabinet was convened that reversed policy on demobilisation, deciding to release conscripts as fast as possible and revert to a much smaller regular army whose loyalty could be guaranteed.[16] By mid-January almost half a million men had been discharged; by the end of the month the figure had reached a million.[17]

For trade unionists this brought the immediate prospect of large scale unemployment – although the returning servicemen were now increasingly seen as potential allies.[18] The fraternisation of workers and soldiers in Russia and Germany was immediately to mind and had a particular resonance in Glasgow where the 3,000-strong Federation of Discharged Soldiers and Sailors was, as Munro noted, "somewhat aggressive". Since early 1918 its elected leaders had been members of the BSP and it routinely marched alongside trade union demonstrations to provide protection.[19] Although elsewhere in Scotland the leadership was less overtly political, the Federation's half yearly Scottish conference in Stirling in December 1918 had unseated its honorary president, the Liberal MP J.M. Hogg, and adopted a Magna Carta of demands including public works, payment of apprentices and the prevention of the exploitation of the labour of discharged men.[20]

It was at this point in early January 1919 that the weekly papers of the BSP, *The Call*, and the SLP, *The Socialist*, shift their focus from reporting developments on the continent to the industrial front and the issue of shorter hours.[21] The Clyde Workers Committee met on 5 January and set up a Ways and Means Committee to work for the rejection of the 47 hour agreement negotiated by the Confederation.[22] This agreement had already run into difficulties because of its detrimental impact on piecework wages among boilermakers, blacksmiths and iron moulders and, more generally, because of the elimination of the breakfast meal break. When the new working arrangements came into force after the New Year holiday there had been a rash of sectional strikes on the Clyde and in other shipbuilding and engineering centres in Scotland, England and Ireland that continued through January. [23]

At this stage there was some jostling for position between the Clyde Workers Committee, the Trades Council and the STUC Parliamentary Committee over the timing of any strike, the number of hours to be demanded and who would lead the action.[24] The Clyde Workers Committee and the Trades Council tended to support 30 hours and a strike date in January; the STUC 40 hours and a strike at the beginning of February. The resolution of differences between the Trades Council and the Clyde Workers Committee saw the creation of a Joint Strike Committee that also included representatives of trade union District Committees backing strike action. The STUC had previously issued a joint statement with Labour Party Advisory Committee calling for strike action to secure legislative action for a 40 hour week. After some hesitation the STUC now agreed to send delegates to the Joint Committee. At a conference on 18 January it won agreement for 40 hours but lost its proposal for the strike to start on 11 February. Instead 27 January was agreed. Shinwell as chair of the Joint Committee was also insistent that all negotiations be through the Joint Committee and not the STUC. These conflicting positions reflected somewhat differing balances within the respective organisations – with a vigorous minority group of right-wingers on the STUC's Parliamentary Committee.[25] The conference on 18 January adopted the following Manifesto:

To the Workers

Call to Arms!

The Joint Committee representing the Official and Unofficial Section of the Industrial Movement, having carefully considered the reports of Shop Stewards and representatives of the various industries, hereby resolves to

DEMAND A 40-HOURS MAXIMUM WORKING WEEK
For all workers, as an experiment with the objective of absorbing the unemployed. If a 40-hour week fails to give the desired result, a more drastic reduction of hours will be demanded.

A GENERAL STRIKE
Has been declared to take place on
MONDAY 27th JANUARY
And all workers are expected to respond

By Order of Joint Committee representing All Industries"
[followed by the names of those representing component organisations].[26]

For the government this call challenged the three central planks of its industrial relations strategy. It demanded government intervention over the heads of management and union leaderships. It undercut the position of the official trade union leaders. And, if successful, it threatened the future use of a 'labour reserve' to reassert management control.

As presented by the Joint Strike Committee the action was to a large extent defensive. It was to defend the wartime time balance of power in the workplace and hence also wages and conditions. It also sought to retain industrial leadership in the hands of shop stewards – with the perspective of asserting wider working class unity – and to develop wider alliances with two particular constituencies: discharged servicemen and women laid off from the munitions factories.

None of the socialists in the Joint Strike Committee saw themselves in a revolutionary situation or anything like it. John Maclean was in Lancashire seeking to win support for the shorter hours movement. On 23 January he wrote in the BSP weekly *The Call*:

> some are suggesting a general strike to enforce a withdrawal
> of British troops from Russia and, I suppose, from Germany...
> That, to some of us on the Clyde, is too idealistic. Were
> the mass of the people in Britain revolutionary socialists
> they would at once see that their well-being depended on
> the peaceful development of Bolshevism in Russia... But
> the workers are not generally of our way of thinking... it
> necessarily follows that we will have no success in urging
> a strike on this issue, especially as the government has the
> majority of trade union leaders in the hollow of its hand.

The key issue for the present, he wrote, was to secure a unity of the unemployed and the employed around the issue of shorter hours. In particular, it was important to bring the shorter hours struggle in heavy engineering into alignment with that of the miners to secure a six-hour day and defend state control of their industry – on which the miners were due to ballot in February.[27]

Arthur McManus, Clyde representative on the shop stewards National Amalgamated Committee, was similarly cautious. At a private meeting in London on 20 January he was doubtful whether the response to the strike call on the Clyde would be "universal" and urged the committee to "wait and see" before convening a national conference.[28]

The first day of the strike was successful but within limits. The call was answered by about half of the engineering and shipbuilding workforce across the Clyde, in Dundee, Arbroath, Aberdeen, at the naval dockyard at Rosyth, in the Edinburgh engineering plants and in Fife where the miners came out.[29] In Glasgow an afternoon rally in St Andrew's Halls was followed by a march to the City Chambers.

This first rally largely set the tone for the conduct of the strike. It was announced, as the decision of the Strike Committee, that only strikers would be allowed to speak: 'the object of such instructions being to keep the political element entirely outside'.[30] This matched the assessment of the organisers about the general temper of workers – they were not in the majority 'of our way of thinking'. Only about half those in the shipyards had turned out that morning. The strike's objectives therefore had to be strictly industrial. The introduction of 'politics' would play into the hands of the employers and the government.

The mass meeting also saw the announcement of important organisational arrangements. Yards and workplaces were being organised into districts, each with its District Committee made up of workplace delegates – with District Committees in turn sending delegates to the Joint Committee. The district committees were to be responsible for picketing, entertainment and the 'relief of necessitous cases'. A significant initiative at District level was to hold meetings for 'women and strikers' wives' and to organise mass pickets of workplaces: 'as many as five thousand females formed one of our mass pickets'.[31] The Monday mass meeting also heard a call for the withholding of the payment of rent and rates till the end of strike and received reports from London, where 10,000 shipyard workers were reported as on strike, and Belfast which began its strike on the preceding Saturday and where the electricians had blacked out the city and rendered the shutdown virtually total.[32]

The Cabinet discussed the situation in the afternoon. The minister of Labour, and Glasgow MP, Horne spoke of the need not to undermine the union executives, who had called for a return to work, and that, although in Glasgow and Belfast the "men totally disregarded the advice of their leaders", there was "no need for undue alarm". The Scottish Secretary Sir Robert Munro stated that he was in touch with "leading citizens" in Glasgow who advised "unofficial propaganda".[33]

On Tuesday mass pickets, now thousands strong and organised on a locality basis, closed most of the remaining workplaces on the Clyde.[34] On the Wednesday, the Lanarkshire miners came out and a further mass meeting was held in St Andrew's Hall. This was followed by a march, described by the pro-Government *Glasgow Herald*, as a mile in length and as "probably the largest demonstration of strikers ever witnessed in Glasgow". This procession halted at the Dundas Street power station in the north of the city and successfully secured a cessation of work – cutting off power supplies to industry. The march then proceeded to the City Chambers where the leaders interviewed the Lord Provost. He agreed to telegram the government asking for its intervention and to report the response on Friday when the workers would again assemble in George Square.[35] Wednesday also saw the local strike committee beginning to issue permits to civic bodies for the limited movement of essential supplies to schools and hospitals.[36]

Thursday saw a further strengthening of the strike on the lower Clyde, the issuing of the first *Strike Bulletin* and a meeting of Clydeside employers, convened jointly by the Engineers and Shipbuilders Associations to hear a report from their executives. Their assessment was that the initial response was no more than 25 per cent and that the subsequent extension had depended on mass pickets. They had asked the Chief Constable for police intervention but he had said that he lacked the resources. They had also called on the union executives of the Engineers and Boilermakers to suspend the local officials who were backing the strike. The meeting agreed that a deputation should interview the Lord Provost the following morning and reprimand him for seeking government intervention.[37] A Cabinet meeting in the afternoon also repudiated any intervention in response to the Lord Provost and reaffirmed the need to "support the position of the union leaders". Contingency plans were discussed for the use of troops if necessary, but not immediately (the Scottish Secretary Munro said he had available 12,000 infantry, six tanks and 100 lorries as transport). It was agreed that immediate steps should be taken to arrest the strike leaders under the Defence of the Realm Act.[38]

On Friday morning the *Glasgow Herald*'s lead editorial reprimanded the Lord Provost for interceding with the government and reproduced a section of the (unpublished) letter written to him by Bonar Law from the Cabinet meeting the previous day:

> Such action could only undermine the authority of those
> who have been chosen by the men to represent them and
> their interests and would destroy the cooperation between
> employers and employed on which the hopes of industrial
> peace depended.[39]

The employers' deputation interviewed the Lord Provost around 11am and, after similarly reprimanding him, demanded to know what he intended to do about the "unruly mob then assembling".[40] It was in these circumstances, after the workers' deputation had entered the City Chambers, that the foot and mounted police concentrated in front of the City Chambers sought to clear the square. Mounted police baton charges were initially successful but were halted when they met the ranks of the ex-servicemen. The police were then driven back across the Square and eventually forced to take refuge inside the courtyard of the City Chambers. At this point the deputation leaders, by then arrested, were allowed onto the balcony to appeal to the workers to form up in columns behind the ex-servicemen and march to Glasgow Green.[41] The leaders clearly understood the intentions of the government. They needed to maintain the wider mobilisation of pro-strike forces and avoid any justification for military intervention.

That afternoon the employers' leaders met to report back to what was a mass meeting of over 120 major Clydeside employers. They reported their discussions with the Lord Provost. They also reported their meeting on Wednesday with the union leaders of the Engineering and Shipbuilding Federation where they pointed out that "they must take steps to have recalcitrant Strikers brought to book; that the first Agreement entered into since the war broke out was in danger of being scrapped and that unless the Unions were able to carry out their terms of the Agreement it was useless to carry on collective bargaining." The meeting then agreed that a deputation should "interview the Press Representatives with the object of a judicious cutting down of statements in the press concerning the unofficial strike and the eliminating from reports the names of the Strike Leaders". The Lord Provost was also to be interviewed again and told to authorise the formation of a "Civic Guard" made up of employers and "loyal workmen" with a "view to opposing the strikers". Discussion also "took place on whether the Employers should issue a manifesto to the effect that two months from this date should there be a number of demobilised soldiers still out of employment, the Employers would either by reduced hours or other means give them employment". This proposal was remitted to the Executive.

Military forces arrived in Glasgow overnight. Machine gun emplacements were set up around George Square. Troops with fixed bayonets occupied bridges, key road junctions, railway stations, the two city power stations and guarded the approaches to major workplaces. The premises of the Trades Council were raided and more arrests took place – including Shinwell, the Chair of the Strike Committee.[42]

Despite this, the strike continued through the following week and the first three days of the third week. It was only twelve days later, on Wednesday, 12 February, that the Joint Strike Committee called for an orderly return to work. The *Strike Bulletin*, which achieved a 20,000 circulation, claimed that the response of military occupation was to strengthen the resolve of the strikers. A delegate conference convened by the Scottish Trades Union Conference the following day on Sunday 2 February resolved to call for a full Scottish wide general strike by 92 votes to 22.[43] Its Parliamentary Committee meeting on the Wednesday following, 5 February, considered that the situation was still moving in their favour as a result of the spread of the strike action to London and parts of South Wales and with Belfast holding firm (Irish military command had warned the government against sending troops against the mainly Protestant workforce).[44]

In Glasgow, where industrial power supplies were restored on Monday 3 February, the employers declared workplaces open for a return. The Glasgow Evening Times reported that, in face of the army patrols, "considerable numbers" of women, some with "children in their arms" had replaced men on the picket lines outside the shipyards.[45] The *Glasgow Herald* lists a few workplaces in South Glasgow with a partial return; in the north "for all practical purposes establishments are idle". The paper's most optimistic subhead, amid much diminished strike reportage, was "Slight improvement in Edinburgh".[46]

The eventual decision taken to end the strike was largely in the context a failure of the strike to spread in England beyond London and the action by the government to use the Defence of Realm Act (and the army) to break the strikes in London by underground train crews, railway workers, electricians and engineers.[47] On the return to work on Clydeside no retaliation was taken against strikers or shop stewards by the employers – their minutes show that they considered any such action dangerously provocative.[48] The employers' case papers also show a rising level of unofficial strike activity in 1919 and continuing disregard for union officials. The unofficial May Day stoppage in 1919, with the demonstrators calling for the release of all political prisoners and the withdrawal of British troops from Russia, was on an even bigger scale than in 1918. In February 1919 Horne presented his more general conclusions to the Cabinet:

> It seems clear that the rank and file, at any rate in our great national industries, having previously been educated up to the idea of complete organisation of some kind, are now becoming capable of similar collective expression to a preference to one form of machinery over another [unofficial as against official]. If this is so, it means that the government has the strongest interest in encouraging efficient trade union machinery.[49]

On Clydeside the rising level of strike militancy through 1919, and the continued industrial leadership by the shop stewards, seems partly to have resulted from experience of the strike itself and partly a consequence of the maintenance of relatively full employment as a result of the sharp reversal of government economic policy in February 1919.[50]

The first draft of the King's Speech was sent to Lloyd George in Paris on 6 February – the day Bonar Law was at his most pessimistic about the spread of the unofficial strike wave, now extending beyond London with the South Western line "almost at a standstill" and the danger that electric power would be turned off in the capital that night.[51] The speech, delivered on 11 February, the day before the return to work in Glasgow, promised "a speedy increase on a large scale of housing accommodation", "the establishment throughout the land of a scientific and enlightened health organisation", investment in transport under government supervision and enhanced provision for unemployment insurance.[52] When the costings for this programme were subsequently debated in Cabinet, Lloyd George described the required £71m as cheap "insurance against Bolshevism".[53] We will return to this policy reversal.

In terms of an analysis of language we lack the verbatim transcripts of 1971 but we do have, up to 31 January, fairly full reportage of strike meetings by the *Glasgow Herald*, the daily *Strike Bulletin* from 30 January onwards and, for the employers, the editorials of the *Herald*.

The key feature of the language of the strike's organisers is its limited range and moderation. The *Strike Bulletin* had eight pages and was issued daily for 18 days. It talks of "workers'" but very rarely mentions "class". At no point is there any reference to the events on the continent which, over the same period, filled the pages of *The Socialist* (whose press was used to print the *Bulletin*). The defeats of Tsarist-British forces in Russia, the temporary successes of socialists in Germany and the subsequent murders of Rosa Luxemburg and Karl Liebknecht were also front page news in the British Socialist Party's *The Call* and the ILP's *Forward* – and from a different standpoint in the *Glasgow Herald*. They were never mentioned in the *Strike*

Bulletin.

Its tone was severely practical. It focuses on the economic arguments for the strike, strike organisation and reports of the spread of the movement in England and Ireland. Its only overseas references are to strikes by Bombay mill workers: "Bombay 150,000 Two men killed. Strike for better conditions. The strikers number 150,000, and are giving a great lead to the downtrodden of India to secure better wages and conditions. A victory in Scotland will help our comrades in India" – and here the word "comrade" appears to be used in the wartime sense of army comrades. [54] After the arrival of the military in Glasgow the *Bulletin* contains a regular satirical column in which army activities are described in the type of language previously used in British military bulletins to describe the operations of the German high command.[55]

The Secretary of the Joint Strike Committee D S Morton subsequently commented in his pamphlet on the strike 'The whole tone of the Yellow Press altered from the day our *Bulletin* appeared'.[56]

The *Glasgow Herald* elaborated the main arguments of the employers in the following stages.

On the morning after the first day of the strike the editorial sought to stress its relative failure: while the strike has caused "very considerable dislocation', the 'ambition to lay the whole labour world idle"... "has failed. The mass of workers held aloof". On the two following days editorials argued that the strike's extension depended on intimidation by mass pickets and that it was led by "agitators who have been openly false to trade union principles". The headlines highlighted "Terrorism". On Thursday the tone changed again. Ordinary workers were being tricked.:

> It is quite certain in our belief that the working men of this
> country have not grasped the meaning of the movement ..
> they have been familiar with the use of the strike weapon..
> They are not familiar with its use as a political weapon and
> dangerous potency in the hands of men whose concerns are
> far less for the immediate improvement in the conditions of
> industry than in a vast political bouleversement .. as in Russia
> at the instance of Lenin..

On Friday, besides the rebuke to the Lord Provost for capitulating to the demand for government intervention, the *Herald* was calling for trade union leaders to intervene and "exercise leadership": the "outcome of passivity is far more serious...may result in the wreck of organisations built up since the repeal of the combination law".

For the following week the *Herald* sought to use the violence of George Square and the tanks on the streets of Glasgow to mobilise opinion against the strike leadership. It was the strike leaders who were made responsible for the violence not the police or the army: "men who from the outset flouted law and order."

The events of the weekend:

> have had the effect of visualising for the workers the
> real tendencies of the leadership under which they have
> voluntarily placed themselves .. it has now been made clear
> that a minor grievance has been utilised for the major purpose
> not only for an attempt on the ordered life of the community
> but also the existing method of trade union organisation.[57]

In an implicit reference to the pro-strike majority at the STUC conference on the Sunday, it appeals to rank and file workers not to let a "superstitious loyalty to ones fellows" act as a deterrent to a return to work and their "higher loyalty to trade union principles".

By the Wednesday of the second week, with the strike continuing unbroken, the *Herald* editorials switch to concerns for cohesion within its own class and, as it does so, the intimate lines of communication between the *Herald*, the Clydeside employers and the hard-line sections of the Cabinet become clear. The *Herald* calls on the government, in face of the growing strike movement in London, to resist "the tendency to panic", not to countenance the "surrender of principles invoked as sacrosanct .. this will multiply the difficulties" and show the "'same firmness as the Clyde".[58]

Shortly afterwards the Clyde Shipbuilders Association agreed a deputation to Lord Pirrie, leader of the Belfast employers, urging him to stand firm in light of the report that he had opened negotiations for a 44-hour week: "a most unfortunate development".[59] The following day the editorial congratulates the government on its declaration of a state of emergency in London and use of the army to keep transport moving. It argues very much the same line as we now know Bonar Law put in the Cabinet: official trade unionism must be defended; there could be no concession to the strikers; but circumstances were such that the government had to promise all-round "amelioration".[60]

By the end of the second week the *Herald* prints new calls from the official trade union movement for an end to the strike: an interview with C.W. Bowerman MP secretary of the Parliamentary Committee of the TUC and statements from Brownlee and Smith of the Confederation and J R Clynes and Colonel Will Thorne of the National Union of General Workers.[61] On the last day of the strike there is a letter signed by Labour MPs and ILP leaders, including Ramsay MacDonald and Clem Edwards, calling on workers of the United Kingdom "to rid themselves of Bolshevik agents in their midst".[62]

Probably the most potent and significant attack in the last week was on the political economy of the strike leaders – this time with a direct material punch. The *Herald* editorial refers to the headlined news story carried the previous day that one of the biggest Clydeside employers, Sir Harold Yarrow, was to shift investment for his new yard to Canada. This is followed by a letter from Sir Lyndon Macassey, formerly the government official in charge of the Ministry of Munitions, underlining the logic of this decision: shorter hours raised costs, would cause an exodus of capital and hence increase unemployment. The following day the *Herald* features a cablegram from Sir Harold Yarrow in New York on the "attitudes of labour in the US": it was "essential in the interests of shipbuilding that the hours of labour are not further reduced".[63]

The *Strike Bulletin*'s own editorials well illustrate the dialogic character of language. Day by day they speak through and challenge the language of the *Herald*:[64]

- 30 January Day 4: The strike not a failure; for a social object; unifying workers, a democratic struggle: "100,000 men are on strike in Scotland for the 40 hour week. This number grows daily... The strike is for a social aim as the forty hours week is meant to benefit all classes of workers. The 40 hours' week will prevent unemployment and maintain the Union rates of wages in all industries. It will enable men and women coming back into civil life to get jobs which will ensure a decent living... everyone who has the interests of democracy at heart must join in the struggle."

- 31 January Day 5: The employers' political economy rebutted (note the dialectic of theme and meaning – unemployment, low wages, ragged hungry): "the government and the bosses don't want unemployment abolished. Hence their opposition to the strike. Unemployment means low wages; low wages means semi-starvation for the workers and big profits for the bosses.. Remember 1908, when the workers were unemployed in large numbers. Wages fell, working hours were increased, Unions went bankrupt; men, women and children went about the streets ragged and hungry".

- 2 February Day 7: government actions illegal; "Machine Guns No Remedy: it is the government breaking the law not the strikers. We defy the government to prove one instance of illegal conduct by the strikers...we challenge them to justify lawfully their use of force against unarmed men, women and children on Friday.. The Czar's government shot down people who asked for votes in 1905 and the British government represses the people who in 1919 ask for a shorter working week".

- 10 February Day 15: "Terrorism Fails ! ..The events of the past ten days must have made it plain, even to them, whose force is based on force, that we will not be driven or terrorised into accepting industrial serfdom.. "

- 11 February Day 16: subservience won't bring jobs and investment – again the dialectic of theme and meaning: 40 hours – work and bread – unemployment – weeping children: "we fight for the 40 hours' week because it is the key that opens the door to economic security and industrial freedom... workers dread unemployment as worse than an epidemic of fever – low wages, hunger, soup kitchens, doles, evictions, fireless grates, ragged clothes, weeping children...During the war there was work and bread for all, and we want that to continue during the peace as well".

- 12 February The final day: strike has achieved industrial unity, won concessions and prepared workers for continued struggle: "If we go back to work, we do so only to change our tactics...The strike already then has burst the infamous 47 hours proposal [referring to Lord Pirrie's initiative in Belfast]. As a result of our agitation workers across the country realise that the 40 hours' week is the one practicable remedy for unemployment .. the barriers of craft have gone over in this conflict, and, henceforth we fight as workers, irrespective of trade or occupation.. nevermore will one section be used against another The knowledge we have gained will not be wasted."

The tone of the *Strike Bulletin* was invariably immediate and practical. There is no mention of socialism or a challenge to the existing social order. The strike is about how workers could retain the advance in bargaining power secured during the full employment of the war. This power had indeed transformed working class lives in a way previously unknown. Workers were able to insist on adequate wages and control the pace of work. Directly elected representatives controlled the workshops. It was the potential loss of this power that was the central focus of the Joint Committee's argument.

In adopting this line the writers of the *Strike Bulletin* clearly understood the configuration of workplace attitudes as they stood in January 1919. A significant degree of political radicalisation had occurred in 1917-18. But it was largely among younger workers. Contemporary accounts and oral history make it clear that the mass pickets at the beginning of the strike were overwhelmingly young: apprentices, the young women who had been conscripted into the munitions factories, and discharged servicemen, mostly in their twenties.[65] This division also corresponds to reports of local campaigning in the general election the month before. The defeated Unionist candidate in Govan, whose meetings had been repeatedly disrupted, complained about 'the young men' who were 'light-heartedly prepared to advocate tomorrow the revolution they had had in Russia'.[66]

But across Clydeside significant numbers of workers, possibly even a majority, voted Conservative and Unionist not Labour or Socialist. These workers would certainly strike to defend sectional gains – and did so in the opening weeks of January 1919 when they struck work against the new shift patterns. But a considerable number, possibly a majority, did not initially come out for 40 hours. For the strike to be effective it was this older generation that had to be won.

The employers were keenly aware of this. In the first week they concentrated on seeking to organise those who remained at work. 'Workers' protest resolutions against 'coercion and picketing' were printed daily in the *Herald*. There was clearly also a calculation that if the mass pickets could be cleared and electrical power restored the strike would quickly collapse. What is remarkable is that it did not. On the Monday of the second week, although the military patrolled the streets, there was no return and the strike continued into the third week – a fact that is even more remarkable when it is remembered that for the majority of workers there was no strike pay. What the employers and the government failed to foresee was the wider symbolism of military occupation. It destroyed the substance of their strongest argument. The opponents of the strike were no longer principally seen as defending collective bargaining and trade union principles operating through 'official' channels. Instead, as the *Strike Bulletin* put it, the opponents of the strike were visibly attempting to terrorise workers into 'industrial serfdom'. As such they were directly attacking the workshop power that all workers, young and old, wanted to defend.

The final issue of the *Strike Bulletin* on 12 February indicates a belief that a turning point had been reached and a considerable degree of class unity achieved. Was this simply bravado ?

It is noteworthy that in the second and third weeks the employers and press sought to revive more traditional sources of working class division. These initiatives appear to have met with little success. Stories were carried that stressed the Jewish origin of Bolshevism and linked this to Shinwell, 'a Jew by race' (before the war anti-Semitism had been fairly prevalent in face of the large Jewish refugee population in the Gorbals). On 7 February the Cabinet was actively canvassed on the propaganda benefits of highlighting the "alien threat"[67] Equally with anti-Irish sectarianism. In the second week of the strike a loyalist meeting calling on workers to return was held in the Protestant area of Whiteinch attended by the Rev David Ness, Grand Master of the Orange Order.[68] Another attempt was made in Govan but this was over-run by strikers.[69] The pro-war Women's Party of Christabel Pankhurst was also mobilised – undoubtedly in response to the thousands of women who had turned out as pickets in face of military occupation. Editorials in the press called on women to make their men 'see sense' alongside a well-publicised delegation to the STUC 'headed by Mrs Flora Drummond of the Women's Party'.[70] She was quickly shown the door.

Yet none of this seems to have been very effective. Good evidence of the new dimensions of working class unity is provided by the local election results for November 1919. Of the ten contested seats Labour won seven, most by leading strikers – five of them net gains. Shinwell, just released from prison, achieved 62 per cent of the vote in Fairfield Ward. Labour won the largely Protestant ward of Ibrox for the first time. The victory jingle ran (referring to the Protestant and Catholic football teams):

> When the Rangers beat the Celtic
> Or the Celtic beat the blues
> We argue and we fight about the game
> But we always can unite
> When Labour's in the fight
> For we know our opponents are the same.[71]

An even more revealing contest took place in Govan Central. There James Docherty contested the seat against a sitting Labour councillor, James Whitehead, a former trade union official who had opposed the strike and who had spoken out against it at the April 1919 Congress of the STUC. Docherty won 64 per cent of the vote. He was backed by the Govan Labour Party, the United Irish Societies of Govan and by another of the sitting Labour councillors, Patrick Dollan, an editor of the *Strike Bulletin*. Whitehead's meetings were described as being disrupted by 'large numbers of young men'.[72]

These results would therefore seem to indicate some level of mass identification with the strike's leaders and a parallel hostility to those who opposed it. They also reveal a conscious attempt to cement class unity in face of historic divisions, particularly those between Catholic and Protestant.[73]

However, the main evidence for a turning-point comes from the more private and candid observations of the employers and their political representatives. In the Cabinet meeting of 4 February Bonar Law stressed the key importance of official trade union structures as "the only thing that stands between us and anarchy". Sir Robert Horne's comment was that "the government cannot hope to win through present and future labour battles unless they have the support of the trade union executives".[74] The repeated stress on the need for propaganda is equally telling. At the meeting of the Glasgow Unionist Association at the end of January Sir Charles Cleland lamented the "universal unrest" and the "ceaseless propaganda being carried on in their midst" while the Unionist MP John Macleod argued the urgency for themselves to create "a system of propaganda".[75] The same theme is repeated in the Intelligence Report from Scottish Command three weeks after the end of the strike: "there is no doubt that a great number of workman are very much unsettled and the greatest importance is attached to proper counter propaganda". [76]

It is the character of the propaganda ultimately adopted that also tells us a great deal about how the threat was perceived. On 13 August 1919 Sir Robert Horne, Minister of Labour, convened at 12 Downing Street, official residence of Bonar Law, "a representative meeting of leading members of the principal banking, industrial and commercial interests of the country" to consider the "urgent need for counter propaganda". The Glasgow industrialist Lord Weir, former air minister, was among those attending and subsequently expressed his serious concern in a letter to Horne.[77] The meeting had been run by the government whips, Lord Talbot and Sir Frederick Guest, who proposed that they, on behalf of the government, should run a propaganda service financed by those attending. Weir felt this to be "profoundly dangerous". Any system must appear quite independent and should dovetail with the system already being developed "by the Engineering Employers Federation, the British Commonwealth Union, the Alliance of Employers and Employed and another Union. The two latter, containing Trade Union interests, appears to me an excellent scheme.. Its propaganda can be almost entirely above board and be legitimately national in character". Weir also prescribed its content. It should focus on industrial economics and the need for competitive production if British workers were to be saved from unemployment and the loss of jobs to America.

It was Weir's scheme that was adopted. An independent organisation was set up named Industrial Information, secretly funded by £100,000 from the Treasury and £100,000 from private sources (the equivalent of £1 billion today), which, among other initiatives, syndicated articles to one thousand newspapers a week, designed school text books in human geography and civics and financed the publication of a range of texts from leading economists combating socialist doctrines.[78] The key requirement for all this material was that it should appear to be independent and unprompted – in line with prescription developed for wartime propaganda by "Colonel John Buchan". The economic arguments of the Left on hours, unemployment and restricted production were to be answered by liberal market economics and such economics should in turn be placed as far as possible in the mouth of the official trade union movement.

It is this focus that is probably the strongest evidence of a reorientation of attitudes on class lines. The political economy argued for by the *Strike Bulletin*, and targeted by this propaganda, combined two elements common to the four year's wartime experience of all trade unionists. The first was that full employment could be secured on the basis of manpower-based planning for war production. The second was that collective action by workers at workplace level, and across grades and trades, could in these circumstances secure major advances in conditions. While the *Strike Bulletin* made no direct reference to state ownership, this was an issue which everyone knew the government had to face later in February 1919: the permanent retention of state control of coal and rail transport and the threatened strike action by miners and railwaymen to secure it. In these circumstances the simple call for a 40 hour week involved a basic re-ordering of assumptions and one which Weir and his colleagues correctly identified as very dangerous. Sir Harold Yarrow's well publicised decision to shift investment abroad marked the first material blow in reasserting the power of market forces and giving real life meaning to the teachings of liberal economics.

Some initial comparisons and conclusions

Leontiev, as cited in our opening quotation, stressed the historically grounded character of meanings ("representations, concepts, ideas") which "dig themselves" into connections with people, into their real life circle of contacts. Choice is not between ideas in the abstract but between "colliding social positions".

So far, our comparisons have, it is hoped, identified some of these contingent and historically grounded meanings at two points, in 1919 and 1971, when workers on Clydeside successfully challenged the languages of control. The narrative has also attempted to demonstrate how, in both cases, the dialectic of theme and meaning could be actively used in an emancipatory way to transform context and hence wider significance.

In terms of comparison there would appear to be in both 1919 and 1971 striking similarities of approach and important differences of circumstantial meaning. On both occasions, for instance, a key aspect of the emancipatory challenge was to win those taking action for an understanding of the immediate practical importance of building alliances. In both cases such alliances enabled striking workers as a group to see their wider position in society in a new way. But the character of the alliances was very different – each grounded historically in distinct phases of development.

In 1971 the alliances Reid and Airlie sought to create were with strata beyond the traditional working class: professionals, management, and those traditionally associated with capital, small and medium business, shopkeepers and local services providers. The terms of this alliance highlighted the centrality of the shipyard workers as producers and hence the centrality of production, and the working class as such, for social development. In doing so it also served to fragment and detach the array of forces on which the government might otherwise have relied: the management in the yards, small businesses across Clydeside, the churches, local government and even that wing of the Conservative Party that relied on Orange working class support. The creation of this alliance also served to paralyse right-wing union leaderships and immobilise the government.

The demand mirrored what was seen as the key structural division within capital emerging through the twentieth century: that of monopolisation and, in various forms and phases, its introduction of fundamental distortions in the distribution of the capitalist surplus.

The alliances of 1919 were quite different. They were essentially intra-class alliances. They were between those who had the power to take strike action and those who did not: the unemployed, women who had previously been employed as munitions workers, demobilised servicemen and those in the home. These were alliances that took the strike beyond the defence of sectional 'rights', the meal break that was the focus of the strikes at the beginning of January, to an understanding of the political economy that determined class power.

The final issue of the *Strike Bulletin* put this very clearly: "the barriers of craft have gone over in this conflict, and, henceforth we fight as workers, irrespective of trade or occupation.. nevermore will one section be used against another ... The strike has taught us our power". The stress from the first day on the role of the locality committees was, it would seem, with the intent of building a unity between different workplaces, between employed and unemployed and between home and the industrial struggle. It was at this level that the mass pickets were organised. This was also the locus for organising the withholding of rent and rates and, over the weekend of 31 January to 2 February, the introduction of patrols to prevent looting. The widespread presence of women on the picket lines on 3 February, the Monday after military occupation, was particularly significant. Described by as thousands strong in each major locality, and mobilised by the locality committees, they stabilised the strike at a critical point – when men would have been subject to military arrest.

The Glasgow *Strike Bulletin* also held up as a model the locality committees in Belfast where the strike started the previous week. It describes these committees as organising food distribution and emergency services, running the dance halls and cinemas and closing down newspapers that printed anti-strike propaganda.[79]

Conversely in 1919, and in contrast to 1971, the grip of large-scale industrial capital over regional institutions and subordinate sections of capital remained monolithic. The Lithgows, Weirs, Yarrows and Beardmores were to be obeyed – whether by newspaper editors, civic authorities or church leaders. In extremis, the 'Civic Guard' was to represent this power in uniform. Their concern at this point was not with the loyalty of managers and foremen. It was, on the contrary, to prevent the consolidation of this new intra-class alliance within the working class. Their key interventions were designed to halt this process and drive wedges between older workers and radicalised younger sections of the workforce, between the strikers and soldiers (the government's package of measures announced on 12 February and the proposed declaration by employers as discussed on 31 January), between men and women and between Protestants and Catholics.

To this extent the wider ideological challenge of 1971 was more "advanced" than that of 1919. The symbolism of the work-in was that it was now the working class that represented and carried forward the productive potential of society. Local capital had bankrupted it. Financial capital concentrated in London was parasitic. A new form of democracy was required – in Scotland a Scottish Assembly or Parliament – that would have the powers by which people would directly rebuild the economy. These were the ideas that by the time of the first Scottish Assembly in January-February 1972 had gained a significant wider support and to that extent had become a material force. Reid's Rectorial Address on Alienation, delivered after his election as Rector of Glasgow University later in 1972, sought to further deepen this critique of capitalism in a way that would, for the stewards, have been actively counterproductive and dangerous a year before.[80]

The ideas that eventually secured a mass base in 1919 were about a more limited exercise of class power. For the majority of workers these ideas were essentially about the class power within a capitalist society. A significant minority did indeed want to go beyond this. Socialism was posed. But the critical ideological battle ground for the years after 1919 was about how the more limited concept of class power and class unity was to develop. Weir and Lithgow, and the politicians they supported like Bonar Law and Horne, were quite clear that the only hope was to work through the structures of the trade union movement. They had to re-win this territory for the concept of a market managed through a (subordinate) partnership of labour with capital.

The plasticity of meanings that marks these ideological battles can be seen in the changing use of the term "democracy". Up to 1918-1919 'democracy' was a demand associated with socialist politics: it carried the assumption that full universal suffrage could and would be used by organised labour to transform the economy. As we saw, the STUC described Britain's military intervention in Russia in September 1918 as a 'challenge to democracy and socialism'. The following month the Labour Party's election manifesto, demanded immediate withdrawal from Russia under the slogan "Hands off Democracy" and "no intervention against democracy in Europe". Conversely, the Conservative objection to a full universal suffrage had until very recently been precisely this: that democracy would lead to socialism.

In December 1918 the suffrage was indeed extended – but it was not by any means fully democratic. It still kept a property-franchise (both Bonar Law and Horne owed their elections in central Glasgow constituencies to votes exercised from offices owned by businessmen and lawyers living elsewhere) and excluded the radicalised generation of younger women who had been conscripted into industry. Any use of the term 'democracy' by government supporters was at this stage very tentative. At the annual general meeting of the Glasgow Unionist Association (the Conservative Party) on 27 January Lord Glenarthur tried it out as follows:

> under a constitution such as ours, with a widely extended franchise, the majority of the People could have their views carried out by constitutional and peaceful means... anyone who advocated resort to other means could be no true democrat, however he may pose".

Three days later the *Herald* carried this as a headline "A challenge to democracy". But on the basis of a "widely extended franchise" this line held too many hostages to fortune and was not repeated. For their part the Joint Strike Committee still continued to associate democracy with the organised class power of working people: "everyone who has the interests of democracy at heart should join the struggle".

On the other hand, by 1971 "democracy" had been significantly redefined and partially stabilised on capitalist terms – effectively as set out by Hayek in 1944. This was that democracy was only genuine and viable if it retained and did not limit the operation of the market. In fact, the very existence of the capitalist market now became the litmus test for Western democracy as defined by Robert Dahl in 1971.[81] It was in this form that Heath sought to use the term in his 1974 election appeal: who governs Britain – democratically elected leaders or trade union activists who threaten political and market freedoms?

While the failure of Heath's appeal in the 1974 election was not necessarily linked to his use of the term democracy, it is important to note that one key element of the challenge posed by the UCS shop stewards in 1971-72 was indeed an implicit critique. Democracy, they argued, had to be extended and deepened. Its existing form was remote from working people and gave dominance to "the faceless men" in Whitehall, implicitly the power of big business. New institutions were needed that could embody the will of working people. At the first Scottish Assembly in January 1972 the General Secretary of the STUC, Jimmy Jack, set out the case for Scottish Parliament on the grounds that it would be a 'workers' parliament' and would act in the collective interests of working people. It was a redefinition that formed a powerful component of the subsequent "class" inflection of Scottishness.

There is one final area of comparison. It concerns the response of the ruling class, for want of a better term, to the setbacks of 1919 and 1971.

In both 1919 and 1971 it can credibly be claimed that history "turned". In October 1971 and also in February 1919 the fear of working class revolt, centred on Clydeside, caused governments to change policies in ways that had fateful consequences for themselves and the strategies they embodied. In 1919 the government had to abandon its plans for a near immediate return to gold payments. The decision to embark on a massive programme of government spending on housing and welfare, and paying for it on the wartime basis of printing of paper money, created an inflationary boom that fatally pushed the pound out of alignment with the dollar. As we will see later, the subsequent ill-fated attempts to retrieve this ground, and reassert the banking primacy for the City of London, saw Lloyd George deposed. In turn the Conservatives sought, first under Bonar Law and then under Baldwin, a ruling partnership with a re-educated Labour Party – one committed to constitutional methods.

The response after 1971 was if anything even more revealing. The immediate reaction of the Heath government was to rebuild tripartite corporate structures between government, business and the unions and to pump money back into the regions. The political impact on the trade union movement and the Labour Party was, at least temporarily, to see a sharp swing to the Left in terms of policy. The programme adopted in summer 1973 called for the famous 'irreversible shift' of wealth and power in favour working people and included the nationalisation of docks, shipbuilding, aerospace and energy, the public control of the top 25 companies, mandatory planning and investment agreements with the rest and, for the first time, power for trade union representatives to call a direct halt to unsafe production procedures. This programme won two general elections in 1974 but was only very partially implemented. Meantime the accompanying 'Social Contract' between government and unions on wage control was used to demobilise the shop stewards movement. The previous motive force for advance now lost its power to mobilise.

The longer-term response was far more fundamental. Under the label "Thatcherism" its general characteristics are well known. It sought to strike directly at the material bases of working class power. But it also had one additional element that should not be forgotten. This was the stress laid on also creating a new social base to implement these policies. Managers, company directors, academics, establishment journalists and key sections of the Conservative Party now had to be won away from a corporate mindset of social democratic partnership.[82] These old assumptions, basically those of 1919, had become ideological barriers and, it was argued, their political weaknesses fully exposed in 1971-2. A new world view was required to give coherence and direction to the subordinate social strata whose work was essential to creating an environment in which the market for labour, though nothing else, was once more to be made fully free and unfettered.

Some interim conclusions on method

One key objective in this study has been to demonstrate the relevance of the Volosinov/Vygotsky/Leontiev approach to the understanding of changes in social consciousness.

Its central contention is that the dialogic character of language opens it to an understanding of how meanings can be changed. The inter-relationship of distinct class-inflected discourses in circumstances of real social conflict, the day by day testing of these 'meanings' in contest with one another, how specific contexts can be used to transform meaning, provides a powerful basis for identifying key turning points and their material origins. As we have seen, this dialogue need not be face to face. In 1919 and 1971 it rarely was. But, in seeking to address and influence the same constituencies, the two conflicting class positions had to speak through, acknowledge and refute the other at the same time as trying to transform and reorder the 'received meanings' which had 'dug' themselves into the consciousness of these social groups. Success depended on knowing these constituencies and their received meanings and the precise level of their development. It also depended on the ability to exploit changes in material circumstance on a day to day basis.

At the same time this approach sees a critical difference between the types of language used on the two sides of this class-inflected dialogue. One will be 'emancipatory; the other not. One will seek to penetrate to the heart of an exploitative social order – even though it may not do so explicitly. The other will seek to reinforce and manipulate the sectional identities by which different groups accommodate themselves to this exploitative order.

Historically it is quite rare for those who have the ability to deploy such emancipatory language to secure a platform from which to do so on a mass scale. 1919 and 1971 are therefore exceptional moments. On both occasions a key concern of those in authority was to minimise the influence of such language and, if possible, to remove those using it altogether. Yet, though rare, such moments, when they do occur, are both deeply revealing and historically of determining importance. Meanings do shift. While the existing order may indeed succeed in re-imposing itself, it will be on the basis of subtly changed dispensations and altered understandings. These new identities and understandings may well become quite as 'non-emancipatory' and sectional as previous received meanings but they will be different and usually materially more demanding.

Both in 1919 and 1971 the circumstances in which challenges become possible occurred when these existing dispensations were under immediate or threatened attack. In 1919 it was the workshop power that had been secured through wartime full employment. In 1971 it was the issue of full employment, the right to work and the attack on the post-1945 model of partially socialised capitalist production.

The particular strength of the methodology used here is that it enables us to identify key turning points in these processes and their material contexts. In 1919 it might have been assumed, given the revolutionary events taking place over previous weeks and months in Russia and Germany, that it was this international stimulus that sparked the challenge on Clydeside. But for the majority of workers it was not. The perceived challenge was to workshop control. The leaders of the Joint Strike Committee were quite clear that the task in hand was to win a much more limited but nonetheless fundamental level of class consciousness: to move from sectional collectivism to that of a class collectivism that united employed and unemployed, men and women, home and workplace and did so around an understanding of political economy that sought in the first instance to limit the capitalist market. In 1971 the shop stewards, and their allies outside the yard, attempted a more profound reordering of meanings involving democracy, alienation and the role of the working class in carrying forward society's productive potential. In both cases these new meanings did at least for a period embed themselves in 'real circles of contact'

We will now go forward to test these more general findings by looking at the parallel general strike in Belfast in 1919 and its aftermath in 1920, at the how the Councils of Action in August-September 1920 directly challenged government and how far the lessons learned were, or were not, carried forward to the 1926 general strike. We will end our case studies with the General Strike of 1842, an episode of working class mobilisation that, as we noted earlier, critically influenced the thinking of Marx and Engels on the character and social role of working-class struggle.

NOTES

1   For the general background see C Wrigley, 'The State and
the Challenge of Labour in Britain 1917-1920' in C. Wrigley,
ed., *Challenges of Labour: Central and Western Europe 1917-1920*
(London,1993).

2   The evolution of post-war economic policy is examined in J. Foster
"What Kind of Crisis ? What Kind of Ruling Class ?", in J. McIlroy
et al. (eds), *Industrial Politics and the 1926 Mining Lock-Out* (Cardiff,
2004) pp. 15-44.

3   *Glasgow Herald* 13 December 1918, p. 7.

4   GH 21 January 1919 for the report of the National Conference of
Shipbuilding and Engineering Trades in Manchester, 24 December
ballot result and GH 25 December 1918 for a report of the joint
meeting of the trades federation and employers.

5   NA CAB 24/71 GT 6427 Memorandum from Sir T Munro 1
December 1918.

6   NA MUN 2/28 Labour Report week ending 29 December 1917
on rank and file repudiation of trade union officials; MUN 5/151
(300/61) memorandum from Sir Stephenson Kent and Humbert
Wolfe 4 October 1918 on how to remedy the loss of authority by
trade union officials.

7   Glasgow University Business Archives DC 96/3/5 Weir to Askwith
7 November 1919 is one example among many. One of Weir's
subsequent campaigns against trade union influence is examined by
Kevin Morgan, 'Cutting the feet from under organised labour? Lord
Weir, mass production and the building trades in the 1920s', *Scottish
Labour History*, Vol. 43, 2008, pp. 47-68.

8   *Glasgow Herald* 21 January 1919, p.4.

9   The fullest and most reliable treatment is still provided by James
Hinton, *The First Shop Stewards Movement* (London, 1973). Iain
McLean's *The Legend of the Red Clyde* (Edinburgh, 1981) is seriously
handicapped by its failure to review the full scope of evidence
on industrial militancy during and immediately after the war as
demonstrated by Joseph Melling, "Whatever Happened to the Red
Clyde ?", IRSH 40, 1991,pp.2-32 and John Foster, "Strike Action and
Working Class Politics on Clydeside", *IRSH*, 40, 1991, 33-70.

10   J. Smyth Labour in *Glasgow 1896-1936: socialism, suffrage, sectarianism*,
a Scottish Historical Society Monograph (Edinburgh,1998) provides
an excellent introduction to local politics.

11   Glasgow Mitchell Library MS Minutes of Glasgow Trades Council,
meeting 17 December 1918 reported 224 affiliated trade union
branches with a membership of 65,774.

12   Angela Tuckett, *The Scottish Trades Union Congress, 1897-1977*

(Edinburgh, 1986).

13   Glasgow Caledonian University Special Collections, Parliamentary Committee of the Scottish Trades Union Congress Minute Book 1914-1920: 6 July 1918, 14 September 1918, 6 November 1918 and 30 November 1918.

14   Wrigley, "The State and the Challenge of Labour" provides background: CAB 23/9 Cabinet minute for 8 January 1919, p. 5, provides details of army unrest.

15   Diary microfilm 1919 Imperial War Museum 2040 73/1/1-9, entries for 3-4 January (mutiny at Folkestone; anger at officers negotiating with men); 6 Jan 'the whole army will turn into a rabble' unless action taken; 10 January: Churchill demands urgent recall of 'all reliable troops' specifying Household and other Cavalry regiments and Home County Rifles.

16   NA CAB 23/9 8 January 1919.

17   NA CAB 24/74 GT 6744 Demobilisation Report for 30 January.

18   This danger was also very much in the minds of the War Cabinet: memo from L. Stone, War Cabinet secretariat, to J.C.C. Davidson, Private Secretary to Bonar Law, 9 January 1919 Parliamentary Archives (PA) DAV/ 89 and also discussion at Interdepartmental Committee on the Pay of the Army of Occupation, 25 January 1919, PA DAV/91.

19   *The Call* 21 February 1918 (letter from W. Caven) and *The Call* 8 August 1918.

20   *Glasgow Herald* 2 December p.4.

21   *The Call* (BSP weekly) Marx Memorial Library , London; *The Socialist* for 1919 Mitchell Library, Glasgow.

22   GH 6 January p. 8 for a report of the meeting; *The Worker*, organ of the Clyde Workers Committee, issue for December reprints materials from *The Socialist,* signed by Arthur McManus, on the establishment of workplace committees and an agenda for industrial democracy: GU Business Archives Highton Collection UGD 102/1/4.

23   GH 6 January 1919, p.8 and 8 January 1919, p.12.

24   GH 9 January 1919, p. 8 and 11 January, p. 6 for position of Trades Council.

25   Minutes of STUC Parliamentary Committee 18 January 1919 and 22 January 1919.

26   Reproduced from Glasgow Trades and Labour Council Annual Report 1918-1919, p. 8 (GCU Special Collections).

27   *The Call*, 23 January 1919 and 30 January 1919; CAB 24/74 GT 6713 'Report on Revolutionary Organisations 28 January 1919' provides further detail on Maclean's speeches in Lancashire.

28   NA CAB 24/74 p. 48 'Report on Revolutionary Organisations: 28

January'.

29 NA CAB 24/74 p. 1 and 2 report from the Minister of Labour Robert Horne dated 29 January but probably based on information up to 28 January: "stoppage of many thousands of workpeople of various trades, principally shipyard workers and engineers, on the Clyde and Forth of Firth and in Edinburgh". Belfast was "at a standstill". Unofficial strikes had brought out ship repair workers in Bristol and on the Thames (12,000). Unofficial strikes have taken place among coal miners in Fife, West Lothian and parts of South Wales although officials were calling for a return to work.

30 D.S. Morton (Joint Secretary of the Strike Committee), *The Forty Hours Strike: An historic Survey of Scotland's First General Strike*, Clydebank Branch SLP, 1919, p.7 (I am grateful to Robert Laurie, Treasurer of the Scottish Labour History Society, for a copy of this pamphlet).

31 Morton, p. 6 and 7.

32 GH 27 January 1919, p.8 and 28 January 1919, p. 5 and 6.

33 NA CAB 23/9 28 January 1919.

34 On Tuesday 28 January Bonar Law telephoned Lloyd George in Paris to say the King was 'in a funk about the labour situation' and was demanding Lloyd George's immediate return in case of "revolution". At this stage Bonar Law remained optimistic that the strike would soon crumble: transcript of message PA LG/F/30/3/9.

35 GH 30 January pp. 4, 5 and 6.

36 GH 31 January p. 7; *Strike Bulletin* 30 January p.1. The size of the demonstration and the cessation of work at the power station seems to have transformed Bonar Law's attitude to the danger. He phoned Lloyd George in Paris three times on 29 January. Lloyd George agreed the situation was now 'very serious' and reported he had had discussions with J. H Thomas: telephone transcripts PA LG/F/30/3/11, 13 and 15; PA BL/96/926.

37 Joint Meeting of the Executive Committee of Engineers and Shipbuilders Association 30 January 1919 Archives, Mitchell Library, Glasgow TD 241/1/18 (the minutes are at the back of the regular minute book of the Shipbuilding Employers Association).

38 NA 23/9 30 January 1919.

39 GH 31 January 1919, p. 6.

40 Joint Meeting of the Executive Committee of Engineers and Shipbuilders Association 31 January 191 Archives, Mitchell Library, Glasgow TD 241/1/18.

41 William Gallacher, *Revolt on the Clyde* (London, 1936). Gallacher's 1936 account generally tallies with his comments in *The Worker* 20 March 1920 and at his trial as cited by John McKay. "William Gallacher 1881-1965", unpublished MS GCU Special Collections.

Gallacher was intent on avoiding further violence and not giving the government a pretext for military intervention.

42   GH 1 February 1919, p.5.

43   STUC Annual Report 1918-19, p. 46.

44   Minute Book STUC Parliamentary Committee, 5 February 1919. Henry Patterson, *Class Conflict and Sectarianism* (Belfast, 1980), Chapter 5, pp. 92-114,

45   *Evening Times*, 3 February 1919, p. 1.

46   GH 4 February, p. 5.

47   Minute Book STUC Parliamentary Committee 8 February assessed situation across Britain as 'now very unsatisfactory' and appointed two delegates to the Joint Strike Committee to consider further steps. Horne's Labour report for 12 February 1919 runs: 'The Joint Committee of the Clyde Strike instructed the workers to resume on Wednesday, 12 February [...] The strike is said to be only postponed until it can be reconvened on a national basis': NA CAB 74/24 f.396.

48   TD 241/1/18 Minutes of Clyde Shipbuilders Association 14 February saw proposals from Beardmores for wholesale sackings of shop stewards rejected as provocative; Minutes of 13 and 25 March show reports of workers repudiating official instructions from the Boilermakers union and saying they accepted instructions only from their shop stewards.

49   NA CAB 74/24 f.394.

50   Susan Howson, 'Slump and Unemployment', *The Economic History of Britain since 1870*, ed., Roderick Floud and Donald McClosky, Cambridge 1981 pp. 265-285 cites the debates of February 1919 as a turning point in policy pp. 274-5 (NA CAB 24/75 GT 6880).

51   PA LG/F/30/3/26 telephone transcript 6 February 1919. Further discussion took place on 10 February 1919: Tom Jones, *Whitehall Diary* (Oxford, 1969) I, p. 78.

52   GH, 12 February 1919, p. 7

53   Tom Jones, Whitehall Diary 1, p. 80, 27 February 1919.

54   *Strike Bulletin* 31 January, p.2.

55   *Strike Bulletin* 8 February p.2 and 9 February, p 2.

56   Morton, *The Forty Hours Strike*, p. 8.

57   GH 3 February 1919.

58   GH 5 February, p. 5.

59   TD 241/1/18 14 February 1919.

60   GH 6 February, p. 4.

61   GH 6 February, p. 5.

62   GH 10 February p. 5.

63   GH 4, 6 and 10 February.

64   Glasgow University Business Records Highton Collection UGD 102/1/6-17.

65 The oral history evidence is cited in J. Foster, 'Strike Action and Working Class Politics on Clydeside 1914-19' *International Review of Social History* 1990, Vol. 35, 1, pp.33-70.

66 *Govan Press* 6 December 1918.

67 GH 3 February p.6.; NA CAB 23/9, 7 February 1919, saw the Minister for Reconstruction, Aukland Geddes, reminding colleagues that 'during the elections the country was very excited on the subject of aliens' and the need, in prosecutions for sedition, to draw a strong distinction between aliens and non-aliens – with the death sentences reserved for aliens.

68 GH 5 February 1919, p. 8.

69 GH 3 February p. 6.; *Govan Press* 7 February 1919.

70 Correspondence between Cristobel Pankhurst and Bonar Law 7 February 1919 PA BL/96/10/1 enclosing an article in the *Daily Sketch* 7 February 1919. The STUC declined to meet Mrs. Drummond's deputation of the grounds that the Women's Party was 'distinctly hostile' to the trade union movement: GCU Special Collections, Minutes of STUC Parliamentary Committee, 5 and 8 February 1919; *Govan Press* editorial 31 January 1919: 'Appeal to Women: Are your children hungry?'. By contrast, Cristobel's sister Sylvia Pankhurst led the solidarity movement in London organizing the 'Hands off Glasgow' rally in the Albert Hall on 9 February.

71 *Govan Press* 7 November 1919.

72 *Govan Press* 25 October 1919.

73 Iain McLean, *Legend*, neglects the November 1919 election results in favour of those in 1920 and 1922. The 1919 results would, however, seem to run directly counter to his contention that the January 1919 strike was a last gasp attempt by privileged skilled workers to defend their positions against non-skilled (mainly Irish) and female workers and that a mass Labour vote only developed after 1919 as Wheatley adopted policies for slum clearance that could bridge the gulf between a trade union identified Labour Party and the Irish. The 1919 election results, as well all our current knowledge of the 1919 strike, would seem to indicate the exact opposite. It was the older generation of skilled workers who were, initially at least, most reluctant to strike. While McLean largely ignores the November 1919 results, he does focus on Labour's failure to win the two earlier by-elections in June 1919, one in a largely middle class area not previously contested, and attributes this to the 'debacles' of the 1919 strike and the 1918 general election. In fact the unsuccessful candidate in largely middle class Jordanhill claimed his 36 per cent of the vote would have been higher had it not been for 'the strong inclination among the workers towards industrial action as they were beginning to despair of politics' (Forward 14 June 1919).

74   NA CAB 23/9/44 War Cabinet 4 February 1919.

75   GH 28 January p. 6.

76   NA Air 1 553 16/15/41 Intelligence Report 4-10 March 1919.

77   GUBA DC 96/3/4 Weir to Sir Robert Horne 14 August 1919; Edmund Talbot and Frederick Guest to Weir 16 August 1919; Talbot and Guest to Weir 23 September 1919.

78   Sidney Walton to Arthur Steel Maitland (at the time Minister of Labour) 17 June 1926 in which Walton, previously Director of Industrial Information, details the activities of the organization (Scottish Record Office GD 193/109/5).

79   *Strike Bulletin* 31 January and 5 February. The concept is very close to the model of "workers' committees" put forward as the new political model for workers democracy in *The Socialist* in January 1919. However, although the *Strike Bulletin* and *The Socialist* were both printed on the SLP printing press, and in part written by the same people, no explicit connection is made.

80   Jimmy Reid, Alienation: Rectorial Address delivered in the University of Glasgow on Friday 28th April 1972 (Glasgow, 1972). At Reid's funeral in July 2010 Scotland's First Minister Alex Salmond announced that the lecture would be distributed to all Scottish schools.

81   F. von Hayek, *The Road to Serfdom*, (London 1944), esp. chapter 7; Robert Dahl, *Polyarchy: Participation and Opposition* (New Haven MA, 1971).

82   Interview with Keith Joseph in *The Director* January 1981. The Institute of Directors saw itself as undertaking an propagandist role in industry on behalf of the Institute of Economic Affairs in opposition to the CBI and the Economist through the late 1970s. The *Daily Telegraph* and *The Spectator* took up similar positions to Joseph from 1976: Richard Cockett, *Thinking the Unthinkable: Think Tanks and Economic Counter Revolution 1931-1983* (London, 1994).

THIS PAGE LEFT INTENTIONALLY BLANK

3

The Belfast General Strike of 1919

> The thin clothing and pale faces of honest Protestant workers
> are still in evidence in Belfast. Let us hope that ere long they
> will be marching again to storm the capitalist system which
> has for so long imprisoned not only the bodies but also the
> souls of their class.
> James Connolly, 1915[1]

onnolly was referring back to the manifesto of the Hearts of Steel in 1772 – Protestant tenant farmers and linen weavers who had marched into Belfast to release comrades jailed for refusing to pay rent to their Protestant landlords. Over the following two decades many of the same men went on, as United Irishmen, to form an alliance with Catholic labourers and to raise an army that, with some initial success, challenged British military control over the North in 1798.

James Connolly himself worked in Belfast between 1911 and 1913 as a trade union organiser – in a period which had seen Catholic and Protestant workers temporarily uniting in the docks in 1907 but also subsequently dividing in sectarian conflict both in 1907 and, more violently, in the shipyards in 1912. Notably Connolly refers to the capitalist system imprisoning 'not only bodies' but also 'the souls of their class'. Probably of all Marxist theorists of his time, Connolly was, as a practical political and trade union organiser, most aware of the street-level dialectics of language – of what Leontiev later described as the dialectic of sense and meaning: of the need to tear apart the generalised but vague and non-concrete sense of words and expose actual meanings in terms of all the contradictions and conflicts of life within capitalism.[2] Working as a trade-union organiser in Belfast up till 1913, Connolly appears to have left behind a generation of trade union pupils, Protestants as well as Catholics, some of whom, like Sam Kyle of the Iron moulders, were to play a leading role in the general strike of 1919 and in the Irish trade union movement thereafter. They included, to a greater or less degree, James Freeland of the Engineers, Charles MacKay, in 1919 local President of the National Engineering and Shipbuilding Federation, and William McMullen of the Irish Transport and General Union and Charles Lockett of the National Amalgamated Union of Labour (NAUL). Of the three branches of the Independent Labour Party (later Belfast Labour Party), the East, dominated by the shipyards, took a pro-Connolly position of support for Irish (socialist) independence as, largely, did the Central Branch backing Home Rule. The North branch was controlled by the supporters of William Walker, strong trade unionists and supporters of the Union and, as they saw it, the wider unity of the Labour movement.[3]

The Industrial and Political Background

In 1919 Belfast's industry displayed many of the same characteristics as that on the Clyde. During the war employment had massively increased. The labour force of Belfast's two big shipyards, Harland and Wolff and Workman, Clark, had expanded to well over 25,000.[4] 10,000 other workers were employed in ancillary engineering works, 'the town shops', mainly located in central/east Belfast or in the west. Belfast's textile industry also expanded. Geographically it was based in the west, almost all in linens, and employed around 20,000 mainly female workers, often from the families of those whose male members worked as labourers and semi-skilled workers in heavy industry. Many of the new workers were from elsewhere in Ireland, mainly it seems from within rural Ulster. Especially among the labourers and semi-skilled trades there were a significant number of Catholics.

Wartime full employment brought, as elsewhere, a sharp rise in unionisation. In the shipyards there were major British unions, such as the Boilermakers, Shipwrights, Engineers and the Electrical Trades Union (ETU), many smaller craft and local unions and a number of large general workers unions, the National Union of Amalgamated Labour (NAUL), the Irish Transport Workers Union, the Workers Union and some unions within the Transport Federation. All were combined in trade union terms within the Federation of Engineering and Shipbuilding Trades (FEST) – as were the workers in the smaller 'town shops'. It was the Federation that provided leadership for the general strike of January-February 1919.

The strike's wider political background, in terms of specifically Irish politics, was potentially very damaging to any attempt to maintain class unity across a divided workforce. The 1916 Easter Rising had taken place less than three years before with Connolly himself playing a leading role. In Belfast, just two weeks before the 1916 Rising, there had been widespread sectarian rioting when Protestant Unionists, at least some from the shipyards, broke up an anti-conscription rally at the traditional open air meeting point, the Custom House Quay, in central Belfast.[5] These years also saw Edward Carson, along with other Ulster politicians who had initiated the Ulster Covenant of 1912, seeking to maintain a mass base for the military defence of Ulster. They were pledged, should the British government seek to implement the legislation for Home Rule, to organise armed resistance to protect Ulster. Military units of the Ulster Volunteer Force, well-armed as a result of the gun running of 1914, existed across the North officered by the Unionist gentry, professionals and businessmen and a rank and file mainly drawn from the Orange Order. While war depleted the ranks of this organisation, the UVF maintained a very significant underground presence.

The December 1918 general election had brought the issue of both Home Rule and independence back onto the immediate agenda. Sinn Fein won the overwhelming majority of seats across the three southern provinces and scored advances in parts of south and west Ulster where there were significant Catholic populations. Elsewhere Unionist dominance continued, at least on the surface, relatively solid. In Belfast Unionist representation included, at the insistence of Edward Carson, four MPs badged as Unionist Labour. In face of these results the Ulster Unionist leadership had, using its block of Westminster MPs entered discussions in January 1919 with the empire supremacists within the Lloyd George cabinet, Bonar Law, Birkenhead and Milner, about how, if it came to it, action could be taken to preserve a 'British' state in the North.[6]

It was in these apparently unpromising circumstances that the leadership of the Federation of Shipbuilding and Engineering Workers in Belfast initiated their campaign for a 44-hour week. Discussions with local employers, mainly it seems the managers of the two big shipyards, had begun in August 1918 but were shelved as war continued.[7] The main movers were leading trade unionists in the Harland and Wolff yard, James Baird and James Freeland. Two further discussions took place in the autumn of 1918 prior to the Confederation of Shipbuilding and Engineering Unions at British level negotiating its proposal for a 47-hour week with the employers. This was put to the ballot in December 1918. As on the Clyde, a significant majority was registered against 47 hours – with Edward Carson having equivocated on the issue in the Ulster Hall meeting prior to the General Election. After the election the local Federation then pressed ahead with negotiations to secure 44 hours. A further ballot was held and the result declared on 14 January. The arguments were very similar to those used on the Clyde. '44 Hours means no Unemployment'; '44 hours means work for demobilised soldiers'. 20,225 voted for strike action and 558 against. The demand was lodged on 16 January – with the notification of a strike to begin on Saturday 25 January.[8] The employers failed to respond, claiming lack of time. The strike commenced on the Saturday and continued for almost four weeks till 19 February, considerably longer than that on the Clyde.

On the first day, on 25 January. Belfast's gas and electricity works were taken over. Transport, in terms of trams, ceased to operate. So did all those workplaces and services, such as the big department stores and some of the newspapers which were dependent on electricity, gas and coal supplies for their operation.

Subsequent assessments of the strike have varied significantly. Probably a majority portray it as primarily economistic, focused on limited objectives relating to conditions of work, significantly more restricted in its wider social objectives than the Clyde, led by the predominantly Protestant/Unionist elite of skilled workers and maintaining close relationships with the City authorities and with the Royal Irish Constabulary. Its organisers, it is argued, kept their distance from the more radical movement on the Clyde, as well as subsequent developments across England. Organisationally, its base within the Federation rather than the more radical and widely-based Belfast Trades Council reflected this moderate and Orange-tinted orientation. Hence, it is argued, its ability to continue so long without military intervention.[9]

The interpretation here is different. It follows that of Fearghal Mac Bhloscaigh and a number of others including those who wrote much closer to the time such as J. D. Clarkson.[10] It is that the strike leadership did consciously seek cross-sectarian class unity, that its leading committee included Catholics as well as Protestants (Charles McKay, the Federation Chair, was, among other leaders, a Catholic) and that the general unions, NAUL and the Workers Union, played a central role in the Federation and in the cohesion of the strike. It will argue that its leaders set their arguments very much in the fashion of Connolly – seeking to highlight class contradictions, requiring unity in action, and actively exposing the divisive role of sectarian stereotyping. It will also argue, and this is the relevance of this episode for our wider exploration, that the Belfast strike of 1919 is an example of a rapid change in consciousness and that, like the Clyde, this was most marked among younger workers. It examines the evidence that this new mass consciousness continued, was manifested in Belfast's 1919 May Day demonstration and even more remarkably in the January 1920 municipal elections. In consequence, it had a very significant impact on the tactics adopted by the British government and by the Unionist elite over following months.

The Strike

The strike began at midday on Saturday 25 January as workers left the shipyards and engineering works. The power stations for gas and electricity were occupied and supplies turned off – though with some supply maintained for hospitals and for the Post Office which was used by workers' families to receive pensions and other financial subventions. Thereafter the streets were in darkness and trams stopped. At midday on the Saturday the first edition of a professionally printed four-page *Strike Bulletin* had appeared and continued, mainly on a daily basis, for the next four weeks. Tuesday saw the first march and mass meeting several thousand strong. On Thursday it was announced that henceforth the Association of Discharged Servicemen would protect marches and demonstrations and that strikers should not pay either rent nor income tax until the strike was concluded (as also on the Clyde). Further workplaces either ceased work or saw their workers leaving. On Friday the shipbuilding and engineering employers issued a statement at the request of the Lord Mayor saying that they were bound to observe the 47 hour settlement agreed between the employers and unions at British level. That day the Strike Committee visited Mr Robert Lynn MP, the editor of the *Northern Whig*, one of the last remaining daily papers printing, and extracted an apology for misleading reportage.[11] On Saturday there was a further mass meeting at the Customs House Steps at which it was announced that the strike would be extended to the Transport Workers Federation and that discussions were taking place to ensure all unions provided strike pay.

The second week began with a mass demonstration on Monday. This was many thousands strong and described by the *Northern Whig* as the 'finest ever'. The demonstration sent a message to the Lord Provost of Glasgow demanding the release of the arrested strike leaders. The Strike Committee also challenged the Lord Mayor and City Council to establish a joint committee to oversee food distribution. The Lord Mayor equivocated, consulted councillors and then failed to respond. The same day Lord Pirrie, ultimate owner of H&W and at that point still the government's Controller of Shipping, returned to the city for the funeral of the managing director of H&W and agreed to meet the Strike Committee. Initial discussions took place on Tuesday. Contrary to a prior agreement, Pirrie issued a statement detailing the discussions on the Wednesday and was denounced in Thursday's *Workers' Bulletin*. Discussions continued on the Friday and were then adjourned. The *Northern Whig* reported several thousand strikers waiting for news outside the strike committee headquarters on the Friday evening.

Negotiations continued over the weekend and on to the Monday. Another mass meeting was held on the Custom House Steps. The Strike Committee was reported as remaining adamant for a 44-hour week. The *Workers Bulletin* claimed that the employers were drawing out the negotiations in the hope that the strike would crack. On the Monday leaders of most national unions arrived in Belfast, declared the strike official and that strike pay would commence – with the one exception of the still right-wing controlled ASE, which refused strike pay and suspended local officials. Monday also saw the outcome of discussions with Pirrie. There would be a ballot of all workers for a settlement by which employers would offer a 'less than 47 hour' settlement contingent on a national (British level) conference. The Strike committee agreed to a ballot – but not to the terms offered which it described as a 'pig in a poke' in the *Workers' Bulletin*. The ballot was, from the Strike Committee's point of view, intended to enable the workers themselves to assert their unity for the original demand. On the Wednesday the Town Council temporarily commandeered the electricity works and restarted the trams. The Strike Committee intervened, ordered the trams back and reasserted control over the power supply. The Town Clerk sent a letter apologising for a misunderstanding.[12] The 'Town Shop' engineering employers protested to the City Council. The *Belfast News-Letter* reported that it understood that 'action' was now imminent. On Friday troops arrived in Belfast and took control of the power stations. At the same time the ballot results were declared. Of the 20,000 voting there was a strong majority for rejecting the offer and continuing the strike. *The Workers' Bulletin* called for a 'fight to the finish' and denounced the 'Town employers' for sabotaging a settlement.

On the Monday the Strike Committee strengthened its mass pickets on the town shops, especially at Mackies, the biggest of the engineering employers. The shipyards remained out. Mass pickets continued round the town shops on the Tuesday – although, it seems, with less success. Most of the town works attempted to restart. On Wednesday the Strike Committee took the decision to terminate the strike for Thursday and issued a call to maintain unity and prepare for further struggle.

This very brief account of the strike begs a number of questions. There is, first, the apparent division within the ranks of the employers – between the two big shipyards on the waterfront and the employers in the city itself. It could have been an invention used by Pirrie and colleagues in the shipyards to justify their failure to meet the Strike Committee's full demands. But the Strike Committee seemed convinced that it was real and that it derived from the wish of the somewhat smaller employers in the 'Town', who employed hundreds rather than thousands and who wanted to prepare, as war work ended, for a far less favourable market environment. They saw themselves as needing the discipline of a much higher labour reserve – while the shipyards had long order books for the resumed building of trans-Atlantic luxury liners.[13]

However, there may also be a simpler and more direct explanation. That is the intervention from Scotland. We noted in our case study of Clydeside the decision of the Scottish employers to send an urgent delegation to Belfast once they heard that Pirrie was proposing a compromise near to 44 hours. Police reports from Belfast to the Colonial Office in London claim that the employers were originally prepared to give the 44 hours but instructed not to by the Scottish employers.[14] Pirrie was no doubt unwilling to reveal such external pressure. Instead, it was town employers, equally unhappy about

44 hours, who got the blame.

The second question concerns the vacillating and equivocal role of the City Council and the Lord Mayor. The third, a related one, is why troops were not called in earlier. As in Glasgow, it would have been easy to organise a show-down with police on the two occasions when the strikers encircled the City Hall – and thereby legitimise a call for military support. The *Workers Bulletin* claims that the closest links of Lord Mayor and his associates in the City Council were not with Pirrie and the shipyards but with the 'town' employers and the land agents and landlords who had interests in maintaining the existing private provision of housing. The Council leaders appear to have been taken by surprise at the scale of the strike and the strikers' ability to close down services. In these circumstances the Mayor was forced to allow his officials to negotiate with the Strike Committee to secure the maintenance of a minimum provision. But the Council leaders themselves, who had been elected as Unionists, with a significant group of populist 'Labour' Unionists, tried hard to avoid being 'taken over' and being seen to be operating on the strikers' terms. It also seems there was indeed a call for troops early on which was refused – partly because of troop shortages (mid-January was the period of very fast, forced demobilisation) and partly, it seems, because of the dangerous symbolism of troops being used against striking workers in the Unionist North. The Ulster Unionist leadership, James Craig and Dawson Bates, strongly deprecated any such action.[15] That the call was eventually conceded is significant. But troops were sent in relatively small numbers – and with rifles and not, as in Glasgow, tanks.

However, the biggest questions remains. How was it that the cohesion of the strike was maintained for so long within what was an ideologically divided workforce, one also where the potential agents of division, even if a minority, were well-organised and well-armed ? Was there, as a result of this relatively short confrontation, any transformation of attitudes and how far was the language of the strike leaders consciously transformative ? The evidence is limited. What we have is the text of the *Worker's Bulletin* and also the reports of strikers' meetings in the commercial press. These are relatively full. As on the Clyde, we see the familiar dialogue between strike leaders and the editorial lines advanced in the commercial press and the positions taken by the City council and the employers. There is also evidence, it seems, of a very carefully calibrated and conscious introduction of 'class' concepts.

The battle of words and ideals

The first issue of *The Workers' Bulletin* was distributed as the workers exited work at midday on Saturday. 'The plunge has been taken. The City is now aware that the workers of Belfast are in earnest about their claim for the simple justice of a fair working day'. The *Bulletin* then attacks the mainstream press for its misrepresentation of the workers' demands. 'Leader after leader has been turned out by the Belfast editors misrepresenting the workers claim'. 'Now', the lead article argues, 'when their duty has been faithfully accomplished they are maligned when they ask for the relief of an Eight Hour Day'. 'The bogy held up by the intelligent Belfast editors is that Belfast cannot demand 44 hours when across the water the request has been for 47.' To repudiate this claim the *Bulletin* prints an interview with Mr Thom of the Clyde Workers Committee, a member of the executive of the Scottish Iron moulders, who describes the widening movement across Scotland supporting their demands: 'the Scottish Workers are out for 40 hours and nothing else will satisfy them'.[16]

The *News-Letter*, hard-line Ulster Unionist, responded on Monday accusing the strike leaders of 'syndicalist Tyranny', of 'unofficial action' to 'force concessions' and holding the whole community to ransom. It again stresses that 'no shipyard 'across the water' has 44 hours and argues that the shipyard firms had been given insufficient notice to respond.[17]

The following day the *Workers Bulletin* takes on the accusation of syndicalism.

> What is immoral in ALL members of a trade union coming
> out when a strike is declared… The municipal electrician
> has exactly the same grievances against the Corporation as
> against any other employer.

It goes on to answer the claim that the demand was made without warning to the employers. 'Seven months ago the demand was first made publicly but owing to war conditions the men postponed their claim'. The main article finishes with an attack on the main mass circulation evening paper, the *Belfast Telegraph*, which 'exists on the workers pennies and then poisons the public against them' and celebrates its demise as its power supply was cut. Later in the *Bulletin* there is a report on the operations of the Strike Committee itself and its growing structure of subcommittees as 'sitting in practically continuous session since Saturday … the stoppage had exceeded all expectation … a splendid feature is the harmony amongst delegates'.[18]

Also in this second issue is a more 'abstract' general article, a continuing feature of the *Bulletin*. We do not know the writer. No articles in the *Bulletin* were identified by author and there appears to have been a convention both for the *Bulletin* and more generally to stress the impersonal unanimity of the strike leadership. The article takes a book entitled 'How to live on 24 hours a day' and then proceeds:

> even those workers who have not …understood the evolution
> of their historical struggle for a higher and better life perceive
> subconsciously that many of the most beautiful things of life

> have been withheld from them … now the worker is rising
> to a consciousness of his personal dignity. He refuses to be a
> 'hand'. He is determined to be a human being…[19]

This theme was continued and deepened in subsequent issues. Tuesday saw the first of the mass demonstrations in support of the strike followed by a mass meeting. The two commercial papers still printing, the *News-Letter* and the *Northern Whig*, gave what were probably somewhat tendentious reports of the speeches which stressed their overbearing and threatening character. The Federation Chair Charles McKay is reported by the *News-Letter* as saying 'the fight would be bitter and some of them had got to suffer …It was better to make it fast and furious, short and sharp …Since Saturday the whole City has been ours' (this phrase 'The Whole City is Ours' was printed as the headline of the report).[20] Earlier McKay stressed the importance of unity. 'The workers had resolved they were a power in the community. The Federation took prompt and decisive action …on Saturday. Inside three quarters of an hour there was not a tramcar on the streets. They had the electricity station at their command.' In the shipyards the clerks and draughtsmen were out. McKay was also reported as stressing the wider social objective of the strike: the 280,000 unemployment figure and 'what would happen when demobilisation comes ?'. The *Whig* reports McKay as saying that their enemies were 'in the City Hall not other parts of Ireland'.[21] The *News-Letter* version puts it more explicitly: 'the Federation had agreed that they should not just refuse to pay rent but also income tax until the 44 was conceded: 'for the people of this country, north, south, east and west. They should not regard the workers in the south and other parts of the country as their enemies. He was a Belfastman with all the traditions of a Belfastman … but I tell you our enemies are in the City Hall not other parts of Ireland'. The second speaker, James Freeland, is reported as claiming the workers were now awake. First it was the shipyards. Next it would be the mills and, after that, the campaign for housing. Samuel Geddes, a further speaker clearly of Protestant origin, challenged the claim that this was not a Belfast movement but engineered by enemies of the city; 'the whole public opinion in the City was behind the men with the exception of the people in there', pointing at the City Hall, and 'the people who did business over there', pointing to the businesses and banks in Donegall Square. The Vice Chair of the Strike Committee, Donaldson of the Plumbers Union, described the new power that could be exerted by a united working class:

> the state of affairs had changed … when six delegates from
> the Federation Committee could walk into the Generating
> Station and the Gas Works and call out the men there and
> when the members of the Corporation, practically on their
> knees, begged them to give them more time.[22]

The *News-Letter* gave the numbers on the march as 4,000. The *Workers Bulletin* reported tens of thousands. 'To dismiss the strike as unofficial is mere trifling ... no wonder the workers of Belfast are rankling under a sense of injustice'.[23]

For the following day, Thursday, the *News-Letter* notes the rapid spread of the strike beyond engineering – partly as a result of the loss of power, partly through mass picketing and partly, it seems, as a result of spontaneous action by workers. It also reports disorder in the blacked out City centre involving 'youths'. One report stresses looting as plate glass windows were smashed. Elsewhere the paper notes a more carnival aspect. 'The noisy element once more made itself felt ...small parties moving along to marching tunes from mouth organs or music hall ditties'. The *Northern Whig* describes the 'thoroughfares of the city paraded by bands of young people of both sexes, many of whom carried lamps. They accompanied their march by stridently sung choruses of popular songs'. The reports, in the *Bulletin* as well as the commercial press, also appear to indicate the degree to which 'youths' were appointing themselves enforcers of the blackout – attacking premises showing lights including the Post Office which was doing so by Strike Committee permit. A representative of the Strike Committee intervened, it seems successfully, stressing that: 'it belonged to the workers'.

Thursday's *Workers Bulletin* deplored acts by 'irresponsible youths' but commented that 'more damage had been done on many an occasion of popular rejoicing', a not-so-veiled reference to the 12th of July. The editorial noted that the *Workers Bulletin* was increasing its pagination: 'we intend to place something in hands of workers but also their heads ... In the early stages Labour was intimidated and apologetic ... Labour in the very act of struggling became conscious of its strength ...Now the worker is claiming the right to have a say of the matter of deciding the hours of his labour'.

The Thursday editions of both the *News-Letter* and *The Northern Whig* highlight an attempt to hold a 'socialist' meeting in front of the City Hall in which there were frequent references to Soviet power. This was led by a 'Mr O'Hagan' (real name Jack Hedley from Liverpool, later an Irish TGWU organiser). This was fairly quickly taken over by representatives of the Strike Committee as unauthorised. The following day, Friday, the *News-Letter* denounced the Strike Committee as an 'Industrial Soviet' and deplored the 'involuntary' acquiescence by the city authorities. 'We do not believe that the people of Belfast recognise the path in which they are being led.[24]

The Saturday at the end of the first week saw the *Worker's Bulletin* broaden the front of attack to the Coalition government. The newly installed Cabinet had, it said, betrayed the wartime promises for a reconstruction programme on housing, health, education and employment. The Strike Committee could not hold back the anger of the workers much longer. It reported messages of support from Manchester workers and stressed the wider social aims of the Glasgow Strike Committee in terms of providing work for demobilised soldiers and women munitions workers – printing extracts from the Glasgow *Strike Bulletin* and details of the speech by Shinwell at the Friday mass meeting.[25]

By the weekend news was reaching Belfast of the military occupation of Clydeside. The Monday editions of the *Whig* and *News-Letter* were full of it – as showing the dangers facing Belfast. The *Whig* fastened on 'the foreign leaders' in Glasgow, led by a 'Polish Jew' (Shinwell) and its 'violent methods' resembling Petrograd. It links this to the call from the Belfast Strike Committee for joint action with the City Council on services and their alleged comment: 'we will run the affairs of the City'. The *News-Letter* resumed its attack on Syndicalism and Socialism as contrary to trade union principles and printed a half page statement from the Grand Master of the Orange Lodge largely written by Dawson Bates, Secretary of the Ulster Unionist Council. This did not directly attack the strikers but claimed they were being manipulated by the socialist labour candidates who had been defeated in December's General Election. Both papers also highlighted what were presented as voices of criticism surfacing at the Custom House Steps briefing organised by the Strike Committee – mainly it seems relating to strike pay and the fact the gas was still reaching some consumers.[26] Such reports were denied by Monday's Workers' *Bulletin* as an attempt to turn the rank and file against the Committee – and explaining that while electricity could be disconnected selectively to allow, for instance, the agreed use by Belfast's hospitals, gas was more difficult to handle. Instead, the *Bulletin* stressed the continuing extension of the strike to include the Transport Workers Federation and also the decision to bring out the apprentices and ensure they were receiving unemployment benefit. The route for a major rally for the following day was detailed.[27]

On the Tuesday the numbers attending ran to tens of thousands, even the *Northern Whig* described it as the 'finest ever'. The reports of speeches, appearing as below in the *Workers' Bulletin*, appear to give at least some indication of a heightened level of class consciousness. Charles McKay: the 'demonstration more effective than speeches'. They were still solid for 44 hours. There was no coercion. It was a voluntary movement. And it was 'no use on the part of the press or any other body to bring in the old wedge that had always divided them in this city'. James Freeland attacked Bonar Law's failure to intervene. The workers' patience had been tried by the misrepresentations of the war period … pianos, furs and other extravagance had been thrown at them in the press when they knew it had been a struggle to make ends meet. Alf Purcell, the strongly Left-wing leader of the Furnishing Trades and an officer of the Confederation at British level had travelled to Belfast to offer solidarity. 'Their stand was leading to simultaneous action across Britain.' For the NAUL Charles Lockett hoped 'they would not end with the 44 and looked upon the present as a transition period to real government by the people. It was their own movement on the

Clydeside despite misrepresentations in the press…'.[28] Reports in the *Whig* and to a lesser extent the *News-Letter* confirm these statements.[29] *The Workers' Bulletin*, as the official organ of the Federation, gives no indication of being a mouthpiece of timid reformism. It concludes its report by celebrating the 'revolt of the Belfast workers against the serfdom of the past … one was keenly reminded of the enemies of the movement when the City Hall came in sight … the puny opposition of the shopkeeping, Commission Agency fraternity, living mainly on the earnings of working people is so ludicrous that a smile must exert itself… We have been too soft and modest. Let the workers rule.'

These excerpts, typical of other meetings, and also reported nonetheless in the commercial press, do seem to indicate a level of change that parallels that on the Clyde. In fact, if anything, the rhetoric seems to have been less restrained. The ten days that followed, difficult ones for the strike leadership as Lord Pirrie and the employers manoeuvred to break the unity of the strike, show no lessening of 'class' analysis and if anything a strengthening. The leadership seems to have shown considerable tactical skill in orchestrating a ballot that reinforced unity behind their original demands. Termination of the strike, after the arrival of troops, also appears to have been conducted in a way that maintained unity and morale. The editorial of the final issue of the *Workers' Bulletin* issued on Wednesday 19 February began:

> The Great Strike is drawing to an end. The '44' has not
> been won YET, but it is appreciably nearer and, best of all,
> the Belfast workers for the first time have come to a faint
> consciousness of the mighty power they wield. This is the real
> victory arising from the struggle. For the first time shipyard
> worker and town worker, skilled and unskilled, fought side
> by side, and have displayed a spirit of comradeship that can
> never be felt except by those who have arrayed themselves
> against a common enemy. The value of the movement lay in
> the struggle and the sacrifices made in the common cause …
> Yielding now is only a matter of tactics …One thing has been
> made abundantly clear by the course of events, viz, – that this
> was a rank and file movement. In the last ballot … the men by
> their free vote decided to continue the struggle …

The anonymous feature writer continued their commentary:

> Let the worker remember this. The issue never was the justice
> of the '44', but simply had he the sufficient power to enforce
> his demand. If Labour is to treat on equal terms with Capital,
> then Labour must be organised and its machinery must be
> perfect. Mr Lloyd George's Industrial Parliament will only

be a sham and a delusion unless there is at the back of it
the ultimate power to cease work and to withhold labour
until justice is conceded ... Has Capital used its power to
dictate? We have the record written in letters of fire in our
slums and in our army of unemployed. Labour will not allow
itself to be condemned for wrongs it MAY do, when *Capital*
stands condemned for gross wrongs openly and shamelessly
flaunted for generations.[30]

'Class politics' in Belfast

There would also seem to be some evidence of a more general change,
across the city's population as a whole, in attitudes to class alignments –
both positive and negative – and to the potential power of an organised
workforce. During the strike itself some retailers, no doubt for good
commercial reasons and only a small minority, did advertise in the Bulletin
– over a dozen, for instance, in the issue for 3 February. Some cinemas were
also permitted to reopen, with electric current restored, on condition that
they offered discounted tickets to the families of strikers. Two cinemas, the
Lyceum and the Alhambra, appear in the *Bulletin* advertising their services.

On 1 February the *Workers Bulletin* contained an even stranger advert
'Ulster Unionist-Labour Association The usual monthly meeting postponed
until further notice'. This could have been a genuine press notice. But
was almost certainly not (there is no signatory) and far more likely a tacit
editorial comment on the fact that this organisation, the main 'labour'
front for the Unionist machine, was nowhere to be seen during the strike.
Apart from the statement from the Orange Lodge Grand Master, itself very
carefully worded to avoid any direct attack, there appears to have been no
open attempt – unlike 1907 – to exploit sectarian loyalties.

Conversely, there also appears by the end of the strike a broader
awareness, outside the working class itself, that 'class', not religious/
national affiliation, was now a major orientating factor in politics. In the week
after the termination of the strike a Ratepayers Association for Belfast was
formed. The *Northern Whig* reports the resolution adopted at the meeting:
'in view of the recent events it is desirable to form a Ratepayers' Protection
Association – non-sectarian and non-political – composed of representatives
of the commercial and professional communities of Belfast'.[31] The *Telegraph*,
finally printing again, editorially stressed, explicitly in terms of class
mobilisation, the importance of supporting the new organisation:

In the political and social convulsions of the time the greatest
sufferers are the middle classes. We have the working classes
so-called exploiting the wealthy classes and the wealthy
classes exploiting the working classes or at least allegations

are made …We have wages increasing and profiteering increasing … the middle classes seem to be without a voice or friend…' The article continued: 'it is possible that such a movement will have its origin as much in connection with the feeling created by the recent action, and inaction, of the City Council as with the desire to protect ratepayers … we all agree there is something wrong somewhere … or the public services would not have been allowed be to be put out of control as they were.[32]

Twelve weeks later, at the beginning of May, there was a further test of how far the mobilisation during the strike had more lasting consequences. It was Belfast's first public May Day demonstration. The *Telegraph* editorially condemned it.

Labour organised and unorganised is being exploited by revolution just now in a way that is cunningly disguised to deceive the working classes. We are to have a Labour Day demonstration in Belfast tomorrow. Who are at the bottom of it? The little band of disgruntled Radical Socialists who opposed the Unionist Labour candidates in the recent General Election and who figured prominently in the strike. The trick is a very shallow one. In the name of the Belfast workers, the vast majority of whom are Unionists, the demonstration will in reality be worked as a manifestation of anti-Unionism. It was not possible to have the demonstration yesterday [I May] at the same time as Nationalist Ireland demonstrated by a general cessation of work. That would have been altogether too transparent an evidence of the inwardness of the connection with Sinn Fein. So the Belfast May Day is fixed for a Saturday afternoon…[33]

The *Telegraph* printed no report of the demonstration itself. *The Belfast News-Letter* did. The demonstration took, it reported, forty minutes to pass any one point. It lists thirty trade union contingents. At the final rally in the Ormeau Park there were three platforms for speakers. All passed identical resolutions.

The rally's first resolution was 'fraternal greetings to workers of all lands … belief in the international solidarity of workers … readiness to join with workers everywhere irrespective of colour or creed in the hope of creating new conditions without help or hindrance from any other class. As an indispensable prelude the government was called upon to institute a shorter working week fixing no limit till the horde of unemployed men and women are reabsorbed again into peaceful pursuits instead of being held in reserve to beat down the standard of living. To achieve all this it was believed that a peace should be speedily be brought about [with Soviet Russia]... an immediate lifting of the blockade and that all pre-war trade union rights, wrung at great cost from our exacting taskmasters should be immediately be restored...'

The second resolution declared adherence to the principle of direct Labour representation on all public bodies, legislative and administrative, for the reason that only undiluted, uncamouflaged representatives, specifically chosen and responsible to the workers, can serve to establish the workers charter, including the complete revolution of the housing question, educational methods and health regulations. For the establishment of these reforms the third resolution demanded that the state should make the necessary grant in aid.

The fourth resolution called for the immediate release of the imprisoned Glasgow striker leaders. The fifth asked for the 'withdrawal of all regulations having for their object the curbing or repression of the fullest and free-est criticism of all the acts bearing on the welfare of the working classes at home and abroad'.

The speakers cited in the report included a number of the strike leaders, Samuel Geddes, James Freeland and Samuel Kyle as well as, representing the Confederation, the left-winger Alf Purcell who had travelled over from London. 'The best page in history that had been written for some time, said Purcell, was when the men of the shipyards had struck for the forty four hour week and had the support of other workers in the city'. Other speakers were D. R. Campbell, Secretary of Belfast Trades Council, who proposed a resolution of support for Wexford strikers, James Kennedy of the Amalgamated Society of Carpenters, Thomas More of the Labour Representation Committee and Herbert Attwood of the Iron Founders. James Freeland 'described the principal resolution as very strong [a voice: 'It is not strong enough']. Referring to the government and their promises he said that the days of Mr Lloyd George and his class were numbered. Samuel Kyle said that the international character of the Labour movement was brought to the front and that question concerned them in Belfast as much as any other place ... the seeds of future wars were being sewn by the actions of France and Italy'. He 'emphasised the need for a speedy lifting of the blockade ... children were starving in the streets of Vienna and dying in Petrograd ... 100,000 cotton operatives were idle for the same reason in Lancashire. In Belfast linen workers were also affected by the blockade. He appealed to the workers of Belfast not to allow another debacle to happen which occurred last December' – a reference to defeat of Labour candidates in Belfast in the general election by 'Labour' Unionists.[34]

The demonstration was big. *The Belfast News-Letter* put it at 100,000. The strike leaders spoke with authority. No rancour was shown against them for strike's effective defeat. The strike was, on the contrary, spoken of as a matter of pride and the language was clearly that of class combativeness and commitment to future advance. The references to Wexford, and to Vienna and Petrograd, were important in constructing a new labour identity that transcended narrow nationalism – though not in any adventurist way. No direct reference was made to the Soviet government – even though Purcell was a leading member of the Hands Off Russia committee. Kyle and his colleagues were indeed pupils of Connolly.

The months immediately after the May Day demonstration appear to show the Ulster Unionist high command at their most apprehensive. In June Bates wrote to Craig: 'the Labour question is becoming acute in Belfast and the North of Ireland … we have got to face this sooner or later'. Two weeks later he was urging Carson to strengthen the Ulster Unionist Labour Association: 'many of the unions are controlled by officials who hold Home Rule views' …which 'leads many younger members of the working class to Socialist i.e. extreme organisations … if nothing is done the association (UULA] will die, because its members feel it is not sufficiently progressive to meet an admittedly felt want'.

Six months later Bates's fears were confirmed by the January 1920 local elections. In the previous Council there had been no Labour councillors: 52 were Unionists and 8 nationalists. This time only 37 seats went to the Unionists (and this was at a time when the suffrage still gave extra votes to office and shop premises and ensured Unionist dominance of the city centre wards). Labour won 13 seats and the Nationalists and Sinn Fein ten between them. Labour made a strong showing in all working class wards. Most remarkably Sam Kyle topped the poll in the Shankhill ward, traditionally seen as a bastion of populist Unionism within West Belfast. No less remarkably his voting base seems to have been political rather than just personal. He was elected with 2,082 votes, 500 ahead of the nearest Unionist. Because the voting system was based on proportional representation (the British administration adopted it in 1920 to stop Sinn Fein seizing control of local government in the South) we know that all but a very few of Kyle's transfers went in a disciplined way to the other Labour candidates and not to Unionists. In Woodvale directly adjacent to Shankhill the Unionists came top of the poll and won four of the six seats – but Labour won the other two. In St Anne's ward, a traditionally unionist stronghold also in the West but further south, the two top votes went to Labour. In Duncairn, a working class ward in the north close to the docks, the elected Labour candidate secured 1,348 against 2,238 for the top unionist. In the east the Victoria ward facing directly on to the shipyards and with more recently built housing that accommodated many of those coming into Belfast for war work, the top vote went to a Nationalist with 1,500. Of the rest Labour secured one seat with 1,160 votes, Sinn Fein one, the Official Unionists two and Unionist Labour one. In Pottinger Ward also in the East but further towards the City centre the Unionists were more dominant and got the Alderman's seat and three others – leaving Labour and the Nationalists with one each.[35]

Overall, therefore, these results seem to confirm a significant shift of political orientation. Across working class Belfast Unionism had lost its monolithic grip. It still maintained a major base but it was definitely no longer a dominant one. In terms of leadership on practical issues the Unionist high command could no longer be sure of their ability to maintain control. This new sense of challenge was demonstrated at the close of the count in the City Hall in January 1920, when Kyle, the other Labour councillors and 'a large crowd of supporters' sang the Red Flag.[36]

The finale

These conclusions run parallel to those of the recently published research of Fearghal Mac Bhloscaidh. By examining the correspondence of Edward Carson, Dawson Bates and James Craig, and also their allies in government in Westminster, Birkenhead, Bonar Law and Milner, Mac Bhloscaidh concludes that as early as 1914 there was uncertainty about how far reliance could be placed on working class Belfast. Any showdown over a Home Rule government, military or otherwise, would depend, at minimum, on the acquiescence of Belfast. These fears deepened as war continued and were seemingly confirmed in the December 1918 general election when significant numbers of votes were registered for Labour candidates in Unionists areas. Kyle himself secured 20 percent in Shankhill, considerably less than in 1920 but still worrying in the heartland of working class Protestantism. The 1919 general strike intensified these concerns.

At this point Carson, Bates and Craig privately took their final decision to abandon the pledges made in the 1912 Ulster Covenant to defend a nine county Ulster. Monaghan, Cavan and Donegal had sizeable Catholic populations. In military terms Bates, Carson and Craig reckoned that they could probably cope with Belfast's unreliable and potentially hostile working class but not, at the same time, three rebellious counties.

It was, it would seem, this uncertainty about the temper of Belfast's protestant workers that explains the very low profile of the UULA during the strike, an organisation, Mac Bhloscaidh argues, that was run top down by Bates with little autonomy or substance of its own. It also explains the very non-committal and hesitant wording of the appeal from the Grand Master of the Orange Lodge, a document worked over in detail by Bates and Carson uncertain of how to respond to the strike without further antagonising those they wished to influence. As in Glasgow, both the statement from the Orange Lodge and the newspapers played up the bogy of Bolshevik bloodshed and enemy aliens – but without centrally attacking the objectives of the strikers. Unlike Glasgow no direct attempt was made to precipitate physical conflict or arrest the strike leadership.

Three months on, May Day 1919 represented a further challenge – as reflected by the *Telegraph* editorial – but a challenge best ignored, at least publicly. The January 1920 elections confirmed the worst fears of Bates and Carson. The wider grip of Ulster Unionism, even with a labour veneer, appeared to be melting away.

Six months later, on 21 July 1920, the Unionist response finally came. It was the start of what has been described as the Belfast 'pogrom'; the prime focus of Mac Bhloscaidh's research: the expulsion of around 10,000 workers from Belfast's shipyards, mainly Catholics but including up to a thousand 'socialists'. This was followed by 24 months of attacks and counter-attacks in which 23,000 Catholics were driven from their homes, many leaving the North for good. 266 were killed.

The mainstream historical explanation, as developed, for instance, by Bew, Gibbon and Patterson, is that this was a spontaneous outburst of anger. It was triggered by Sinn Fein outrages over the previous weeks, both in the South but also within Ulster, which were seen to threaten a Protestant working class that possessed its own quite distinct values: a quasi-national identity that saw itself as defending progressive perspectives quite distinct from the regressive bigotry of Catholicism. These authors therefore argue that it is delusionary (and discriminatory) for some historians to argue that this identity could somehow transform itself, as Connolly and his followers believed, into an ideal 'class consciousness' devoid of such cultural and ideological grounding.

It was this 'spontaneous expression of anger' explanation that was at the time promoted by the Unionist press to explain the shipyard expulsions. The *News-Letter* reported 'Notice of yesterday's meeting [outside the shipyard] had been given by means of posters and there was a very large attendance of workers, who enthusiastically cheered the speeches that were delivered. In consequence of the feeling which prevailed a number of workers who were known to be in active sympathy with Sinn Fein were told that in their own best interest it would be advisable for them to return to their homes. This advice was received with indignation by the men to whom it was tendered and one of them, apparently by way of challenge, was foolish enough to shout 'Up the Rebels'. The cry was the signal for an outbreak that spread like wildfire. Men, blinded by rage, struck out fiercely...'. [37]

Mac Bhloscaidh demonstrates that the origin was much less spontaneous[38] At the 12 July parade in Belfast Carson made calls for action. These calls were repeated in the press thereafter. But the response itself was organised by the unionist high command. The UULA was mobilised in detail. The Harland and Wolff meeting itself was not one called by shop stewards. It was mobilised from outside the yards by 'posters'. It was also held some distance from the yard itself – with the mobilised unionists then marching to the Harland and Wolff yard.[39] Many of those attending were not shipyards workers and had come prepared, some armed with revolvers. Mac Bhloscaidh uses the disciplinary papers of the UULA as evidence. One of its members had failed to carry through instructions to organise a meeting on Queen's Island when called upon to do so on the day of the pogrom and had additionally failed to condemn a statement that 'the days of the Orange flag and big drum were over'. Those leading the action were mobilised members of the UULA together with the UULA controlled Ulster Ex-servicemen's Association (UESA, a quite different body to the Association of Discharged Servicemen which had protected the strikers' processions in 1919 and which at British level was largely under BSP leadership).

The pogrom was therefore effectively enforced by the mobilised paramilitaries of the UVF. On 24 July the *Westminster Gazette* commented: 'it is common knowledge in Belfast ... that plans were matured at least two months ago to drive all Home Rule workmen in the shipyards out of their employment.'[40] Eighteen months later, after the UVF had been given official status as the B Special regiment within the new Northern Ireland state, Lloyd George commented that Mussolini's Fascisti served as 'an exact analogy' for the 48,000 UVF members then being given official state sanction to enforce detailed local control – a control they had been enforcing less officially since July 1920.[41]

Nor was the timing, July 1920, itself random. May-July 1920 were the months during which Carson, Dawson Bates and Craig came to the conclusion that action to seize effective control of the six counties could no longer be postponed. In the House of Commons home rule legislation was continuing its progress. If implemented, it would give control over the police, among other powers, to a legislature in Dublin. On the ground in Ireland Sinn Fein had in June established Courts of Arbitration for land disputes, and a rival legal system, that covered most of the country including the southern and western three counties within Ulster. In the county council elections in the first week of June Sinn Fein had captured control of Tyrone and Fermanagh (as well as Donegal, Cavan and Monaghan). And in the military struggle, mainly conducted in the South and West, British military commanders were demanding more troops. On 28 June Sir Henry Wilson, chief of imperial military staff, wrote 'I really believe that we shall be kicked out'.[42]

But Britain did not have the troops to send. More were needed in India. The Amritsar massacre in April had been followed by the mutiny of the Connaught Rangers in June 1920. More troops were also needed in the Middle East after the June rising in Mesopotamia (Iraq). In Russia British-supported forces were facing military disaster, and, as we will see in the next chapter, the government was fearful of further denuding troop numbers in Britain. Carson and his colleagues knew this. In securing their own base in the north, militarily as well as politically, some sort of action could no longer be postponed and the use of paramilitary force was the only option. Within that the choice of the shipyards as their first target was not accidental – not because the workforce was inherently sectarian but the reverse: because it was not.

Assessment

This was, therefore, a very different outcome to that on Clydeside. But it is also an outcome that has obscured what actually triggered this response: the relatively fast development of class consciousness within Belfast's working class, one which, for a period of up to two years, was seen as a serious challenge by the region's rulers. Correspondingly also, in terms of modern interpretations, the tendency of historians to see classes and class formation in structuralist terms, and the failure to comprehend the dialectic of oppression and alienation and the potential for rapid change, has given credence to static culturalist interpretations of Irish history.

What therefore has Belfast's 1919 strike to tell us about the character of this class consciousness as compared to developments on the Clyde? First, it seems that, like the Clyde, the development of class attitudes seems to have been most marked among the young. This is evidenced in Bates's correspondence during the strike itself in which he called for action to 'enrol [in the UULA] the younger members of the community who are liable to be influenced by the opponents of our cause'.[43] In June 1919, after the mass May Day demonstration, bigger, it seems, than the usual 12 July Orange march, Bates was still more pessimistic. 'If nothing is done the Association [the UULA] will die'.[44] During the strike itself we have the reports of young men and women appointing themselves enforcers of blackouts in the city centre. The 'strident' singing of music hall songs, not party anthems, may, or may not, have been part of this protest but would certainly not have appealed to Carson, Bates and Craig. At the same time, unlike Glasgow, all workers in the shipyards came out on the first day. The older generation of shipyard workers did not remain – even though picketing was required for some other workplaces.

This leads us to the conclusion that the shipyards were not the weak link within Belfast's working-class movement but in fact, at that time, seen as the basis of its strength. The expulsion of over a thousand non-Catholics in July 1920 would also lead us in that direction. These workers would represent the politically mobilised core of the workforce, in fact a remarkably large number, who had been identified in detail by the UULA organisers and whose wider influence had stabilised and carried forward the strike action in 1919. This issue of a mobilised core is one to which, theoretically, we will need to return.

If there was a difference with Clydeside, it was not that Belfast was more reformist or dominated by a cautious trade unionism. The words of its leaders refute this. It was more in the coherence and unity of the Belfast leadership and the degree to which its members were collectively aware of the risks being taken in face of an enemy that would, if it got the chance, not scruple to mobilise both racist passions and paramilitary violence. One example would be *The Workers Bulletin*, with its careful anonymity and slow, modulated development of 'class' arguments. Another would be the interventions to curtail O'Hagan and his evocations of Bolshevik revolution – exactly mimicking the claims advanced by the press and in the Orange Order proclamation. But most important of all was the explicit handling of the issue of sectarian division. Repeatedly, and using very much the same rhetorical devices, speakers would refer to sectarian conflict as a disabling division of the past, something blocking workers advance and point to the real enemies in class terms and the need for a solidarity that encompassed all workers both in the north and elsewhere (and by May 1919 including Petrograd – or at least its children). Alf Purcell's presence at two of the most important rallies demonstrates this underlying agenda. Purcell represented the Confederation at British level – but he also personally represented, by his position on Hands Off Russia committee, an unspoken commitment to the wider social changes for which James Connolly stood.[45]

Their opponents were equally aware of the importance of words spoken in the 'practical moment' – fictitiously conjuring up just three words 'Up the rebels' to explain (and justify as 'spontaneous') a bloody pogrom they themselves had organised over the previous weeks.

We should also remember that, just ten years later in 1931, workers from both the 'Protestant' Shankhill and the 'Catholic' Falls Road united in protest against mass unemployment – and that the machine gunners in the Stormont government's armoured cars managed, with unintended symbolism, to shoot dead one Catholic and one Protestant (as well as injuring many more).

NOTES

1   James Connolly, The Reconquest of Ireland, *Collected Works* (New Books Dublin 1987) Vol 1, p.206.

2   A.N. Leontiev, *Activity, Consciousness and Personality*, pp. 91-92.

3   Terry Cradden, 'Labour in Britain and the Northern Irish Labour Party 1900-1970' in P. Catterall and S. McDougall, eds, *The Northern Ireland Question in British Politics* (Macmillan, Basingstoke 1996).

4   The Labour Gazette XXVII 1919 gives the number of insured workers in shipbuilding in Ireland as 23,476 on 3 January 1919 of whom 4.3 percent were unemployed. The percentage unemployed rises to 11.68 percent by June 1919 but the number then declines from 2709 to 2066 in November 1919. By May 1920 the number had declined further to 1208 (5.9 percent) and remained at roughly this level over the summer of 1920. There would in addition have been further workers in casual employment. John Lynch, 'Harland and Wolff: its labour force and industrial relations' *Soathar*, Volume, 22, 1993 gives an overall figure including all grades at Harland and Wolff in 1919 as 27,000 with more at Workman's and ancillary workshops.

5   Emmet O'Connor, '"Rotten Prod": James Baird and Belfast Labour', *Socialist History*, Vol.60/1, 2021.

6   Fearghal Mac Bhloscaidh, 'The Belfast Pogrom and the Interminable Irish Question', *Studi Irlandesi: a journal of Irish Studies*, 12, 2022.

7   This account is mainly taken from the Belfast *Strike Bulletin* (subsequently retitled *The Workers Bulletin*) from 25 January 1919 onwards. It is supplemented with material from the *Belfast Telegraph*, the *BelfastNews-Letter* and the *Northern Whig*. Austen Morgan's *Labour and Partition: the Belfast working class 1905-23* (Pluto London 1996) provides some very useful detail although its conclusions are different from those of Mac Bhloscaidh and those argued here. Graham Walker, writing in *Soathar* 10, 1984, 'The Northern Ireland Labour Party in the 1920s' contests Morgan's claim in his 1978 PhD thesis, 'The Working Class in Belfast 1905-1923' that the Connolyite presence was largely absent in the 1920s (p.23-4).

8   *Belfast Strike Bulletin* 28 January 1919 page 1, and continued, provides a background to the pre-strike negotiations.

9   The classic text for this assessment would be Paul Bew, Peter Gibbon and Henry Paterson, *The State in Northern Ireland 1921-1972* (Manchester 1979) heavily influenced by an Althusserian reading of Marx and particularly Balibar on the State. In terms of a specific assessment of the 1919 strike leadership Emmet O'Connor, as cited, and also in *Syndicalism in Ireland 1917-1923* (Cork 1988) tends to portray the strike leadership as cautious, dominated by craft unions and distancing itself from the strike on the Clyde. This is also, as noted, the position of Austen Morgan. More recently Olivier Cochequelin, '"Le 'Soviet' de grevistes a Belfast'? La Grande Greve de Belfast de 1919', *Les Etudes irlandaises*, 48/1, 2023 similarly tends to see the Belfast strike as aligned to British unions, to be relatively cautious, avoiding any identification with Soviet models and in that regard unlike the 'Producer Soviets' used as a bargaining tactic by the Irish TGWU in 1920-21.

10 J. Dunsmore Clarkson, *Labour and Nationalism in Ireland* (New York 1926).

11 *Workers Bulletin*, 31 January 1919.

12 *Northern Whig* 12 February 1919.

13 *Workers Bulletin* 12 February cites Mr S.C. Davidson, representing the non-shipyard employers, as stating that they will stick to 47 hours even if the shipyards go for 44.

14 TNA CO 904/108 January 1919. The Clydeside employers decided to send its deputation to Pirrie on 14 February: TD 241/1/18 14 February 1919.

15 Mac Bhloschaidh, p.177 cites correspondence between Dawson Bates and James Craig for 1 February counselling against any military intervention as 'embittering' workers and being likely to precipitate a junction with the workers movement in the south. Dawson Bates and James Craig, as leaders of the Ulster Unionist Party, would have been in detailed and daily contact with the UUP members in the City Council, the Lord Mayor and other councillors as well as with the editors of the Belfast press.

16 Belfast *Strike Bulletin* 25 January 1919.

17 *News-Letter*, Monday 27 January 1919.

18 Belfast *Strike Bulletin*, 28 January 1919.

19 Fearghal Mac Bhloscaidh suggests that this matches the style of Robert McClung, another of those strongly influenced by James Connolly.

20 *News-Letter* Wednesday 29 January.

21 *Northern Whig* Wednesday 29 January.

22 *News-Letter* 30 January.

23 Belfast *Strike Bulletin* 30 January.

24 *News-Letter* Friday 31 January 1919.

25 *Workers Bulletin* Saturday 1 February.

26 *News-Letter* and *Northern Whig*, Monday 3 February.

27 *Workers Bulletin* Monday 3 February.

28 *Workers Bulletin* Wednesday 5 February.

29 *Northern Whig* and News-Letter for Wednesday 5 February.

30 *Workers Bulletin* Wednesday 5 February.

31 *Northern Whig* 18 February.

32 *Belfast Telegraph* 24 February 1919.

33 *Belfast Telegraph* 3 May 1919. The 'disgruntled socialists' reference is

to the Belfast Labour Party.

34 Belfast *News-Letter* 5 May 1919.

35 *Belfast News-Letter* 17 January 1919 and 19 January 1919.

36 *Belfast News-Letter* Monday 19 January 1920.

37 *Belfast Telegraph* 22 July 1922.

38 Mac Bhloscaidh pp.183-185 cites the relevant correspondence between Bates, Craig and Carson.

39 *Daily Herald*, 30 July 1920, statement from expelled workers: 'the attackers were directed from the meeting to march on Harland and Woolf's East Yard'.

40 Dorothy McCardle, *The Irish Republic* (Dublin 1951 edition) p. 357.

41 Mac Bhloscaidh p.187. The *Daily Herald* for Tuesday 27 July 1920 quoted Joseph Devlin MP speaking in the Commons on 26 July denying that the events of 21 July were a response to the killing of Colonel Smyth: 'they had been planned long before', 'the organisation of a Unionist mob' followed Carson's 12 July announcement of the re-organisation of the Ulster Volunteers. It might also be noted that a somewhat similar tactics were employed fifty years later during the 'Ulster Workers' lockout in 1974. Opponents of the power-sharing government sought but failed to win the votes for the lockout at duly convened meetings in Harland and Wolff. They responded by burning the stewards' cars and then using paramilitary forces to block motorways and access roads to workplaces: Foster, The Great Tradition of Independent Working Class Power, *Unite History,* volume 4 (Liverpool 2023) pp.126-127.

42 McCardle, *Irish Republic*, p. 377.

43 Mac Bhloscaidh, p. 178 – citing letter dated 27 January 1919,

44 Mac Bhloscaidh, p.178 – citing Bates to Carson 30 June 1919.

45 The following year Purcell became a founder member of the Communist Party.

4

The Councils of Action 1920

One of the most formidable challenges ever given to
democracy … The government will fight back with all its
resources
Lloyd George in the Commons on 16 August 1920 speaking
on the Councils of Action[1]

They must recapture the public mind and counter the
formidable body of young men whose aim it is to destroy
the present industrial and parliamentary system and replace
it with a workers' state – and whose advocacy of Soviet
government drew strength from popular impatience with the
parliamentary mode of government.
Lloyd George, summer 1920 as cited by Ken Coates and Tony
Topham, *The Making of the Transport and General Workers Union*
(London 1991) p.715.

A t the end of May 1920 two small news items were carried in the
Daily Herald. On 28 May it reported on escalating strike action in
Oxford, a city at that point not normally seen as a centre of industrial
militancy. Bus drivers had managed to secure an increase of 1p an hour.
The same increase had been refused to garage workers. All bus workers
then immediately came out on strike. Other vehicle workers then gave a
week's notice of strike action. The Trades and Labour Council (combining
both trade unions and the Labour Party) had then met to discuss calling a
general strike across the city. In its issue for the following day the *Herald*
reported another incident. This was in Balham, a lower middle-class area
of South London. It was addressed by the local MP. 'There were turbulent
scenes last night in the LCC School, Balham when Dr Cato Worsfold MP

delivered a lantern slide on Bolshevism ... He was challenged on practically every statement ... 'India, Egypt, Ireland' were flung at him whenever he mentioned the word 'Freedom'. Worsfold, a local solicitor, had been elected by an overwhelming majority 18 months before. On this occasion he had to be rescued by the police.

These two incidents, not necessarily typical as we only know about them because they were highlighted by the *Daily Herald*, nonetheless illustrate something of the political climate in the early summer 1920 two months before the Councils of Action crisis in August. Without this background it is now difficult to comprehend the events two months later: how it was that the Trades Union Congress and the Labour Party jointly created a Council of Action to organise a general strike should the government continue with war preparations against Soviet Russia and, in doing so, also sought to mobilise local communities to create their own alternative structures of popular government across the country.

Unlike the mobilisations described in earlier case studies – whether immediately after the First World War or in the 1970s – the mobilisations in August 1920 did not depend, or at least not so much, on carefully considered statements designed to win otherwise sceptical working class audiences suspicious of socialists and agitators. The necessary arguments appear to have been won some time before within a significant section of the working population, particularly the younger generation. It is otherwise difficult to explain how it was that previously committed right-wingers, and friends of the government, such as the rail union leader JH Thomas, or cautious middle of the road labour leaders, like Arthur Henderson and Margaret Bondfield, did not resist, and actually supported, the decision to proceed with preparations to establish across the country Councils of Action ready to usurp the powers of constitutional government. They gave support, it would seem, because they were acutely aware of how opinions had changed. Special Branch itself made this point in its report to the Cabinet in early August. The formation of the Councils of Action had, it noted, served to:

> rehabilitate the moderate labour leaders with their extreme
> supporters and to weld the whole temporarily into one body
> .,. moderate leaders whose popularity is on the wane have
> seized the opportunity of giving the lie to accusations of
> treachery (Home Office 12 August).[2]

This chapter will examine the evidence for this transformation. It will consider how it was achieved and how it was, at least temporarily, given organisational form in terms of 'councils of action'. At this point in 1920 it would appear that a significant section of working people had expectations of rapid social change. One participant in these events, the labour historian G.D.H Cole, wrote during that summer:

> we are co-ordinating the forces of Labour not simply in
> order to increase Labour's strength in negotiations, strikes
> and elections. We are marshalling our battalions for an actual
> assault on capitalism, to be followed by an actual assumption
> of power.[3]

Half a century later the analyst of industrial society, Keith Middlemas, by no means a left winger, wrote:

> the Councils of Action represented in tangible form, and on
> an issue of immense appeal, the last manifestation of that
> popular democracy which the shop stewards' movement
> had always claimed existed'. He also noted that it was the
> 'fear of the popular appeal of shop stewards, BSP and the
> rest, particularly in local Labour Parties and Trades Councils,
> that induce[d] Labour and the TUC to approve extra-
> parliamentary resistance[4]

This chapter will first set the scene in terms of the post-war balance of class power, of how the contest between capital and labour moved on from the uncertain stalemate of early 1919 to a stage a year later when organised labour directly challenged the government and the class forces it represented. Our focus will be on the character of the resulting popular mobilisation.

At the end we will briefly carry the narrative forward to the General Strike of 1926 and to look at the reverse process: the restoration of right-wing control in the labour movement. It is argued here that the government's original aim in setting up this confrontation was to end permanently such processes of class mobilisation. It sought to do so by consolidating a new constitutionalist leadership within the Labour Movement that itself saw its main purpose as defending a liberal economic order – largely in partnership with large-scale capital. This objective was not entirely reached. The memory of 1920, and of the new organisational forms then developed as the basis of working class rule, was still too immediate. Yet the outcome did effectively end this period of large-scale class mobilisation. Some comments on how it was done seek to illuminate both its character and the wider social processes involved in capitalist re-stabilisation.

1 Setting the scene

On 7 August 1920 the Parliamentary Committee of the TUC and the NEC of the Labour Party did something quite remarkable. They directly challenged the constitution – jointly convening a Council of Action with a remit to organise a general strike to halt any move by the British government to declare war on Soviet Russia or, short of that, to supply troops or munitions to its enemies. Over the following days over 300 local Councils of Action were called into being to provide the organisational base for the strike. These were almost all based either on Trades Councils or the still extant joint Trades and Labour Councils and covered virtually all areas in England, Scotland and Wales. Over the following week the government decided not to proceed and instead backed Soviet proposals for a peace treaty with the principal aggressor, Poland.

In his review of British industrial relations James Cronin identifies 1920 as marking the peak of the third of the three great waves of industrial militancy that played a formative role in the creation of Britain's modern Labour Movement – the previous two being 'new unionism' between 1888 to 1890 and the 'great unrest' of 1910 to 1913.[5]

This third wave, empowered by the full employment of the war years, saw the first full unionisation of unskilled workers, brought women workers into the mainstream of the trade union movement and, most significantly of all, produced a powerful and increasingly radical shop stewards movement. Politically the official trade union leadership had taken a pro-war position and entered a pact with the government to suspend industrial action – in a period of steeply rising inflation, a crisis in housing supply and growing food shortages. This, as we noted earlier, left a vacuum in leadership filled by those socialists who had taken an anti-war position and whose workplace militancy increasingly provided support for wider community struggles on rents, rationing and conscription. In industrial and mining areas trades councils and, in Scotland 'workers' committees', assumed a wider leadership that for the first time created a mass community base for the Labour Party. [6]

Immediately after war the official pro-war leaderships maintained their positions in the major trade unions. They also did so in the Labour Party which the trade unions funded and largely controlled – although, in response to the wartime radicalisation, the Labour Party had in January 1918 adopted a new constitution. This included the socialist Clause IV but also an individual party membership which provided the basis for a new local branch structure separate from the left-wing dominated trades councils. During the shop steward-led strike wave of January-February 1919 the official leadership of the trade union movement had, as we have noted, effectively sided with the government. The same equivocation was seen in face of the demand for coal nationalisation in the spring of 1919. Although ostensibly backing the miners, the TUC leadership and that of the Labour Party, under Jimmy Thomas of the railway workers, had been wary of remobilising the pre-war Triple Alliance of miners, transport workers and rails. Through the first nine months of 1919 the TUC leadership repeatedly allowed itself to be outmanoeuvred by the coalition government still intent on returning the mines to private ownership.

Yet 1919 was also a year of increasing militancy and rising political expectations on the Left. The number of strike days, as we noted earlier, rose to 34 million, the highest figure ever. The local elections saw strong gains for the Left – with Labour capturing 12 councils in London and advancing in South Wales, the North and Scotland. Internationally the year saw a short-lived Soviet government in Hungary, Soviets temporarily established in northern Italy and the workers' movement in Germany recovering from the murders of its leadership in January 1919. Within Britain's formal and informal empire, powerful movements of resistance developed in what are now Iraq, Egypt and Iran, in China and, most worryingly for the authorities, in Ireland and India.

1920 saw these tensions escalate. Inflation increased to 15 per cent, the issue of coal nationalisation remained unresolved and the conflict in Ireland moved into a far more active phase.[7] Conflicts within the government also intensified. The post-war coalition brought together two distinct groupings of Conservatives. The dominant group remained those committed to sustain the pound as the dominant world banking currency. They included the two Chamberlains, Austen and Neville, the Geddes brothers, Reginald McKenna and Baldwin. Those who saw the future in terms of a more protectionist bloc of empire territories, now much expanded, included Bonar Law, Milner and Birkenhead and, less emphatically, Curzon. Organisationally the Conservative Party remained intact. The Liberal Party had splintered. Lloyd George, the victorious war-time leader, remained a useful figurehead for a Conservative-dominated government, particularly to contain labour radicalisation. But he was, as he knew, increasingly a hostage and ultimately dispensable.

Outside both groups, but inclined to the former, was the wartime defector from the Liberal Party, Churchill, who by 1918-1919 had placed himself at the head of an informal international anti-Bolshevik alliance largely fronted by the French government.

It is important to note that this alliance was not entirely or even primarily motivated by anti-Bolshevik politics. The Bolsheviks were indeed seen as a political threat – both to Britain's empire possessions in India and China and to domestic stability. But there was also a key economic aspect. The repayment of Russia's massive war debts to Britain and France was seen as essential if these countries were to resume their dominant positions within the post-war international economy – and particularly for Britain's bid to get sterling back on the gold standard at its 1914 parity to the dollar. More that this. A dependent puppet government in Russia, committed to the repayment of Tsarist war debts, would fully open up that country's massive mineral resources, of oil, coal and gold, to external exploitation. If Britain was to regain its dominance of international banking, in face of the United States, Russia had to be secured. Hence, the three years of continuing and expensive war carried on in Russia itself. Churchill's role as war minister was not therefore politically maverick. While it suited the Cabinet for it to be seen as a personal crusade, it was a key element within post-war economic stabilisation – as it was for Britain's key allies, France and Italy.

It was this issue of re-establishing sterling as the dominant international currency that also caused the biggest internal conflict within the government. The pound's reversion to the gold standard at or near its 1914 level was seen by the City of London, and its cabinet supporters, as an essential step if the pound was to regain its position as the world banking currency in face of US competition. However, such a course would require massive cuts in real wages and government spending. Other Conservatives, the empire loyalists, were more fearful of domestic unrest and advocated a closed empire economy operating behind tariff barriers that would sustain wages and employment in Britain.[8]

In 1919 Lloyd George had successfully played these factions off against one another. In face of Treasury demands for cutting back of the promised post-war reconstruction, Lloyd George had exploited the mass strikes of January-February 1919 to push for a reflationary budget delivering the promised expenditure on housing and health. He described it, as we noted earlier, as 'cheap insurance against Bolshevism'.[9] As a result, inflation continued through 1919 – compromising the drive for the gold standard, sustaining high levels of employment and stoking labour militancy.

Towards the end of 1919 the Bank of England, with Treasury support, had started to push up interests rates. By early 1920 it was clear that a majority in the Cabinet were backing a deflationary budget that would drive up unemployment, prepare the way for the necessary assault on wages (particularly in mining) and at the same time destroy Lloyd George's reformist credibility. By February 1920 Lloyd George was putting out feelers to the Labour Party and the Webbs as to the feasibility of an alternative Coalition.[10] Nothing came of this – possibly because the Labour right-wingers already saw themselves as politically endangered – and events took their course. Spring 1920 saw a savagely deflationary budget. Interest rates were increased to 8 per cent. Ministers began preparations for a showdown with the miners in the autumn of 1920, by which time unemployment was expected to rise sharply. However, for the moment unemployment continued to decline, reaching its lowest post-war level of 2.6 per cent in June 1920. Inflation also rose, to 15 per cent, and for the first six months of 1920 union membership continued to increase – to a peak of 8.3 million.[11] Strike action also reached a new high – much of it 'unofficial', initiated at workplace and shop steward level without official sanction.[12]

2 The Labour Movement swings towards direct action

On 13-14 July a specially-convened TUC voted by 2.7m to 1.6m in favour of balloting members for direct action if the government continued its policies of direct or indirect intervention in Russia and its use of military force in

Ireland.[13] It instructed the General Council to make detailed preparations for national moblisation.[14] The TUC also reaffirmed its support for the public ownership of the mines. Three days before, on 10 July, the Scottish Trades Union Congress had also taken a decision for 'direct action' in August to force a reversal of the government's decision to deregulate rents – combining an all-Scottish general strike with a withholding of rent.[15]

These developments took the government by surprise. Neither the Ministry of Labour nor the Home Office had predicted such outcomes. Very quickly authoritative figures were warning of the dangers. Sir Lynden Macassey KC, the government's Director of Labour for munitions during the war, wrote in the *Sunday Times* for 18 July under the headline 'Force versus Freedom' detailing the scale of the reversal in attitudes and rebuking the 'official' Labour leaders for vacillation. He cited the Webbs as previously arguing that a general strike for political ends was highly unlikely in Britain: 'The unexpected', he wrote, 'has now happened'.[16] Two days later the Minister of Labour apologised to his cabinet colleagues for troubling them at the beginning of the summer recess but felt it necessary to warn them that a 'difficult situation may have to be faced in the comparatively near future'. The most 'disquieting feature', he wrote, was the scale of unofficial strike action and the 'lack of control' by the officers of the trade unions. He instanced the Labour leader, J R Clynes, 'who has shown such courage in the past', as compromising in a way that was 'fatal to all discipline'.

> We have been able to tide over a great many difficult
> situations over the past eighteen months. But there is a limit
> as to what can be done by conciliation.[17]

All this occurred some weeks before the Polish crisis. Four converging developments would seem to explain it.

The first was triggered back in January 1920. This was the fall from grace of the principal bastion of right-wing influence in the Labour movement, Jimmy Thomas, leader of the rail union NUR. Despite support from other Triple alliance members for continued strike action, JH Thomas almost publicly connived with the government to terminate strike action intended to defend real wages and the state control of the rail industry. This led to a storm of protest within the NUR, a public rebuke from Arthur Henderson representing the Labour Party and tacit and sometimes public condemnation by leaders of the Transport Federation and the miners. By the end of April widespread unofficial action on wages was being taken by NUR members. Thomas condemned it but it was backed by his deputy Jim Cramp. This was followed by an open revolt by the union's executive on 20 May over the issue of the transport of arms for Poland. Conflict continued within the NUR executive into June over arms – now involving Ireland as well as Poland. This conflict over the transport of arms was the subject of a special congress on 18 June. This failed to back Thomas – who had been shouted down at a public meeting in Battersea the previous week. At the union's annual conference in Belfast in early July 1920 Thomas suffered a final defeat. The conference endorsed direct action – in this case backing the refusal by its Irish members to carry British troops or munitions for war purposes against the Sinn Fein government.[18] Cramp, the acting general secretary declared that he believed that a 'Soviet government on the Russian plan' might be introduced in Britain without bloodshed.[19] The President WJ Abraham called for united action with the transport workers federation and the miners federation to halt British moves to support the enemies of Soviet Russia.

With this the last remaining bastion of right-wing influence collapsed. Still up till late May 'moderates' had just managed to maintain control of the Parliamentary Committee of the TUC – frustrating at its 22 May meeting calls from the Triple Alliance executives for a conference to challenge the government on its new conscription Bill. Once Thomas had been ousted from effective control of the NUR and Tom Mann had taken over as general secretary of the engineers in early June, all other major trade union groups were under left-wing leadership. This included the miners (Robert Smillie), transport (Robert Williams) and shipbuilding and engineering (Alf Purcell and John Hill). All had policy to oppose British government support for the enemies of Soviet Russia.

The second major development was the decision to move for the organisational unity of the political and trade union wings of the movement to facilitate joint action. On 17 June the Political Committee of the TUC called a special congress for 7/8 July (later changed to 13 July to avoid a clash with the miners conference) on the supply of munitions both for British forces in Ireland and for the enemies of Soviet Russia. Three weeks before that conference, on 25 June, the Labour Party's own conference, effectively controlled by trade union votes, called for the creation of one overall committee representing both the political and industrial sides of the movement to coordinate joint action. The special TUC congress on 13-14 July, as noted earlier, finally voted on the resolution to call a general strike should the government not step back from further military action in both Russia and Ireland.

These organisational changes came on top of the slow organisational build-up of support for Soviet Russia within the country at large. This had begun in early 1919 with the establishment of Hands Off Russia when British armies were still in action in North Russia and Siberia. By early 1920 the committee had the backing from a comprehensive range of trade union leaders: William Straker of the Miners Federation, Purcell of the Furnishing Trades (and Federation of Shipbuilding and Engineering Unions), Cramp of the NUR, Tom Mann of the Engineers, John Hill of the Boilermakers, John Bromley of ASLEF and Alex Gossip of the Furnishing Trades and the ILP.[20] It also had the support in local communities and workplaces organised through the National Shop Stewards Committee, the Clyde Workers Committee and, especially in London's docklands, through Sylvia Pankhurst's *Workers Dreadnought*. It was principally through the work of Sylvia Pankhurst's organisation and London shop stewards that the continuing scale of British government munitions shipments in was first exposed and then stopped. Initially starting with sabotage of the vessels carrying arms for Poland in April 1920, the dockers finally took official strike action on 9 May to halt the coaling of the *Jolly George*, ladened with aircraft and heavy guns, all labelled OHMS.[21] The government, which had always denied it was supplying munitions, was not in a position to intervene.[22]

This campaign in the London docks coincided with the decision of the Labour Party to send an official delegation to Soviet Russia. It left on 28 April and returned on 1 July. It included two dozen leading figures from the Parliamentary Labour Party and the trade union movement. Initial responses were published in the *Herald*. Even from previously cautious middle of the road Labour Party leaders responses varied from acceptance to enthusiastic. Margaret Bondfield:

> the movement will never regret it sent the deputation to
> Russia. Those who have been privileged to visit Russia
> have certainly realised the complexity of the problems and
> we come back in firm opposition to the Entente policy and
> convinced that the safety of Western Europe as well as that of
> the Russian people demands peace and goodwill with Russia.

Mrs Snowden:

> In Russia the men and women work together in everything
> and under the same conditions. They consider they have
> solved what we call the women question by establishing
> equality in every profession … paid exactly the same income.

Committed left-wingers like Purcell and Robert Williams saw the delegation as vindicating their previous positions. Purcell, now president of the Shipbuilding and Engineering Federation, told the press, 'All power to the Soviets...and here in England I say all power to the soviets everywhere'.

This development was of particular importance for ideological alignments. Previously attitudes to the Soviet revolution, and particularly condemnation of its 'unconstitutional' character, had formed a key dividing line between left and right. That line no longer held. There was general anger at Britain's duplicity together with demands for an immediate end to the economic blockade and any further military assistance to anti-Soviet forces.[23]

The fourth development was a widening fear, within the general population, of a major new war as Britain struggled to subdue the new territories it had acquired and to hold those it already possessed. In the early months of 1920 troops were actively engaged in China and on India's northwest frontier. In the new territory of Mesopotamia (Iraq) British military garrisons were under siege and equally so in the oil-bearing territories of Iran, in the remaining British enclaves on the Caspian and the Black Sea, in Egypt and increasingly in Ireland. On 25 June the government issued a call for reservists to return to the army and three days later British troops were on their way to support Greece in its war with Turkey.

Of key importance in politically deepening what might otherwise have been simply resistance to renewed war was the role of the *Daily Herald*. This was organisationally and financially sustained by a range of trade unions. Of these the transport workers federation, led by Williams and Ernest Bevin, was foremost. The paper's journalists were mainly members of the ILP and the BSP and the Guild Socialists – and quite a number would join the united Communist Party in August 1920. By the spring of 1920 the paper had a mass circulation of over 300,000 and took a strongly pro-Soviet position. It led the way in detailing the government's duplicitous role in the empire, exposing the Amritsar massacre in early summer 1920 as well as the continuing role of British forces in Russia. In summer 1919 the government had claimed that it was withdrawing British forces from active service in North Russia and in December 1919 that it was ending all military and financial support for the remaining White forces. The comprehensive defeat of the Whites in the early months of 1920 saw their archives falling into Soviet hands – revealing, as reproduced in the *Herald*, the falseness of government claims.

Cumulatively, it was these four developments, the failure of the Right, the creation of a new organisational unity led by the Left, the transformation of attitudes to Soviet Russia and the development of a politicised peace movement, that led the Minister of Labour to issue his warning to Cabinet colleagues on 20 July.

Returning to James Cronin's waves of militancy, it was this relatively brief period, the summer of 1920 with record levels of both employment and unofficial strike action, that marked the peak of the third wave. Already in the weeks before the Polish crisis, the Home Office was reporting significant levels of political expectation – especially in mining communities – with the belief that the coming miners' strike would see a showdown between organised labour and the government. The country's one million miners, constituting one sixth of the total male workforce, remained determined to ensure that their industry remained under state control. In Yorkshire, it was reported, 'every village pub was a debating society'. In Scotland the 'younger unmarried miners' were described as looking forward to the strike as 'the precursor to revolution'. The formation of the National Union of Ex-Servicemen in July, holding a ten-thousand strong demonstration in

Liverpool, was viewed as a matter of great concern by the authorities. With 36,000 members MI5 referred to it as the nucleus of a future Red Army.[24] The Home Office commentary concluded:

> 'the situation has become far more menacing. All the
> indications point to a strike of the miners, if not the engineers,
> during the second half of September and this may develop
> into a real struggle. The plans of the strikers, in collusion
> with the Cooperative Society, are far better laid than they
> were last year and it is essential that no time should be lost in
> maturing plans for the safety of food supplies, public services
> and means of communication, especially as the Transport
> Workers, or sections of them, may join the strike.'

All this occurred prior to the Polish crisis.

3 The Polish Crisis and the formation of the Councils of Action

In April 1920 Polish forces had launched a surprise attack on Soviet Russia. Supplied with tanks and aircraft by the British and French, they made fast advances and captured Kiev in May.[25] By June, however, they were coming under heavy pressure from the Red Army. By July they were in full retreat. The end of the month saw Soviet forces driving towards Warsaw – with Soviet troops reaching the German enclave of East Prussia on 31 July. On 1 August the *Sunday Times* reported fraternisation between Soviet and German soldiers. In Danzig, the only supply route for British and French arms to Poland, the German dockers were refusing to unload further munitions and British troops sent to intervene. [26]

For the British government this represented a most dangerous development. Although the Versailles Treaty had been signed the previous summer, the details of the financial reparations remained under negotiation. The British were fearful that the penal terms demanded by the French were destabilising Germany and threatening the fragile control exercised by its right-wing government. The imminent arrival of Soviet troops at the German frontier was seen as an almost existential threat to the stability of the continent. [27]

Churchill and Curzon backed the French in wanting an immediate declaration of war. Lloyd George vacillated. On 2 August Churchill had an article in the *Evening Times* putting the case for war and the remobilisation of the German forces – the day after the Poles had broken off peace negotiations with the Soviet government. On 3 August Lloyd George sought to distance himself from Churchill's article but on 5 August sent an ultimatum threatening war unless the Soviet advance was halted. Four battle cruisers were despatched to Danzig.[28]

On Friday 6 August Robert Williams for the Transport Workers demanded the implementation of the 13 July TUC resolution. The miners' federation leader Robert Smillie, at the time attending an international meeting of miners' trade unions in Geneva, telegrammed his union's decision that all mines should stop. Arthur Henderson, as leader of the Labour Party, then issued a call for weekend demonstrations against war and sent a letter calling for a meeting of the Labour Party NEC and the TUC Parliamentary Committee on Monday 9th.[29] The Communist Party, formed just seven days before and based mainly on the Labour Party-affiliated British Socialist Party, sent a telegram to all branches calling for the formation of local 'action committees'.[30]

The Labour Party and the TUC duly met at 6 p.m. on Monday and issued a joint call saying that the movement's 'whole industrial power' would be used to halt war and summoned a national conference, a Council of Action, to implement the 13 July decision.[31] At 7pm this decision was communicated to the prime minister. At the Cabinet meeting later that evening Lloyd George secured agreement to open negotiations with the Soviet delegation on the terms then being offered: that Soviet troops would withdraw to the previous border in return for an end to the blockade and the start of discussions on trade.[32] Three days later, 1,400 delegates met at the conference convened by the national Council of Action and issued instructions for all trades councils and local Labour Party branches (many still joint organisations as Trades and Labour Councils) to constitute themselves as local Councils of Action.[33] In the event of a strike call they were to take over responsibility for providing community services and maintaining order. The *Herald*'s headlines for the weekend 13-14 August were 'All Power to the Council' and 'Britain will have Peace – or Revolution'.[34]

The lead article for *The Communist* appearing the previous day ran:

> Russia has sent out a call to the workers but her call has been heard beyond the boundaries of Poland. Her splendid fight these last three years, the general education of the proletarian intellect by its own experience to distrust its rulers, the great drive of Communists and Socialists, especially though the "Hands Off Russia" committees – all these factors are bearing their fruit at last. British Labour has risen as one man to the task. The actions of the Labour Party executive on the second day of the present crisis, of the Parliamentary Committee on the fourth are symptomatic, in their way as eloquent of the vast flood of rank and file protests... The constitution of a 'Council of Action' to direct the general strike against the blockade and the war is an inevitable step if the workers wish to win this fight.[35]

THE COUNCILS OF ACTION 1920

4 Did the threat of a general strike halt the drift to war?

The *Daily Herald*, the Left and the Labour Party claimed that Lloyd George's decision to back Soviet peace proposals on 9 August was the result of this mass mobilisation for strike action. The *Herald* headline on 11 August was 'Triumph for Labour's Council of Action: Premier Climbs Down'. Lloyd George later denied that it had been the threat of a general strike that had swayed the government's decision. They were 'pushing at an open door'. Most historians since, Macfarlane, Stephen White and, to an extent, Chris Wrigley, have tended to support this line and to present popular opposition to war as pacifist rather than pro-socialist.[36] For them the mobilisation, though real enough, was of limited potential precisely because it was called officially by the Labour Party and by the TUC leaderships and hence, they suggest, the right-wing must always have been ultimately in control.

The weakness of this interpretation is that it abstracts the Councils of Action from the wider crisis of industrial relations in the summer of 1920. As the government and its advisers knew only too well, the Labour Party right-wing had at least temporarily lost control of the TUC and hence effectively of the Labour Party's executive and done so amid a general swing towards direct action. As we have noted, a significant part of the leadership of the movement was, for these brief months, either Communist, Tom Mann of the engineers, Alf Purcell of the Shipbuilding and Engineering Federation and Robert Williams of the transport workers, or strongly pro-Soviet, Bob Smillie of the miners. Even the railway workers were now under the leadership of Cramp who at that point had declared Soviet sympathies.

The Home Office and MI5, though sometimes inclined to exaggerate, had no particular reason to do so on this occasion. The *Herald* for 10 August reports a court hearing on the 9 August with a police inspector giving evidence on events over the weekend. 'A crowd of quite 4,000 persons completely blocked Edgeware Road' shouting 'hands off Russia' and 'we don't want any war'. Despite a 'large body of police', the constabulary were temporarily overpowered, two injured and a man earlier arrested released. Further police reinforcements ultimately enabled the arrest of two men. The Home Office report for 12 August describes people attending anti-war meetings in their thousands, the police being attacked and, very different from any time between 1914 and 1918, pro-war speakers from the government-subsidised People's League being thrown off their platforms. 'Never have we known such excitement'. The *Daily Herald*, it was reported, had achieved an importance 'which it has never had since the railway strike'. The Home Office report notes the degree to which the calling of the Council of Action had served to 'rehabilitate the moderate labour leaders with their extreme supporters and to weld the whole temporarily into one body.' 'Left and Right have joined forces .. moderate leaders whose popularity is on the wane have seized the opportunity of giving the lie to accusations of "treachery"'.[37]

The Pall Mall Gazette, with close links to Conservative members of the cabinet, expressed extreme concern through the second and third weeks of August at the loss of control by Clynes and the Labour right-wingers: 'smoothing the way for the Bolshevik steamroller' (7 August), 'pawn of the Bolsheviks' (10 August), Thomas implicated in a 'direct challenge to the constitution' (13 August), 'our very own Soviet: a declaration of war against democracy' (14 August) and on 16 August a report that 'the government has in its hands' information on the revolutionary intent on the Councils of Action' and that the 'Labour crisis which is threatening' may assume a much graver aspect. The *Gazette* announced on 12 August 'The King postpones holiday' – no doubt mindful of the consequences of his Russian cousin's absence on vacation three years before.

This chronology itself indicates the weakness of the 'pushing at an open door' thesis – that already before 9 August Lloyd George and his government had decided not to go to war. While on 9 August the government had publicly backed away from such a course, it remained an option. The French government, with whom Churchill was in constant contact, was actively committed to intervention via Poland. On 10 August the French government officially recognised Wrangel, then occupying South Russia and armed and supplied mainly by Britain. In the following days, particularly during Lloyd George's discussions with the Italian government, military intervention was actively canvassed but again abandoned in face of the domestic situation and the lack of government preparation. The postponement of the King's departure from London on 11 August, two days after the notional turning point, indicates the depth of the crisis. Still on 16 August Lloyd George was calling in the Commons for a common front against the threat to the constitution.[38]

Beatrice and Sidney Webb, at the time strongly hostile to the militant Left, doubted Lloyd George's claim that the Councils of Action had no effect.[39] Alan Clinton, who has made the most comprehensive analysis of trades council records, comes to a similar conclusion. He considers these weeks in 1920 to be the high water mark of the organisational influence of trades councils in the 20th century. [40] In many cases trades council members saw themselves to be preparing institutions which, they thought, would sooner or later provide the local basis for working class state power. The Home Office reports for the last two weeks of August and the beginning of September describe the preparations being made in South Wales, the North East, Birmingham, Glasgow and London's East End. The cooperative movement, trade union divisional councils alongside Trades and Labour Councils were actively mobilising. 'The real danger is the very rapid growth in revolutionary feeling that has followed the establishment of the Council of Action … Just as the formation of the National Council united for the first time, Left and Right leaders, so the local councils are permeating that great mass of workers that is usually apathetic. My correspondents report that audiences grow bigger almost daily and there is no opposition. Bolshevism is openly advocated and enormous quantities of extremist literature are distributed. In the Glasgow district alone nearly a million leaflets and pamphlets were distributed during the last weekend.'[41]

The Council of Action's own reports on home security were supplied by the Police Union. Although the union had been declared illegal after the national police strike in 1918 it retained a rump of clandestine membership organised to sustain the hundreds of police personnel dismissed. Its leadership maintained pre-existing links with colleagues in the intelligence section. Their reports indicated that all army leave had been cancelled, troops concentrated at key points, the police armed and an emergency conference of Chief Constables held on 15 August. 'Basil Thomson [head MI5] and the War Office have absolute charge of policy in dealing with the newspapers'.[42] All this was a week after the notional 'turning point'.

The Home Office report to Cabinet for the beginning of September describes the 'revolutionary tendency of the local Councils of Action are becoming more pronounced'.[43] A week later Noah Ablett, S O Davies and A J Cook are described as developing detailed local organisations in Merthyr and the Rhonda valley for 'a soviet system of government'.[44] Similar developments are described in the North East where a federation had been created incorporating twenty-one Labour constituencies. The Ministry of Labour report for the beginning of September describes the industrial situation, particularly as regards the miners and engineers, as 'becoming more serious'.[45]

5 How was this level of working-class challenge achieved?

At this point it is useful to break off from the narrative and return to the wider issue of how such mass mobilisation develops and is sustained. The mobilisation was clearly at a different level to that eighteen months before. Left-wing leaders no longer felt they needed to exercise caution in discussing long-term objectives.

Increasingly also the means were phrased in terms of 'popular democracy' as Middlemas put it, or new systems of locally-based workers committees as advocated by Gallacher and JR Campbell and also, in a slightly different form, by GDH Cole and the Guild Socialists. It is also clear that these terms enjoyed a resonance among a significant cadre of workers and that arguments for socialism no longer resulted in counter-productive responses. To that extent the government's elaborate scheme for counterpropaganda, developed in autumn 1919, seems to have had very little effect. Despite the daily syndication of features across hundreds of local and regional publications, Bolshevism was no longer a bogy. And this was particularly so among the younger sections of the workforce. Home Office reports stress the radicalisation of young workers such as those miners 'without family responsibilities'. Lloyd George also highlighted 'young men' when he set out the government's priorities somewhat earlier:

'They must recapture the public mind and counter that formidable body of young men whose aim it is to destroy the present industrial and parliamentary system and replace it with a workers' state – and whose advocacy of Soviet government drew strength from popular impatience with the parliamentary mode of government. Grievances, principally profiteering, must be met ... the making of money has become a craze...' [46]

These younger workers were drawn from a generation that, if they were not essential workers, would have gone through the war or been close to others who had. Some at least would have been radicalised by this experience – particularly during the final months of chaotic demobilisation and troop mutinies. It was these radicalised ex-soldiers who formed the core of the Discharged Servicemen. Few among the remainder would have welcomed a return of conscription – nor would their families, a fair majority of whom would already have suffered grievous losses. Then, on top of this there were, and not to be minimised, the immediate economic circumstances. For most of 1920, up till the early autumn, very high levels of employment had been coupled with 15 percent inflation, popularly seen as the 'profiteering' referred to by Lloyd George. By then, and for the best part of two years previously, unofficial, workplace action had been the main route for maintaining living standards – increasingly also involving solidarity action between different groups of workers.

All these factors had in fact been summed up earlier in 1920 by the head of Home Intelligence in a report to the Cabinet. As he listed them, they were 'profiteering', bad housing, 'class hatred aggravated by the foolish ostentation of the rich', 'education by Labour colleges ... and better circulation of literature on Marxist economics', 'influence by extremist trade union leaders' (he named some of them: 'Mann, Cramp, Smillie, Hodges, Bromley, Hill, Williams, Turner'), the Labour press 'particularly the *Daily Herald*', and 'external influences – Russia, Ireland, Egypt, India'.[47]

These last words were almost exactly the same as those thrown at Cato Worsfold MP during his ill-fated lantern slide lecture in Balham in June 1920.

Yet there was also another factor not to be underestimated. This was the active winning of wider support over previous years, detailed, practical local discussion, and the organisation which had sustained this. The transformations of late spring, early summer 1920 were not spontaneous or automatic. The initial storm centre was the London docks back in April-May. Harry Pollitt later wrote that 'the strike was the result of two years of tremendously hard and unremitting work on the part of a devoted band of comrades in East London' – including the detailed organisation undertaken by Sylvia Pankhurst's *Workers Dreadnought* principally among the women workers. One of the key players in the move to direct action, the secretary of the Transport Workers Federation Robert Williams, wrote the following year: 'the formation of the Council of Action in 1920 was the result of the painstaking and serious propaganda in favour of revolutionary direct action throughout 1919 on behalf of the Triple Alliance'.[48]

Without such constant, detailed argument, by what Pollitt described as a 'dedicated band of comrades', no informed and directed change of attitudes is likely to have taken place. Pre-existing prejudices, the manifold cocoons of 'reified' consciousness, would have continued and been effectively exploited by the government's own, by now, massive and very sophisticated propaganda offensive.

By 1920, however, something of a turning point seems to have been reached. We have earlier seen the attempts to use anti-Semitism during the events of 1919 – at a time when immigrant Jewish populations comprised a significant section of unskilled workers in London's east end and in port cities such as Glasgow and Liverpool. This was equally the case within and against Irish immigrant populations. But it was, it would appear, increasingly ineffective. In 1919 attempts to do so in Belfast were manifestly counter-productive and continued to be so through most of 1920. Very significantly the ultimate character of the intervention in Belfast in July 1920 was 'external', the violent actions of an armed militia. Its scale, particularly the detailed identification of a thousand 'Protestant' workers in the city's biggest workplace, also indicates something of more general importance. By 1920, even in Belfast, 'active' socialists, or those generally seen to be loyal to such positions, were not limited to a few dozen. They composed a very significant section of the workforce. Two years later the employer lockouts in Britain tell a similar story. In conditions of high unemployment, they effectively enforced a purge of socialists – first from among all skilled trades in Scottish shipbuilding and later among electricians and engineers across Britain by requiring all returning workers to sign 'the document': a legal commitment never to engage in unofficial strike action. A significant core of workers, those committed to a class perspective, were thereby excluded within what were seen as the most militant occupations.

'Emancipatory' language, and its active use, was therefore important. But so also were the organisations that sustained it such as the Shop Stewards National Amalgamated Committee and the range of socialist parties.These ensured the constant interchanges of information, the discussion of tactics and, no less important, the human contact such as the journeys of individuals like Purcell and John Hill across to Belfast in 1919. Little of this was accidental or spontaneous. Debates on tactics took place incessantly – both within the British Socialist Party and the smaller Socialist Labour Party, the left of the Independent Labour Party and the Guild Socialists. These organisations supplied the people who led the work of the *Daily Herald* and who also occupied key positions within the top structures of the Labour Party both directly as members and also as members of affiliated organisations. Page

Arnot, then Secretary of the Labour Party's Research Department working closely with Cole developing the structure of the Councils of Action. From 1 August 1920 he was also part of the core leadership of the Communist Party. The Labour Party's International Committee in Spring 1920 was dominated by people who a few weeks later were also members of the Communist Party's leadership, Emile Burns and Palme Dutt. And, as we have seen, key positions were held in the Labour Party executive by trade union leaders who were either members of the BSP and on the Left of the ILP or very close. Almost all became members of the Communist Party from 1 August 1920 as the component sections of the ILP and the SLP began the process of merging with the BSP/CPGB.

This merger has to be seen in this light and was undoubtedly accelerated by the unfolding events of June and July and the need for a consolidated and coherent leadership. So also does the decision of the new party's founding Congress to carry forward the BSP's affiliation to the Labour Party. The party's leading figures, particularly those in the trade union movement, were already members of the Labour Party's leading committees as leaders of the component unions. The *Daily Herald*'s comment on the day of the party's founding convention, was that 'the founding of such a party we emphatically count as a gain to the movement in this country. It is not a new split. It is indeed a fusion. But it is more than this. It is the creation of an organisation for the expression in action of a definite and existent body of revolutionary thought.'[49]

We will come back to the issue of organisation, of 'the expression in action of a definite and existent body of revolutionary thought' in the concluding chapter. For the moment we will return to the crisis of late summer 1920 and its outcome over the following months.

6 The climax of opposition to war with Soviet Russia – and the counter-attack

The period of mass mobilisation ran on through August as Lloyd George's Coalition government continued to tack and manoeuvre – still seeking to find ways of aiding the enemies of Soviet Russia either through Poland or by support for the remaining White forces under Wrangel that controlled much of south Russia. As we have seen, popular mobilisation against the war was massively extended on 13 August when the joint Labour Party-TUC conference, with its 1,400 delegates, called for the formation of Councils of Action at local level. The 300 local Councils of Action brought together, usually under the banner of trades and labour councils, local political parties of the Left, cooperatives, women's guilds, trade union branches, unemployed organisations and organised ex-servicemen. Their remit was, immediately, to prepare local organisation that could take over the running of towns and cities once the strike call had been made.

The ruling class response came with escalating force through the autumn and winter. It was mass unemployment. While the April 1920 increase in interest rates to 8 percent had taken longer than expected to impact, it was devastating when it did. By March 1921 twenty percent of the working population was unemployed.

Meanwhile, however, the momentum of the summer's working class mobilisations was intensified by the formation of local organisation on the ground through local councils of action. It is important to stress the impact of this on local working class communities, its scale and also the wider context. On 11 August, as the Red Army continued to advance on Warsaw, the day after Lloyd George claimed to have changed course, France had recognised Wrangel in south Russia as the legitimate Russian government. While Lloyd George declared that the British government had no knowledge of this, France confirmed that Britain had been consulted in advance.[50]

This was the immediate background to the Friday 13 August conference in London and its unprecedently high attendance. On the previous Wednesday and Thursday, the *Daily Herald* reported, 'the public in cities, towns and villages have attended meetings generally called by Labour bodies …in many centres the full Labour policy of direct action has been endorsed … the men on which the first brunt of such action would fall have been foremost in calling for it'. The conference was unanimous. Robert Williams for the transport federation set the tone: 'it was better to make peace unconstitutionally than to go to war and to kill in the name of the British constitution'. Robert Smillie, for the miners' federation, called for a boycott of all coal exports to France. Ernest Bevin demanded that the Council of Action remain in being until 'they secured an absolute guarantee that British forces would not be used against the Soviet government', the withdrawal of all British naval forces and the recognition of the Soviet government. 'This country refuses to be associated with any alliance between Great Britain and France or any other country which commits to any support for Wrangel, Poland or the supply of munitions … and calls for the withdrawal of labour in support'. The parliamentary correspondent of The *Herald* commented: 'prejudice simply rolled away like a fog'.

Demonstrations were called over the weekend across the country. On Monday (16 August) the *Herald* reported that the numbers of meetings were too great to provide full reports. In the Commons, still in emergency session, Lloyd George refused to give any assurances and instead denounced the Councils of Action as 'one of the most formidable challenges ever given to democracy' and pledged that the government would fight back 'with all its resources'. The previous day, it will be remembered, the government had convened a meeting of Chief Constables to discuss internal security. All army and police leave had been cancelled. And there was a further attempt to relaunch the Bolshevik bogy. On 17 August the Admiralty announced that it had decoded Soviet cables indicating financial support for the *Herald*

– followed by an avalanche of press attacks on the threat to the constitutional order posed by the Councils. These accusations seem to have little immediate effect. Even more mass meetings were held across the country the following weekend. At a meeting in Wigan Bevin challenged Lloyd George on the issue of the constitution: he did not believe that the work of the Councils of Act was over. 'It had only just begun'. Over the following weeks the *Herald*'s circulation, according to MI5, increased by 20,000.

An analysis of the local councils of action, based on their correspondence held in the Labour Party archives, has been published elsewhere.[51] Checked against evidence from the press, the *Herald* and MI5 records it finds that most local Councils of Action continued into the autumn. In terms of political orientation it finds a majority took the line of the *Herald* (and the Communist Party): around 170 of the 300. For many of the others there was no relevant correspondence and it be reasonable to assume that most would also have taken a Left position. Others may simply have dropped out of activity.Those actively on the Left, evidenced by continuing correspondence, called, over the following weeks, for general strike action in the support of the miners and against military coercion in Ireland. These councils continuing in active session were largely in mining areas (at a time when mining employed one in six of all male workers) or the big cities, London, Birmingham, Manchester. The highest percentages of known 'Left' councils were: North East 90 per cent of recorded Councils, Wales 87 per cent, Scotland 83 per cent and Yorkshire 81 per cent – as against the East Midlands 38 per cent and the South East 32 per cent. As we noted earlier, it was in the mining areas also that the most elaborate local organisation took place – effectively creating a shadow structure of government across parts of South Wales and Tyneside.

It was, it would seem, largely because of this depth of wider solidarity in mining areas that the government eventually backed away from an immediate confrontation with miners in September 1920. By October it had negotiated a compromise wage settlement. The government had already been warned in mid-September by Sir Henry Wilson, Chief of Imperial General Staff, that its call for the withdrawal of ten battalions from Ireland would mean abandoning most of that country to Sinn Fein.[52] Equally in terms of the police. The Home Office was concerned that, after the mass sackings following the 1918 police strike, the remaining force was undertrained and 'for the first time ever' would, in case of serious disturbance, face adversaries in the shape of the National Union of Ex-Servicemen who were better trained (at the same time MI5 monitored, as best it could, discussions on military training involving Sinn Fein officers, the chair of Communist Party Arthur McManus and Colonel Malone.[53])

How far then can the Councils of Action movement be described as one that involved a wider, if only very temporary, challenge to capitalist state power – one with a socialist content? Or was it essentially pacifist, a mobilisation for peace by a generation that had already seen more than enough war?

The argument for peace itself was a powerful one. But it seems to have been seen by The *Herald*, and those leading the Left, more as a strategic bridge for the specific purpose of building wider support within what the *Herald* described as the 'middle classes'. On Sunday 22 August, the day reserved for protest meetings across the country, the transport workers' leader Harry Gosling told a rally in the south-east London middle class suburb of Erith that there was 'no difference of opinion on the part of workers across the country and that the middle classes were behind them.' Even here, however, red flags were displayed and when 'a soldier' tried to remove one he was 'roughly handled by a section of the crowd'. Across the country red flags were routinely displayed at the meetings.

Much more directly the movement was now about social change. The biggest rally that day, held in Trafalgar Square, swamped surrounding streets and squares with close on 100,000 attending. The organisers almost flaunted the potential for a fundamental transformation. The ranks of the Ex-Servicemen were drawn up across one side of the square. The ranks of the (now illegal) Police Union lined up across the other. The third side was covered by the National Federation of Women Workers. 'Everyone seemed to be wearing some red emblem'. Unlike January 1919 just eighteen months before, there was now no hesitation about mentioning Soviet power. The Chair, Councillor E Friend, 'told the meeting we were now suffering from dictatorship from Downing Street. If there was to be a dictatorship better have a working class dictatorship'. Margaret Bondfield reported on her earlier visit to Soviet Russia and moved the resolution to secure recognition for the socialist republic – sending fraternal greetings to the workers of the world. The main speaker was Lansbury. He began by calling for 'three cheers for internationalism and thanking the government and the capitalist press for the splendid advertisement they had given the *Daily Herald* and the tremendous increase in circulation' (by revealing the claimed Soviet subsidies). Lansbury called for an end to war in Turkey, Russia and Ireland and the release of the Lord Mayor of Cork, shortly to die in Brixton jail. 'The people of Russia had done what the English workers should have done long ago ... the right, left and middle wings of the socialist movement had disappeared: they were now a solid body for peace with Russia, peace with Ireland, peace with India and peace at home'. Fred Bramley, one of the three joint secretaries of the Council of Action and later, in 1923-25, the strongly left-wing general secretary of the TUC, described the Council as 'one of the most remarkable movements in working class history'.[54]

In the reports of dozens of other meetings up and down the country that weekend, talk of revolution or even a dictatorship of the working class was no longer seen as a handicap to mass mobilisation. Attitudes had shifted sharply. What were the key arguments now ? Peace remained. But, after the victory over the government in early August, it was more than peace. It was about the 'next step' which is what Bramley meant by one of the 'most remarkable movements in working class history'. This was about the demand for ownership: immediately for the public control of Britain's biggest industry, coal, and then more later.

In 1920 coal still remained under state control. As everyone knew, the government's commitment was to privatise it as part of its wider strategy to return to the gold standard. Cutting wages in the pits was the first step in a more general reduction in wages and fully reasserting the power of capitalist market forces over working people. It had been the government's intention to start this move in autumn 1920.

Hence across Britain's coal mining areas – from Fife, Lanarkshire and Ayrshire, through the north-east, Yorkshire, Lancashire, Nottinghamshire to South Wales – the Councils of Action were viewed as having a much broader role in building for resistance and cementing solidarity action at local level with other workers. In doing so, and in taking control of local communities, the Councils would provide the structures for working people to collectively take control of the means of production. G.D.H. Cole, from his position in the Labour Party's Research Department in charge of organising the Councils, put it in almost exactly these terms in September 1926: 'we are coordinating the forces of Labour not simply in order to increase Labour's strength in negotiations but for an actual assault of capitalism, to be followed an actual assumption of power'.[55]

However, in September-October 1920 there was no show-down. While unemployment had started to bite, it had only done so only patchily, and the government decided to temporise. It negotiated the compromise Datum Line agreement with the miners in October-November 1920 and took a further six months to prepare the ground. At the TUC in early September the Left had remained dominant. The proposal to replace its parliamentary committee by a more powerful 'general staff' was carried despite opposition from Clynes. Resolutions for peace with Russia and self-rule for Ireland were passed without opposition. Alf Purcell's final report on the Russian delegation was given enthusiastic approval. J H Thomas at this stage said that the position on the Councils of Action was fully justified.

In the following weeks of September and October 1920 there was clearly some hesitancy in both the Cabinet and the right-wing of the Labour Party about further action. Unemployment was seen as providing, as in the past, a potential for control – but this was combined with the fear that in the new circumstances it might also bring still further radicalisation. The Intelligence report for 7 October reports 'agitators are inciting the unemployed to seize the means of production...the worst feature are that the men are told that unemployment is an artificial condition, a mere move in the campaign of the employers against labour'. Two weeks later the report for 21 October noted that 'there is a feeling, assiduously fanned by the revolutionary press, that the government and employers are leagued together' and goes on to quote John Hill, Secretary of the Boilermakers, writing in his union journal: 'our employers deliberately brought about [unemployment] with malice aforethought. Our industry is run for profit and for profit only. The first thing essential to this end is to have a surplus of labour.'[56] A few days before the Minister of Labour had informed the Cabinet that 'the Labour movement has shown keen interest in recent industrial developments in Italy … principally, of course, in the reports of the seizure of workplaces by workers on strike in the north of Italy'.[57]

The battle for the control of language and, through this, for the interpretation of how the economy operated was clearly, by the autumn of 1920, a central concern for the government. Would more unemployment 'control', as in the past, or stimulate further revolt? However, effectively the Treasury and the Bank of England had already set the course: the rate of unemployment rose without cease to 20 percent by April 1921.

Meantime the right-wing within the Labour Party began to test the waters. In late September the right-wing mustered a majority on the Labour Party executive to reject the application of the Communist Party for affiliation. Its action was editorially condemned in the *Herald*: 'we protest against this decision. There is no greater division of line or method between the Labour Party and the Communist Party than there was between the Labour Party and the British Socialist Party [which] forms a very large proportion of the Communist Party.' It also noted the continuing anomaly that local Communist branches were still fully accepted as affiliates of local Constituency Labour Parties.[58]

The same week, on 28 September, a motion was moved at the National Council to wind up the Councils of Action at the full meeting of the National Council. It was defeated with just the mover and seconder supporting.[59] A subsequent move by J H Thomas in October was defeated 32 to 18, on a counter motion by Robert Williams that the Council remain in being till 'the Russia question has been settled'.[60] Mid-November saw North East Councils sending out a call for all local councils to demand a National Conference. This was quickly backed by Birmingham with a similar circular. On 15 November, again at the initiative of Robert Williams, the TUC and NEC of the Labour Party called for the remobilisation of the councils to demand that the government end its prevarications on opening trade and fully recognise Soviet Russia.[61] The *Herald*'s headline was 'The Council of Action Awakens'. December saw a spate of resolutions from local Councils on the issue of trade with Russia, unemployment and Ireland and on 23 December the National Council met to discuss developing pressure on the government. By January 1921, however, the National Council was dismissing further demands for action as 'Communist inspired' – even though some local Councils continued to send resolutions demanding action on unemployment and Irish coercion up till April (36 Councils did so then with the biggest number in London).[62]

By March, with unemployment nearing its peak of 20 percent, the government was finally ready to act. It moved to isolate and defeat the miners over the fundamental issue of returning the mines to private ownership. The promised backing from the other members of the Triple Alliance failed to materialise. The NUR, with Thomas's influence resurgent, withdrew its support at the final moment. This was followed, though less predictably, by the Transport Federation. This federation was still very much a loose association. Many of its small individual unions, already faced with massive membership loss, were now fighting for their existence. The Federation's secretary, Robert Williams, was isolated as Bevin took control of the situation. 'Black Friday' effectively closed this period of intense labour militancy. During these final weeks the *Daily Herald* had tried to reconfigure linguistic understandings of trade union alignments in line with those previously applied in Russia. The government and all those – in the Labour Party and elsewhere – giving them tacit support were described as 'The Whites'. All those supporting continuing solidarity with the miners were 'The Reds'.

But with mass unemployment and the Left now displaced from its control in key unions, particularly Robert Williams in transport, the right-wing had taken over the *Daily Herald*, replaced its editor and sacked almost all its journalists. The government and its supporters inside and outside the Labour movement fully understood the power of language – including the press. The period of intense challenge was over.

Interim conclusions

What conclusions can be drawn ? First, for the government. There were, as we have seen, significant divisions. But for the dominant grouping the main concern was always how to manage the labour movement. This was why the Tories tolerated Lloyd George for so long. Social stability came first. If it eventually required abandoning the Poles, Wrangel and Russian debts, so be it. If it required mass unemployment and a shuddering brake on the economy, that also was a necessary cost – even if it condemned the country to a decade of low growth, far lower than that in comparable economies. As the Cabinet Secretary Sir Maurice Hankey warned in early August, the government's strategic focus must be domestic: 'to tame the labour movement and rescue the pound.' These two objectives were not compatible with a new war.[63]

The second conclusion concerns the way the Labour Party was now seen by the guardians of the established order. After March 1921 and the restoration of right-wing control it was viewed as an essential support for continued stability – as long as it remained under the correct leadership. Organised labour could be chastened by mass unemployment. But it could not safely be repressed as a political movement. This was now the settled conviction of the key centrist figures in the Conservative Party such as Baldwin, Bonar Law and their principal adviser J.C.C. Davidson.[64] And, if this was the case, its leadership could not be left to visibly corrupt carpet baggers like JH Thomas. It required new leaders with credibility among the younger, upcoming generation of trade unionists. Ernest Bevin was seen as the best potential candidate.

The third conclusion concerns the politics of Labour itself. Our earlier study of Clydeside after 1919 demonstrated the shift which occurred electorally in the 1920 local elections and then in the 1922 general election. A base of mass support had finally emerged – one that did not particularly discriminate between the Communist left, the ILP Left and the trade union left, all of which, at that stage (including the émigré Scot Ramsay Macdonald) paid tribute to Karl Marx as the movement's founding father. After the summer of 1920 the same applied to most parts of England and Wales. Parallel to the identification of 1920 as a key turning point for a mass trade union movement so also the analysts of generational shifts in political alignment identify these months as marking the emergence of mass support for the Labour Party.[65] The 1922 election saw a 9 percent swing in its favour – now giving Labour four million votes against an unchanged 5.2 million for the Conservatives and a significantly reduced share to the Liberals.

Our fourth conclusion, an interim one, concerns the language of class mobilisation, its power and its limits. The slogans of the Bolshevik revolution were Peace, Land and Bread. That of 1920 was singular: that of Peace – even if it was peace with Soviet Russia. Attempts later in 1920 to add 'unemployment' were blocked by the right-wing. Even 'peace in Ireland', although included in June-July 1920, failed to get backing from those who had re-established control over the Labour Party later in the autumn. Both MI5 reports and the wider press coverage show the power of 'peace' as a mass, popular demand through July and August, a demand that clearly also went, as we have seen, beyond a simple 'pacifist' opposition to war and was infused with an explicit opposition to British imperialism: 'India, Egypt, Ireland'. More directly, through the summer of 1920 it was peace with Soviet Russia, with a far sharper ideological challenge, and was directly linked to the visible creation, at local level across Britain, of new forms of power by workplace representatives and working class community organisations, forms directly echoing Russian soviets. In the growing confrontation with the government over the control of the mines these did indeed symbolise potential working class power, particularly in mining areas and also in the working class areas of some of the big cities, London, Birmingham, Manchester and Newcastle. It was this challenge that seems to have been powerful enough to persuade the government to postpone its assault on the miners by six months.

But the government still retained in its own hands sufficiently powerful levers, economic and political, above all unemployment, to transform the economic environment, gut the shop stewards movement, split the Triple Alliance and ensure that a wider confrontation did not take place – even though, for the government, these dangerous months did see a turning point in attitudes to the Labour Party and a decisive shift towards fully incorporating it within the two-party system. This transformation of attitude was to be significantly more central to the politics of Britain through the twentieth century than the 'insurance against Bolshevism' paid out in February 1919 – even though, as we have seen, the resulting sixteen months of full employment up till the summer of 1920 did play a major part in the transformation of the political balance in the trade union and labour movement.

Postscript on the Councils of Action

It is unclear where the term 'Councils of Action' came from. Alan Clinton claims it was used during the 1919 strike in Belfast.[66] However, as we have seen, although the concept may have been present, the term itself was not. The organising body was the 'Strike Committee'. Nor was it used on the Clyde. The central body, bringing together the STUC, the Trades Council and the Clyde Workers Committee, was the 'Joint Committee'. Neighbourhood Locality Committees were set up – at the instigation of Gallacher, it seems – but they were not called either Committees or Councils of Action.

Subsequently Gallacher did further develop the idea in his pamphlet 'Direct Action', jointly written with JR Campbell, and published by the 'Scottish Workers Committees', in December 1919. This built on the experience of the Clyde Workers Committee during the war and the subsequent experience gained during the January 1919 general strike. It stressed the future importance of committees that combined workplace shop stewards with representation from working class neighbourhoods. Gallacher uses the term 'Social Committees' and stresses particularly what he calls the 'repressive role' of these committees in taking over the functions of state power – but in the interests of workers – through the control over the supply of power, food and other necessities and the issuing of permits to local businesses to provide for working class needs. 'The greater the repressive power of the workers, the feebler the resistance'. But again the term Committees of Action is not used. Nor is it used by D.S. Morton, Joint Secretary of the 1919 Strike Committee, in his pamphlet The 40 Hours Strike – although, as noted earlier, Morton does stress the wider community base of strike and the importance of 'Locality Committees', particularly for the role of women.

It seems likely therefore that the actual term 'Council of Action' was coined in July-August 1920, and originated with those tasked to map out the organisational structure of the new organisation. Central here, it would seem, were the academic GDH Cole and Robin Page Arnot, the full-time officer of the Labour Party's Research Department. Both were members of the National Guilds League, sometimes called the 'Guild Socialists', formed late in 1915, which had welcomed the Russian socialist revolution at its 1918 conference and by 1920 had, as Page Arnot puts it, developed a 'revolutionary wing' of which he was a leading member.

The term 'Councils of Action' was carried forward to the 1926 general strike largely at the initiative of the Communist Party and its Left Labour allies in the Minority Movement – a movement established in 1924 to re-create the basis for a militant shop steward-led trade union movement.

The General Strike of 1926: some notes

Mobilisation for the 1926 General Strike does indeed have some potential to reveal the dynamics of class consciousness as developing in specific localities. But as an episode within any wider process, it is more problematic. It has been well analysed elsewhere and it is difficult to represent it in any coherent way as a direct challenge to state power. It could have led in that direction. Page Arnot and Palme Dutt recognised this potential. But even for them its defined aims were, correctly, those of solidarity with the miners which, if successful, would indeed have challenged the existing balance of forces.[67]

The strike itself lasted only nine days. It ended in shameful capitulation, defeat and widespread victimisation – and over 8,000 arrests – and left the miners themselves isolated and forced into ultimate surrender. Overall, it resulted in the dominance, for well over a decade, of the right-wing within both the trade union movement and the Labour Party. For all these reasons it cannot be claimed as a clear inheritor of the wave of mobilisation that began in January 1919. Nor is it easy to identify 'practical moments', or triggers, in which arguments were won for intensified mobilisation. There is indeed potential here for further study in particular localities. But the most relevant focus is in the reverse direction: how, during the strike but even more afterwards, such arguments were lost or, more precisely, suppressed. What was the background ?

A renewed assault on the miners was launched in 1925. That year Britain had returned to the gold standard at 1914 parity to the dollar. To secure international competitiveness the price of coal had to be reduced by at least 10 percent – and thereby also miners' wages. The mine owners, now restored to full ownership, sought these reductions and relied on Baldwin's Conservative government to support them.

The Communist-led Minority Movement of Left-aligned trade unions campaigned throughout 1925 for the TUC to adopt a similar approach to that in 1920 in preparing for solidarity strike action in defence of the miners. It had considerable initial success in mobilising support for a new Quadruple Alliance (Transport, Rails and Engineers alongside the Miners). In March 1925, on 'Red Friday', the threat of a new general strike halted any reduction in miners' wages and forced the government to provide a subsidy for nine months while a Royal Commission deliberated.

The Left, buoyed by this success, was also able to carry through a number of resolutions in favour a collective defence of the miners, as well as trade with the Soviet Union, at the following TUC in September 1925. But there the success of the Left ended. That autumn saw, as a result of right-wing trade union leaders returning to their positions after serving in the first Labour government, a swing to the right in the composition of the TUC General Council. This was followed by the death of its left-wing general secretary, Ted Bramley, and his replacement by the right-winger Walter Citrine. In consequence the TUC made no organisational preparations for a general strike – and spent all its energies in fruitless negotiations to avoid a situation in which it would be obliged to meet its commitment to support the miners.

In the event it was the Communist Party and its not insubstantial group of trade union allies in the Minority Movement that called for the local establishment of Councils of Action during the strike itself. Mainly these were in mining areas (South Wales, the North East, parts of Yorkshire and Fife), in some working class areas of London and, late on in the strike and after a battle with pro-TUC right-wingers, in Glasgow. On Tyneside Robin Page Arnot was a leading figure within the Federation of sixteen Councils of Action and in that capacity was able to lay down terms, in negotiations with local military commanders, for the supply of food to troops. This was, however, exceptional.

Across the country as a whole the areas that adopted Councils of Action were not, it would seem, the majority – certainly at the outset. Elsewhere strike committees were established more directly under the leadership of the TUC and following the organisational direction of Bevin, for the TGWU and Citrine as TUC general secretary. These local strike committees did also seek to exercise control over transport and the distribution of food supplies and issued permits. However, unlike the Councils of Action, they did not extend membership more widely to the National Unemployed Workers Movement or seek comprehensive inclusion of local tenants associations and cooperatives. Nor did they establish, as was the case in Fife, South Wales and parts of Yorkshire, workers' defence corps.

How do we explain this fatal lack of mobilising power? It was because the TUC leadership did not want a strike and feared its consequences.

The decision to call the general strike was effectively forced by the government on an unprepared TUC leadership. By the spring of 1926 it was Baldwin who wanted a strike – on his terms. He saw its inevitable failure as providing a key political opportunity to take forward, and complete in terms of the incorporation of the unions as well as the parliamentary Labour Party, his long-term plan to 'educate' and constitutionalise the entire Labour movement and incorporate its leaders within the constitutional conventions of a 'parliamentary democracy'. After weeks of behind-the-scenes discussions Baldwin broke off negotiations on the eve of the threatened strike and did so at just the point when the TUC general council was willing to offer compromise terms – even though these terms were unlikely to have been acceptable to the miners.

In the event the immediate response to the strike call, involving the 'first wave' of workers in rails, docks, freight and bus transport, was beyond the expectations of both the government and the TUC leadership. By Day 5 the level of organisation and mass support in the east end of London and its docks was endangering supplies of petrol and food for the capital and home counties. Baldwin then had to take a step he had previously resisted: calling out the Territorial Army. With memories of the impact of using the military on the Clyde in 1919 Baldwin had strongly opposed any direct use of military personnel on the streets. The Territorial Army was now mobilised with the proviso that its members be enrolled as special constables and not in uniform. The 'specials' were then used to clear mass pickets in the major cities, London and Glasgow in particular. They did so with only with limited success. By days 7 and 8 there may have been some weakening of the strike in areas of the Midlands and the home counties. But elsewhere the strike was strengthening – with some members of the 'second wave' unions, in manufacturing, shipbuilding and heavy engineering, now coming out before the call was due on day 10. In some mining areas such as South Wales, Yorkshire, Durham and Fife local administration was increasingly taken over, as noted earlier, by strike committees, often as Councils of Action. For a very brief period, just a few days, these working class communities, although probably still a minority, were fully under working class control. Employers queued outside committee rooms 'their hats trembling in their hands' – as one miner remembered – to get permission to operate.

However, on Day 9 the TUC capitulated. On the basis of a false claim by Thomas that he had secured a compromise deal for the miners, the TUC leadership sought a meeting with the prime minister after first having met his condition that they call off the strike (a move in part also motivated by the knowledge that on the ground the leadership of the strike was slipping into the hands of the Left). At the consequent meeting with Baldwin and his Cabinet colleagues they discovered that there had been no deal agreed. Baldwin simply accepted their capitulation. The following morning returning workers found that many employers, particularly in transport and the docks, were demanding no strike commitments and sometimes additional concessions on pay and conditions. Bevin for the TGWU and some other unions immediately issued orders for renewed strike action – forcing Baldwin to call on employers to allow a return on old conditions. But this concession went no further. No deal was secured for the miners. Instead they fought on in isolation for another six months.

The strike's outcome was therefore largely one of defeat, widespread victimisation, disillusion and division and one which opened the way for Baldwin and his immediate allies to secure their basic long-term objective of 'constitutionalising' the full 'labour movement', the trade unions as well as the parliamentary party. However, this latter course was by no means easy or straightforward and, although the outcome of the General Strike marked a significant defeat for the Left and the working class movement as a whole, it was a defeat that was also very costly, politically and economically, for Britain's ruling class.

Within this outcome the control of language, and its class inflexion, played a central role – and involved, it would seem, at least some informal contact between the government and right-wing Labour leaders.

The first stage took place in October 1925 after the right-wing had regained control of the TUC in September 1925. It was to redefine the boundaries of the legitimate political action. The Labour Party conference of October 1925, now dominated by the big right-wing-led general unions, adopted two new policy documents. The first, *Labour and the Nation*, redefined the movement's political objectives and, more specifically, how they were to be achieved. It stressed the party's obligation to work within existing constitutional structures 'for national reconstruction and reform by parliamentary means and within progressive stages.' This was complemented by another resolution *Labour Policy for the British Commonwealth of Nations* which outlined the empire's positive interim benefits for both the colonial territories and for British workers.

The adoption of these policy documents in 1925 then opened the way for a vote to exclude members of the Communist Party from further participation in Labour movement policy-making. Up that point Communists remained individual members of the Labour Party and, within trade unions and Trades Union and Labour Councils, correspondingly retained the right to represent members at Labour Party conference. Many did so. Now, in line with these new policy positions, it was proposed that they be excluded on the grounds that they were doctrinally opposed to Labour Party's new constitutional position. Although resisted by a significant number of smaller skilled unions – and the Labour Left – the ban was enforced by the block votes of the major general unions, Thomas's NUR, Clyne's GMW and Bevin's TGWU. Extra-parliamentary action now illegitimate. This opened the way, just two weeks later, for the government itself to move against the Communist Party. The party's executive was arrested and charged under the 1797 Incitement to Mutiny Act. Sentencing members to prison terms of up to a year the presiding judge described them as 'members of an illegal party carrying out illegal work in this country'.[68]

These interventions set the immediate ideological guidelines for the subsequent general strike. The government immediately declared the strike unconstitutional and technically illegal. The TUC, having been trapped into declaring the strike, defined it as a trades dispute and hence legal – a cessation of work in support of the miners who had been locked out by their employers. But for the TUC it was no more than this. Local leadership was to be retained in the hands of responsible unions. Little guidance was issued as to how organisation was to be developed locally – except that it should be strictly by and through trade unions and exclude Left-wing organisations. Any action had to be seen as 'constitutional'. No challenge should be made to the rights of government itself.

On the ground, as noted earlier, the response was much stronger than expected and there seems have been an almost spontaneous reversion to the types of local organisation established six years before. This momentum grew as the strike continued. The leader of the GMW, Charles Dukes, told the conference of trades union executives in 1927 – as justification for calling it off – 'every day that the strike proceeded the control and authority of that dispute was passing out of the hands of responsible Executives and into the hands of men who had no authority'.[69]

What were the arguments of these 'men of no authority'? These were, as already noted, quite limited. It was to force the government to meet the terms advanced by the miners and to use the full strength of organised labour to do so. Wages should not be reduced. Hours should not be increased. And also, and critically, the Left placed this demand in its wider political context. If the miners were beaten, the way would be open for all wages to come down as Baldwin had said himself in 1925. This was the logic of the government's return to the gold standard and the bid by Britain's ruling class to restore the pound to its pre-war status as the world banking currency.

A miners' victory would not therefore mean socialism. But it would decisively change the balance of class forces and, within the working class movement, re-assert the legitimacy of using the united class power of working people. For all these reasons the miners had to be supported by the full strength of the Labour movement and of working class communities locally. These were the arguments of the Left and what the government feared most.

Its response was censorship and repression. The BBC was commandeered. Wavering members of the establishment, such as the Archbishop of Canterbury, were banned from speaking. Newsprint was seized. Unauthorised possession of printing paper became a criminal offence under the Emergency Powers Act. The TUC's strike bulletin was permitted – carefully restricting itself to calls for strictly constitutional action. But all other publications were suppressed. Special Branch and the police focussed their attention almost obsessively on seizing duplicators and arresting those involved in distributing cyclostyled local news-sheets putting the position of the Left. Something like half the membership of the Communist Party, among others, were arrested on such charges.

Nonetheless, it was, as we saw, the assessment of the Labour right-wing that this policy of suppression was not working. Local control was increasingly being lost. And this also seems to have been the assessment of the government – hence the opening of the fraudulent back-stairs negotiations involving J H Thomas.

Three pieces of evidence might be cited in support of this shift of opinion during the strike.

First, electoral. Just five days after the end of the general strike there was a by-election in Hammersmith West, a largely while collar constituency in West London. Previously comfortably held by the Conservatives, it was won by Labour with 54 percent of the vote and a 15 percent swing in an election fought on the constitutional rights and wrongs of a general strike.[70]

The second piece of evidence is from industry. Six weeks after the end of the strike the Engineering Employers Federation sent a memorandum to the government arguing against proposals for punitive anti-strike legislation at least for the moment. The EEF reported that, although the trade union movement was 'somewhat disintegrated', it was likely to be reconstituted 'stronger than ever'. Any hasty move would be a mistake. 'Nothing would do more to consolidate the whole Trade Union and Labour Movement.' Particular concern was expressed at the local power of Trades and Labour Councils. As a result of this intervention and similar ones by the Minister of Labour, the Trades Dispute Act was delayed for several months.[71]

The other evidence comes from the Cabinet itself. During the strike, on 7 May, Lord Robert Cecil wrote:

> the government has failed to overcome the distrust of the
> working class ... as soon as the strike is conclusively won,
> the government needs to compromise on social issues such as
> profit sharing ...[72]

Five days after the end of the strike his brother, the much more hard-line Lord Salisbury, submitted a paper entitled 'Education, Trades Disputes Act and Partnership'. He wrote:

> Suspicion is not only widespread but has gradually grown
> in power and now developed into a settled conviction to
> have a change and since the war has assumed an urgent and
> dangerous character.. Up to that date the workers sought their
> end in parliament...The favourite method is now direct action,
> which is in its logical development revolution.. Unless the
> government and parliament be-stir themselves this change of
> method may become stereotyped, revolution may become a
> conviction. The worst of it is that unconstitutional pressure
> and direct action has been proved to be effective and the
> present triumph of the forces of order is an exception. If we
> look at the attitude of the workers and at their intentions – no
> doubt largely subconscious but no less formidable for that
> reason – the situation is essentially unstable. The worker is

THE COUNCILS OF ACTION 1920

> no longer content to be merely a hired machine of somebody
> else to do somebody else's work. He will be told, and he
> will partly believe it, that if the means of production are
> nationalised the work will be the nation's work and, as he is
> part of the nation, his own work.[73]

Here we see a member of the government adopting the linguistic conventions of the Communist left in order to advance his argument – and then going on to propose forms of industrial cooperation and joint management in industry to overcome what he quite effectively described as a process of alienation.

After the strike Baldwin and his Minister of Labour Steel-Maitland moved quickly, though on an informal basis, with plans to involve selected trade union leaders in the discussion of industrial policy. A continuing round-table conference was planned to bring together leaders of the major industrial conglomerates and selected union leaders – with Ernest Bevin seen as the key figure on the Labour side. The first moves were initiated only three months after the strike. At this stage Bevin and the other selected trade union leaders postponed any immediate involvement fearful of a backlash from their members – again evidence of the degree to which the strike had resulted in at least a limited radicalisation. For the same reason discussion of the strike was vetoed at the 1926 TUC on the grounds that the miners' lock-out was continuing.[74]

However, by the 1927 TUC, with the miners defeated and overall trade union membership sharply in decline, Bevin and other members of the general council were ready to take on the Left. Rejecting any accusations of betrayal of the miners, they secured agreement for the General Council to develop 'interim' policies for economic development including, as Bevin argued, trade treaties that brought together European markets and Britain's empire territories. Socialism was no longer even a medium term objective. Instead the new policies demanded joint initiatives with employers – setting the scene for the discussions between the TUC and leading British industrialists headed by Lord Mond of Imperial Chemical Industries that began three months later.[75]

In the event little concrete came out of these talks. But the symbolism was important. Labour and capital were working together. Common approaches were being discussed on issues of industrial rationalisation and international trade. Many of the same themes were carried forward by the 'National' government through the 1930s led by the former Labour prime minister, Ramsay MacDonald and JH Thomas as Colonial Secretary. Britain's Commonwealth and Empire, including 'India, Egypt' (though no longer 'Ireland') were now portrayed as enabling British workers, at least in the Midlands and South East, to survive the world crisis of the 1930s far better than those in the United States or Germany.

In 1938, just a year before the outbreak of the second world war, Baldwin told a private meeting of Conservatives in the Athenaeum Club in London that he considered his greatest political achievement had been to 'educate' Labour and incorporate its collective institutions within the processes of constitutional government.[76]

But it was at a cost. The drive in 1925-26 to reduce wages across all industries had to be abandoned and, within a few years, so also had the gold standard itself. In its place a new commonwealth and empire sterling currency and trading area provided a profitable framework for the British business through the 1930s. However, this had highly untoward longer-term consequences. 1938 was also the year Chamberlain signed his non-aggression pact with Nazi Germany. He did so after refusing proposals for a common anti-Nazi front with France, the Soviet Union and the United States – at least implicitly because such a front would involve ceding to the US market access to Britain's empire territories and the wider sterling area.

So, as in 1919 and 1920, working class mobilisation, though short-lived, was powerful enough for the guardians of capital to make major shifts of policy.

1919-1926 Languages of Mobilisation

Before going back to the Chartist General Strike of 1842 and its impact on Marx's own theoretical development, let us first consider some interim conclusions about language and class mobilisation.

In Scotland in 1919 the 'practical moment' seems to have involved three factors: the impact of the sudden end to war, attempts by employers and the government to reimpose pre-1914 terms of employment and the threat this posed to the workshop power established by shop stewards over the previous four years. It was a challenge taken up principally by a shop stewards leadership and was politically shared between three or four competing socialist groupings. Its wider support, at least initially, was mainly based among the younger generation of workers – both men and women. The older generation, it seems, still tended towards a cautious deference to established authority as shown by the December 1918 election results. For these workers 'circles of immediate contact' would still largely be determined by trade, grade and religious affiliation. Their potential response, however, was seen as of determining importance by both the strike organisers and the government.

The language used by the strike leadership appears to have been carefully structured to match this environment. It avoided any reference to the contemporary revolutionary turmoil in Germany and Austria or to events in Dublin. The horizons projected were those of the British labour movement. Critical importance was attached to parallel actions taken elsewhere – in Barrow, South Wales, industrial Lancashire and towards the end by electricians and rail workers in London. Equally Belfast. These struggles gave wider practical meaning in terms of 'class' mobilisation, to the exercise of power against the employers and government – and hope of victory.

For the government the deployment of troops on Clydeside appears to have been a major tactical mistake which changed the political dynamics overnight. Military occupation of working class neighbourhoods exposed the government's alignment with the employers.The mass picketing by women, in their thousands, symbolised the wider class response. At this point, if not before, the allegiance of the older generation shifted and the language of the strike leaders increasingly reverted to the bitter industrial battles of the pre-1914 period. The 1919 local election results demonstrated the consequences.

Belfast reveals a parallel process but with three additional points of importance. The first is the political maturity of the strike leadership. It seems to have known precisely what it was doing in terms of addressing underlying sectarian alignments – presenting them as something of the past, divisions which had previously been used to erode rights and living standards but which were now seen for what they were. Class unity trumped sectarianism. The second was its ability to exploit divisions within the ranks of the employers, a strategic understanding of differing economic priorities of the shipyards (disruption of production schedules) and those of the smaller engineering firms (labour costs). The third is more difficult to gauge: its ability to carry forward this strategic 'knowledge' in adverse circumstances. Organisations would be important here, the Trades Council, Left political parties, the ILP and the legacy of Connolly's IRSP. So also would be people – as, for instance, Sam Kyle. What is clear, however, is that the class cohesion achieved in the strike was sustained and strengthened over the following year and that its base was seen, by its enemies, to be entrenched in the biggest workplace, Harland and Wolff, and too strong to be dealt with by anything other than paramilitary force.

In Britain in 1919 the government failed to achieve any resolution. Unlike 1926-27 there was no turning point. Working class mobilisation continued despite, or more precisely because of, Lloyd George's 'cheap insurance against Bolshevism' in the February 1919 budget – with money for housing, education and (limited) health services – sustaining employment and as well as being matched the following month, in March 1919, by the postponement of any showdown with the miners on privatisation and the establishment of a Royal Commission. These government initiatives sought to re-establish its credentials as a government 'of the people'. They visibly failed. So also did the government elaborate and very costly plans for counter propaganda. Unofficial rank and file strike action increased. The standing and influence of local Left leaderships in workplaces was confirmed while at the same time the Left in local councils, quite often the same people, challenged the government on poor relief and housing.

The years 1919 and early 1920 was a critical period for the Left. The full employment that resulted from the economic concessions of February 1919 maintained the impetus of unofficial, shop steward-led trade union militancy. At the same time inflation, largely driven by speculative finance, peaked. It was over these 12 months that the anti-capitalist Left matured, strengthened its workplace organisation and its wider influence, notably through the *Daily Herald*. The Left also engaged, as Williams and Pollitt themselves demonstrated, in strenuous, detailed interventions in localities and workplaces to win wider anti-capitalist and anti-imperialist understanding.

Conversely right-wing trade union leaders – now exposed as blocking immediate working-class interests – suffered a major loss of influence. The consequences were seen between June and August 1920 and even in September when the government postponed any showdown with the miners. Over these months it would probably be correct to say that, as against 1919, the level of class mobilisation and class consciousness in 1920 reached its 20th century peak and, though different in context and character, beyond that secured in 1972-74.

It built on five years of shop-steward mobilisation and workplace politicisation. It did so in period, internationally, of revolutionary challenge. Though this, as we saw, was initially exploited nationalistically by supporters of the existing order, this was no longer the case in 1920. By then the forces of the state had themselves suffered severe dislocation. Most important of all, the Left itself had secured a level of internal coherence, developed a mass circulation daily newspaper and been able to create an organisational form, the Councils of Action, that gave visible reality to an alternative form of class rule, one run directly working people, across virtually the whole country.

However, as we saw, it could not last. Britain's rulers retained state power. By late autumn, winter 1920-21, they had used it to impose brutal levels of unemployment, broke Left control, stabilised the Right and enabled the expulsion of many left-wing stewards. 1924 to 1925 did see a temporary resurgence as the government sought to secure a 'strong pound' through an absolute reduction of wages across all export industries. A new potential 'practical moment' emerged.

To this extent 1926 did bring, as we have just noted, a more fundamental shift of strategy for Britain's ruling class. In immediate terms it revealed the continuing combative strength of the Left, strengthened by the organisational lessons that had been learnt over the previous decade. This highlighted all the dangers posed to the new 'constitutionalist' leadership in the trade unions and Labour Party. Rescuing this leadership and sustaining it became the new priority for Britain's rulers. Within six years the gold standard itself had been abandoned – finally ending the international hegemony of sterling and surrendering banking primacy to the United States. Instead, the world economic crisis of 1931-32 saw priority given to the survival of this new political settlement and the creation of a 'National Government' ostensibly led by key figures from the Labour Party.

This retreat to Britain's vast empire-based trading area sustained new industries in motors, electricals and consumer durables and provided levels of employment well beyond those in the United States and Germany. Where these new industries were concentrated, mainly across the Midlands and south-east, new consumerist identities crystallised. Skilled workers – in largely non-union workplaces – could now (just) afford mortgages and the associated consumer goods. At the same time, at national level, the new concordat established with trade union and Labour leaders between 1926 and 1929 once more enabled the isolation of those who wished to challenge capitalist state power. As we will see next, a not dissimilar process occurred between 1842 and 1846.

However, in closing this section, it is useful to make a final point about language and the emergence of 'practical moments'.

Such moments stemmed, as we have seen, from the 'dull compulsion of economic relations', the unfolding contradictions of capitalism as a system – though always as moderated and directed by the owners and representatives of capital. These moments involved, some way or other, the erosion of existing standards of life and the undermining of defined identities within the alienated landscape of stable capitalism. But, as we have seen, the response also required something else. There had to be people who would make the arguments for resistance. The speed and depth of the response relied on this – and, moreover, on how far such 'people' were organised: how far the scale of their organisation matched the geographical reach of the state power and how far it carried forward the knowledge gained from previous struggles. We will next examine the importance of this in 1842.

NOTES

1   Hansard, 16 August 1920.
2   Home Office Report.
3   Home Office Report 16 September 1920 CAB 24/111/63.
4   Middlemas, *Politics of Industrial Society*, p.167.
5   James E Cronin, *Industrial Conflict in Modern Britain* (London, 1979) p. 93. Equally Butler and Stokes, *Political Change in Britain* (second edition: Macmillan 1974) p. 174. identify the generation maturing during the first world war as marking 'profound alteration of party allegiance among manual workers'. The war 'disturbed the social order … and brought a vast growth in trade unionism'. Quite how this happened Butler and Stokes don't say.
6   Chris Wrigley, ed. *The Challenge of Labour* (London, 1993), chapter 14.
7   J. O'Donoghue, '*Consumer Price Inflation since 1750'*, *Economic Trends, No. 64*, pp. 38-46 (ISSN 0013-0400); R. Middlemas, *Politics in Industrial Society* (London, 1979) provides a resume of the political background.
8   Susan Howson, 'Dear Money 1920', *Economic History Review*, February 1974. Treasury Bills were increased from 3.5 percent to 4.5 percent in October 1919 to 6 percent in November and 6.5 percent in April 1920.
9   T. Jones, *Whitehall Diaries* (Oxford, 1969), 1, p. 80.
10   T. Jones, *Whitehall Diary*, 1, 99-104; N and J Mackenzie, *The Diary of Beatrice Webb* (London, 1984), III, 331-338.
11   By December 1920 unemployment had reached 7.9 per cent and by April 1921 20 per cent *www.ons.gov.uk/ons/rel/lms/labour-market…/unemployment-since-1881.pdf.*
12   Ministry of Labour Report 17 June 1920 National Archives CAB 24/109/53.
13   The Ministry of Labour report for 23 June (CAB 24/108/32) notes, over the period prior to the special TUC, the focus by the socialist press on direct action – with the *Daily Herald*'s support being contested by the *Cotton Factory Times* and the *New Statesman*.
14   Home Office Intelligence Report for 15 July 1920 CAB 24/109/35 attributes the victory to the votes of the three big unions (miners, engineers and transport workers) with the others divided. The report describes it as the intention of Smillie and Williams to force a strike for the Hands Off Russia and Ireland movements in August. It also refers to a scheme for a 'General Staff' for Labour: 'if this comes into being it may become an important factor in the internal affairs of the country'. Home Office Intelligence Report CAB 24/110/6 29 July 1920 refers to the Labour Research Bureau, where Page Arnot was secretary, as gradually becoming the 'General Staff for Labour'.

15 Ministry of Labour Report, 7 July 1920, CAB 24/109/53.
16 L. Macassey, 'Force v. Freedom', *Sunday Times*, 18 July 1920.
17 Macnamara to War Cabinet, 29 July 1920: CAB 24/110/6; the
Ministry of Labour Weekly Report for 17 July (CAB 24/109/53)
reported that the 'most disturbing feature' was the scale of unofficial
strikes against officially agreed JIC settlements.
18 The conference agreed to seek assistance from Triple Alliance
allies and also to support the call for a special TUC: P. Bagwell, *The
Railwaymen* (London, 1963) p. 445-448.
19 Home Office Intelligence Report 8 July 1920 CAB 24/108/92 reports
the NUR conference and Crump's speech.
20 People's History Museum, Salford: Labour Party Records: CA
GEN/296 headed notepaper of Hands Off Russia.
21 OHMS (On his majesty's service): DH 6 and 7 May 1920 reported
the loading of munitions and attempts by the London district
secretary of the dockers' union to locate and stop. The *Workers
Dreadnought* for 8 May reports the wreck at Gravesend of the
Neptune carrying aircraft and siege guns. Harry Pollitt, *Serving My
Time* (London, 1940) p. 111-117, notes that this was engineered by
'two revolutionary firemen'. John Mahon's *Harry Pollitt*, pp. 80-81
(London, 1976) recounts the demise of the *Neptune* and before that,
he claims, of two barges in the North Sea as a result of interventions
by dock workers. Munitions were offloaded from the *Jolly George* on
12 May (DH 13 May).
22 *Daily Herald* 3 and 6 July 1920.
23 *Daily Herald* 8 July 1920.
24 Home Office Intelligence Report 8 July 1920 makes this comment
and gives current membership as 36,000: CAB 24/108/92. The
leadership were in close contact with Arthur McManus, who was
from 1 August chair of the new Communist Party, and through him
with both Sinn Fein officers and Cecil Malone MP. Malone, a cousin
of Countess Markievicz, had been a rising star within the British
army leading work on the military use of aviation, promoted to
Colonel at the age of 29. He resigned his positions, as he put it at the
Hands Off Russia rally in the Albert Hall in March 1920, in protest at
the use of British aircraft in the aerial bombing of Russian civilians
with poison gas – 'one of the greatest crimes in history'.
25 R. Jackson, *At War with the Bolsheviks* (London, 1972); C. Kinvig,
Churchill's Crusade (London, 2006).
26 *Sunday Times* 1 August 1920.
27 Churchill to War Cabinet 3 August 1920 Cab 24/110/27.
28 DH 3, 5 and 6 August 1920.
29 CA GEN 9 and 10.
30 DH 7 August 1920.

31   CA ADM 1 and CA ADM 14 i.
32   Lloyd George, 'Note of Text handed to Kameneff', 6 August 1920, Cab 24/110/51; DH 9 and 11 August 1920
33   CA/ADM 26.
34   DH 13 and 14 August 1920.
35   *The Communist* 12 August 1920: the author was Andrew Rothstein.
36   L. Macfarlane, 'Hands Off Russia in 1920', *Past and Present*, 38, December 1967; S. White, *Britain and the Bolshevik Revolution: a Study in the Politics of Diplomacy 1920-24* (London, 1979) 9-11 and 32-50; S. White, 'Labour's Council of Action 1920', *Journal of Contemporary History*, October 1974; C. Wrigley, *Lloyd George and the Challenge of Labour: the Post-War Coalition 1918-1920* (Harvester, 1990).
37   Home Office 12 August 1920 CAB 24/110/72.
38   This paragraph relies heavily on the account of Robin Page Arnot, *The Impact of the Russian Revolution in Britain* (London 1967) pp.170-178. In July-August 1920 Page Arnot was Secretary of the Labour Party's Research Department and had administrative responsibility for the Councils of Action.
39   Mackenzie, *Diary of Beatrice Webb*, III 363.
40   Alan Clinton, *The Trade Union Rank and File: Trades Councils in Britain 1900-1940* (Manchester 1977) 225 and footnotes 24 and 27.
41   Home Office Intelligence Report CAB 24/111/5, 26 August 1920.
42   Police Union to Council of Action (no date): CA ADM 58 i.
43   Home Office Intelligence Report 2 September 1920 CAB 24/111/30.
44   Home Office intelligence Report 9 September 1920 CAB 24/111/49.
45   Ministry of Labour Report 4 September 1920 CAB 24/111/27 .
46   War Office, 606A, cited by K. Coates and K. Topham, *The Making of the Transport and General Workers Union* (London 1991), p. 715.
47   Cited by J Cronin, 'Coping with Labour 1916-1926', in Cronin and J. Schneer (eds), *Social Conflict and the Political Order in Modern Britain* (London 1982), pp. 113-145.
48   Cited by Coates and Topham, *The Making*, p.751, from Williams, *The New Labour Outlook*, 1921 p.127.
49   DH 31 July 1920.
50   Page Arnot, *Impact*, p. 176.
51   J. Foster, *The Councils of Action 1920 and the British Labour Movement's Defence of Soviet Russia* (Manifesto Press for Marx Memorial Library, 2017).
52   Henry Wilson to War Cabinet, 14 September 1920: CAB 24/111/5.
53   For Malone see above footnote 199.
54   *Daily Herald*, 23 August 1920.
55   Home Office Intelligence Report 16 September 1920 CAB 24/111/63.
56   CAB 24/112/29 Intelligence Report 21 October 1920.
57   CAB 24/112/74 Ministry of Labour 16 October 1920.

58   DH 14 September 1920.

59   CA ADM/23 i 28 September 1920.

60   CA ADM /24 i House of Commons meeting.

61   DH 16 November 1920.

62   CA ADM/51 circular dated 6 January 1921.

63   Maurice Hankey to War Cabinet, 3 August 1920: NA CAB 24/110/24.

64   R.R. James, *J.C.C Davidson's Memoirs* (London 1969). Lord Davidson, in turn PPS to Bonar Law and Baldwin and in 1922 Chancellor of the Duchy of Lancaster had a significant role in developing the intelligence services in the early 1920s and in building links with the Labour Party. Along with Baldwin and Bonar Law, Davidson mobilised support inside the Conservative Party for ending the coalition government and integrating the Labour Party as the second party in a two-party system. Bevin is described as becoming 'a very close friend of the Davidson family' (p.416).

65   D. Butler and D. Stokes, *Political Change in Britain* (second edition: Macmillan 1974) p. 174.

66   Alan Clinton, *The Trade Union Rank and File: Trades Councils in Britain* (Manchester 1977), pp. 183-171.

67   R. Palme Dutt, *Communist International*, June 1926; Robin Page Arnot, *Communist International* October 1926. There are many histories of the general strike. Those used here include A Bullock, *The Life and Times of Ernest Bevin*, Volume 1 (pp. 279-336) (London 1960); Margaret Morris, *The General Strike* (London 1976), K. Laybourn, *The General Strike of 1926* (Manchester 1993). It also draws on J. Foster, 'British Imperialism and the Labour Aristocracy' in *The General Strike 1926*, ed. J. Skelly (London 1976) pp 3-57 and the new materials in M. Davis, *Unite History*, Volume 1 1888-1931 (Liverpool University Press 2021).

68   James Klugmann, *History of the Communist Party of Great Britain*, Vol 2 (London 1969), Chapter 2.

69   'Report of the National Strike Special Conference' in *The Mining Crisis and the National Strike* (TUC London 1927) p.58.

70   *Lansbury's Labour Weekly*, 5 June 1926.

71   Glasgow University Business Archives Weir papers DC 096/16/26 July 1926.

72   TNA CAB 178/88 R. Cecil to Cabinet, 7 May 1926.

73   TNA CAB Paper 207, Salisbury, 18 May 1926 (CAB 24/180).

74   M. Davis, *Unite History* Vol I 1880-1931 (Liverpool 2021) pp 89-90.

75   M. Davis, as cited, pp. 104 ff.

76   G. Young, Stanley Baldwin (London 1952) p. 246.

THIS PAGE LEFT INTENTIONALLY BLANK

5

The General Strike of 1842

… the terrible tide of thought and energy that is now flowing
fast…
Address of the Chartist Executive, 17 August 1842[1]

However much the individual manufacturer might give rein
to his old lust for gain, the spokesmen and political leaders of
the manufacturing class ordered a change of front and speech
towards the workpeople…
Karl Marx, *Capital* I[2]

Britain's general strike of 1842 is the first clear example of a working-
class movement briefly but fundamentally challenging capitalist state
power. It was a political strike demanding universal male suffrage – a
demand that in British circumstances would, as Marx and Engels pointed
out in the *Communist Manifesto*. have effectively meant a transfer of state
power to working people. The strike continued for over a month and
covered virtually all industrial areas of England, Scotland and Wales from
Dundee down to Merthyr. It ended in military occupation, mass arrests,
transportations and exile. But its challenge redefined the way in which the
ruling class governed and led to profound politico-economic changes. It
was also significant in another way – theoretically. It played a key part in
the development of Marx's own understanding of class and class struggle.
Marx's classic writings establishing the centrality of class and class struggle,
The German Ideology (1846), his letter to Annenkov (1846) and *The Poverty of
Philosophy* (1847) were written over the years following his second encounter
with Frederick Engels in 1844 and Engels's reports on the working-class
movement in Britain. Engels himself had moved to Manchester in December

1842 just a couple of months after the end of the strike – writing his study of the English working class over the following year. In 1845 Marx himself visited Manchester. The quotation which opened this study, 'ridding itself of the muck of ages', came from their joint work written in 1845-1846, *The German Ideology*.

This chapter will not attempt to retell the story of the strike. This has been done most fully by Mick Jenkins in his study published in 1980, building on the work of GDH Cole, F.C. Mather and Naomi and TDW Reid, and since amplified, among others, by Malcolm Chase, Robert Fyson, Peter Gurney, Theodore Koditschek, Paul Pickering, Anthony Smith and Robert Sykes.[3]

Its focus will be on the themes already identified as relevant to the development of class consciousness and, no less important, how the ruling class will endeavour to overcome it. We will seek to identify what made this revolutionary strike possible, how the arguments needed to trigger it were won, that is, the 'practical moment' – and correspondingly how such mass class consciousness was ultimately countered by those defending the existing order and, further, how these responses re-defined economic and social relations.

A brief outline of the course of the strike

Although the General Strike of 1842 was the 'first', it was also – looking back – strange and untypical of any other. Action was taken by an organised movement – but it was taken against the majority decision of its elected leadership. The strike itself gives the appearance of developing chaotically. Yet its hallmark was discipline – marching columns of workers defying bayonets and rifles and with local working-class communities maintaining order and discipline for weeks after the arrests of their leaders. This chapter seeks to position and explain this exceptionality and relate it to the equally exceptional character of the working-class movement in early industrial Britain.

The strike wave began among the Staffordshire miners in the last ten days of July 1842. Miners' delegates voted on 16 July for a strike to oppose further wage reductions. Miners marched from pit to pit through the Staffordshire coalfield and then on through the south Lancashire pits to gather support. By the end of July all miners in this area were out. At this stage the political demand for the People's Charter was not at the forefront of the miners' demands. Resolutions in support of the People's Charter were passed at some of the mass meetings but the principal demand was on pay, to halt further reductions.

In the adjacent textile towns mass meetings of workers began a few days later. These were explicitly for the Charter though linked to opposition to wage cuts. On 26 July the first of these mass meetings took place in Ashton under Lyne in South Lancashire and was followed on 29 July by one six miles away, across the Derbyshire border, in Stalybridge. On Monday 1

August there was a further meeting at Hyde and on 2 August at Dukinfield. These four towns were all within seven or eight miles of each other. In all towns the employers had announced wage reductions. At the meetings local Chartist leaders spoke alongside workplace and trades union leaders. In all the meetings the proposal for a strike for the Charter was adopted. On Sunday 7 August there was a mass meeting on Mottram Moor, immediately adjacent to these four towns, the traditional meeting place for radical and Chartist meetings. At this it was announced that a general strike was to begin the following day, Monday 8 August and it would be both for the Charter and to resist reductions. On the Monday columns of strikers marched north to Oldham, bringing out workers there and also to Hyde. On the Tuesday, 9 August the strikers marched into Manchester halting its cotton mills and other workplaces. Over the following three days columns of workers moved north to the textile towns of Rochdale, Bolton and Preston, west to Wigan – and on, with reinforcements, to meet other strikers in Halifax and the industrial towns of Yorkshire.

In all cases, as strikers marched in, there was dialogue with local trade union and Chartist leaders. Votes were taken at mass meetings. In most cases all trades, including metal trades, engineering, chemicals, dying and ancillary textiles trades, came out. By the second week of August the strike was British-wide. In Scotland the mining areas were out and some textiles. In England the strike extended across the North, Lancashire, Yorkshire, Tyneside, to the potteries, the Black Country and Birmingham and on to parts of South Wales. New areas, Carlisle, Norwich, Nottinghamshire, continued to join through the fourth week of August. As the government raced to reinforce troop numbers in the north, crowds massed in front of London's railway stations calling on the rank and file to desert. Bayonets were mounted to clear the way.

Very quickly, on Tuesday 9 August, the first steps were taken by the strikers to constitute a delegated leadership. This was based on the representation of trades, that is, trade union organisations. Power loom weavers in Manchester met that day to elect delegates. The following day 10 August the five Manchester metal trades did the same. On 11 August a delegate meeting for all trades took place in Manchester with delegates arriving from other centres. They voted to organise a meeting for all trades and localities already on strike for the following day 12 August. This meeting in turn convened a General Delegate Meeting of all trades, across the country, for Monday 15 August – the day before the executive of the National Charter Association was due to meet in Manchester to mark the anniversary of the Peterloo massacre.

These detailed organisational steps were undertaken in face of repeated intervention by the military with arrests, violent dispersals of meetings and the seizure of halls. However, the 15 August delegate meeting took place despite having to reconvene twice – on the day before the planned

Manchester meeting of the National Chartist Association (NCA) Executive. Its 500 delegates voted by a very significant majority to endorse a general strike to secure the Charter. When the NCA Executive met the following day, on 16 August, it had little alternative but to endorse this call. The strike was already in full force – and it was for the Charter. The Address of the NCA, officially calling the strike, was published the following day, 17 August.

The explanation for this rather strange path of development goes back four months – although in some important ways far longer – and arose from the tension between the advocates of 'constitutional' and 'unconstitutional' methods, to a large extent also between the 'older' and younger generations of leaders.

The year 1839 had seen the climax of the first phase of the Chartist movement – marked by the building of an alliance between a mass working-class movement, one developed and consolidated during the industrial struggles of 1834, and petty bourgeois radicals based mainly in London and Birmingham. The government rejected the resulting mass petition, played on the movement's internal divisions, and in December – with some good luck – was able to put down an armed uprising in South Wales and circumvent planned actions of support elsewhere. Almost all the leaders of the Chartist movement, including O'Connor, were arrested and imprisoned.

However, basic organisation was maintained. The movement's paper continued to appear – though weekly and no longer daily. Local support was consolidated and a new organisational structure created. In July 1840, before O'Connor and other leaders had been released, local leaders in the industrial north, led, it seems by James Leach of Manchester, a long-time working-class activist and later friend of Engels, initiated the creation of a new type of mass membership organisation, the National Chartist Association, NCA, explicitly to represent working people. The NCA was structured on democratic centralist lines. Delegates were mandated by local constituencies. But the resulting decisions of the NCA Executive were binding – to overcome the confusion of alliances and leaders that had plagued the movement in 1839.

Over the following months through 1841 a further step was taken. Leach, at that point NCA president, John Campbell, the NCA Secretary and Richard Pilling, a power-loom weaver and long-term working-class activist based at the time in Ashton, South Lancashire, sought to consolidate this identification with the organised working class by winning the affiliation of trade unions. In this they were joined, when he was released from prison, by Peter McDouall, one of the national leaders arrested in 1839, a doctor from Ramsbottom, a factory village near Manchester. By winter 1841-42 the work of securing trade union affiliations had been largely achieved, at least in the country's industrial heartland. At this point the NCA's individual membership had reached 50,000 in 400 local branches.

By then O'Connor and the principal Chartist leaders had also been released from prison. O'Connor opposed the new line. His strategy was to mobilise a popular mass movement through another petition. By spring 1842 three million signatures had been secured and the petition was presented to Parliament in May with the support of 42 MPs. It was rejected. The subsequent May meeting of the NCA debated further action. O'Connor supported by William Hill, the editor of the *Northern Star*, called for a Remonstrance to the Queen, involving further mass petitioning. This was to be linked to public work in constituencies with view to the next parliamentary elections and securing enough MPs pledged to support the Charter to hold the balance of power between the two parties.

James Leach and Peter McDouall, with the support, it seems, of delegates from the industrial North, put a supplementary proposal. This was that the movement use its new industrial strength to call a general strike for the Charter – combining it with a demand for a reversal of the wage cuts arising from the current industrial depression. O'Connor and the advocates of constitutional action opposed and the proposal was voted down. Not just this. Any mention of the proposal was excluded from the columns of the *Northern Star* over the following weeks.

However, one motion from the north-west could not easily be opposed. It came from Alexander Hutchison, an ironsmith and leading trade unionist in the Manchester metal trades. It was that the next meeting of the NCA Executive be held in Manchester and that it be on 16 August to mark the anniversary of Peterloo and the unveiling of a monument to Henry Hunt.

The practical moment?

> 'They must stand firm for the Charter and no surrender …
> this time they could get it but if they did not, they need never
> try again.'
> William Moorhouse to workers at Compstall on 11 August (as
> cited at his trial)[4]

It is, therefore, quite difficult to define the 'practical moment' that triggered the general strike of 1842. It some ways the key arguments were those that took place within the NCA leadership – not between leaders and workers locally in factories and communities. However, such arguments certainly did take place at this local level over May, June and July – and were won by those supporting general strike action.

What, therefore, were these arguments that won the call for a general strike and how can we define the material context of this 'practical moment' in the months leading up to August 1842?

There was a directly economic factor. The years 1838 to 1842 were ones of deepening industrial crisis, probably the worst in the 19th century. As profits fell, wages were driven down – a crisis that was visibly, as the Owenites and other socialists had long argued, the result of chaotic investment and internal competition – and particularly so within Britain's dominant industry, cotton textiles. Although Britain was by far the biggest world producer (consuming up to three times as much cotton as the rest of the world combined), internal competition was driving prices down year by year – in turn feeding through to the coal industry, which supplied the power, and the engineering industry which supplied the machinery. Though less acute, other industrialising sectors of the economy in wool and linens suffered similar problems – with the combined impact on incomes in turn depressing consumer demand.

The factory employers blamed the intensity of the crisis on the artificially high cost of food. Grain imports had been restricted since 1816 to protect the profits of commercial farming, the dominant lobby within the Tory party. The factory employers argued that a repeal of the corn laws would not just cut the price of food but also open the corn-producing countries for commercial development, for British investment and for British goods.

Cotton trade unionists had long put forward their own solution. Short of running the industry on cooperative lines with socially planned investment, as argued by the Owenites, the hours of labour should be radically reduced. Cutting the working day would limit overproduction, reduce unemployment and enhance labour's bargaining power. This had been the workers' argument since the 1810s and they sought to use the gross exploitation of young children to add strength to their demands. In 1833, however, the employers' lobby circumvented this campaign by securing legislation that instead required two successive shifts of child workers. For the employers this not only avoided any limitation of the working day but increased the financial pressure on the spinners who themselves paid their juvenile helpers. It was one of a number of legislative interventions through the 1830s that played a major part in re-mobilising the long-standing demand for universal suffrage. Others included the introduction of a far more penal system of poor relief from 1834 and the strengthening of the state's coercive force at local level. This involved, from 1839, reorganising policing under the jurisdiction of the County Sessions largely made up of large-scale local employers and gentry – circumventing existing arrangements through vestries and police commissions.

The intense industrial crisis of spring and early summer of 1842 heightened all these tensions. Employers demanded a fresh round of very significant wage cuts, in some cases up to 25 percent, and laid off workers. Their leaders in the Anti-Corn Law League (ACLL) sought to mobilise the cotton workforce as part of a mass campaign of protest to secure their own demands – potentially diverting workers from the long-standing and unifying demands for universal suffrage.

It was this economic crisis, and the political intervention made by the ACLL that provided the immediate background to the abortive proposal made at the May meeting of the NCA for a general strike. Subsequently calls were made for a strike for the Charter later in May at in north Lancashire, in Colne, Preston and Burnley as well as in South Lancashire. A month later similar calls were made at the funeral in June of the Chartist Samuel Holberry, imprisoned since 1839, across the Pennines in Halifax. O'Connor himself toured the north in June, it seems, to put the counter arguments – although no mentions of the debate at the May EC or of subsequent calls for strike action were allowed to appear in the *Northern Star*. In fact no mention of the strikes appeared until the issue of 22 August after the decision had been taken at the 16 August meeting of the NCA Executive.

Where did the idea of a general strike for come from ? It was by no means new. The general idea of some form of strike action to secure universal suffrage had been raised during the period of Jacobin-inspired resistance in the 1790s. It was a continuing demand of the Spencean socialists and became a central part of the abortive insurrectionary plans for 1820. Across the West of Scotland, where news of cancellation was not received in time, there had indeed been a mass general strike lasting two days. The idea was given more precise form with Benbow's 'Plan' of 1832 while the Grand National Consolidated Trade Union of 1834 invoked somewhat similar ideas. Five years later the concept was again, but briefly, incorporated in the Chartist 'National Holiday' of summer 1839.[5]

However, the scale and timing of the 1842 strike can only be understood by reference to more basic structural factors arising from Britain's unique experience of capitalist proletarianisation, its impact on local social structures along with political developments immediately preceding the crisis of 1841-42.

Proletarian Britain: an exceptional society

Britain's pioneer transition to a capitalist economy was by the 1840s more than two centuries old. Uniquely in Europe land was enclosed, owned in big rent-generating estates, and commercially farmed by tenant farmers employing landless agricultural workers – an arrangement that also generated a reservoir of labour power which fed the country's growing industries and, no less important, the armies and navies that enforced Britain's control of a new global capitalist market. Much industrial production was still at a handicraft level – though organised and controlled by large wholesalers to feed this global market. However, the distinguishing feature of Britain's economy was its power-driven textile industries that by 1840 had already dominated world markets for sixty years. Textiles were, in turn, complemented, and sustained by, engineering industries that provided the machinery and by steam technology which had additionally revolutionised transport on land and sea over the preceding 20 years.

Britain's industrialisation was, however, also unique in another sense. Because it was the first it was also highly labour intensive. Technology, though pioneering, was primitive. The amount of labour required in the 1820s and 30s was double that required as industrialisation gathered pace a generation later in continental Europe and the United States. This in turn determined the social structures of the industrial towns and cities that were clustered on either side of the Pennines (supplying water power and coal) – as well as for the industrial valleys in Wales and the textile towns adjacent to Scotland's coalfields. Typically, these industrial communities would have two or three dozen families that owned the factories and mines, another hundred to service them, clergy, managers, postmasters, solicitors and doctors, and a hundred or so 'small masters' in ancillary trades. But then there would be, quite disproportionately, 10,000 working families and another 200 or so shopkeepers, publicans, teachers that were largely dependent on their custom. In the semi-rural mining areas the ratio between workers and owners was even more extreme. In these economic and social circumstances the political struggles of the 1840s had an important pre-history. stretching back two or three generations, to the initial replacement of hand-production and the first development of trade union organisation in the challenging economic circumstances of the 1780s and 90s. These first key movements for collective organisation had, moreover, taken place amid the wider horizons of political engagement engendered by the independence struggles in the American colonies and, closer to home, Ireland as well as the politically still more challenging influence of the French revolution.

By 1842 Britain's industrial towns and villages possessed long established radical leaderships. They also sustained trade union organisation of a particular kind which had, by necessity, to operate largely outside the law. It nonetheless did so on a mass scale. Even in rural areas agricultural labourers had from the early 1830s challenged both agricultural mechanisation and the ban on trade union organisation. By the 1840s Britain's rulers were only too aware of these imbalances within the country's social structure and of the political dangers they posed. Britain had no landowning peasantry and, outside the metropolitan cities and the rural market towns of the south, the petty bourgeoisie was small and unreliable in its loyalty.

Conversely, this particular social structure, and the specific sequence of political experience, had by the 1810s and 1820s seen the development of a relatively strong culture of resistance which – though certainly stronger in some areas than others – seems to have held back and eroded processes of 'social accommodation' or 'reification'. In some areas at least an organised working class had used its numerical strength, and its purchasing power over local shopkeepers, to secure political control over the distribution of poor relief by electing its own nominees to the vestry and similarly over policing and in some areas even over parliamentary elections – explaining why at least some of the 42 MPs voted for the People's Charter in May 1842. It was this base also that supported a mass circulation radical press. Through the 1820s and 1830s this illegal press, mainly based in London, operated on the basis of an underground distribution network across the country but was particularly strong in the industrial north. From the later 1830s the *Northern Star* operated commercially despite the imposition of a financially punitive stamp tax. Conversely what held back Tory and Whig leaders from any concessions on the electoral franchise was an awareness of this level of political working-class mobilisation quite as much as the sheer size of the working population.

Such class mobilisation was correspondingly important for local structures of social and cultural identification, that is, for the actual circles of social reference, returning to Vygotsky and Leontiev, within which people lived their lives and understood their society.

In many places, but particularly in the industrial north, the principles of working-class solidarity did indeed possess material force. As already noted, the exercise of any form of collective trade union power had, for over half a century, required illegal organisation and activity. Over the same period, but intensifying since the end of the Napoleonic wars, any radical political activity, the circulation of radical newspapers and the organisation of protests and demonstrations, required clandestine organisation. And, although such political activity was necessarily distinct from trade union activity, the circles of people involved usually overlapped. Particularly important, perhaps, for the mass reach and impact of such organisation was the practice of 'exclusive dealing' to which reference has already been made. This involved workers patronising only those shopkeepers who voted for candidates backed by the radicals and enabled control to be exercised, at least in some contexts, both in parliamentary elections and more frequently over elections to the vestry and thereby control over poor relief and town police. The possession of arms was also relatively endemic in the industrial communities of the North – with regular challenges to the state authorities from the 1790s, through 1812, 1818 and 1819-20 and thereafter.

The result, in many places, was a local culture of secrecy, mass organisation and disciplined compliance – and it took place in communities where ideas of solidarity and resistance were by the early 1840s deeply embedded. Employers, backed in any crisis by military force, were seen as the enemy.

Recent research by Tom Scriven, Gregory Varga, Matthew Roberts and John Saunders has amply exposed the depth of the resulting popular culture. They demonstrate the role of radical libraries, 'chapels' and schools, of regular commemorative dinners celebrating radical heroes and martyrs, the visual culture of banners and, not least, how far this work locally commanded, at least to some extent, an equality of the sexes.[6] This pattern was not necessarily universal. There were some industrial towns where detailed intervention by the factory owners seems, as in Stockport, to have already eroded this autonomous working-class culture by the early 1840s.[7] But in general, this transition seems to have come later. In Oldham, where some level of detailed neighbourhood analysis has been made, there is pretty firm evidence of this. At the very beginning of the century, in the 1800s, the Sunday 'education' of children was still conducted in 'mill' schools directly run by local employers. By the 1810s, 1820s and 1830s this pattern had been broken. Virtually all such schooling was secular, not under millowner control and conducted by those who in general supported the radical objectives of the local working-class communities. It was only from the later 1840s, after the breaking of the Chartist movement, that schooling on Sundays (the only 'free' day) was again provided on a sponsored basis, now mainly by the non-conformist denominations associated with mill-owners.[8] This seems to have been the pattern in other aspects of working-class social life and provision. It was, with its underground newspapers, clubs, illegal union organisation, clandestine arms possession, a society culturally and ideologically quite apart from that of the owners, one where secrecy was essential, where there needed to be a constant guard against informers, but also where martyrs were celebrated and a rich culture of songs, poetry and writing flourished.[9]

it was this depth of coherent working-class organisation, and its disciplined character – but also the immediate threats to it – that explains much that would otherwise be inexplicable about the general strike of 1842. O'Connor and his supporters had, after their release early in 1842, and using their control of the *Northern Star* paper, been able to win back a majority on the NCA executive and successfully oppose the line being developed by Leech, Campbell, McDouall and the leaders from the industrial north. Further action, they argued, had to be within legal, constitutional limits.

Their opponents argued that the political situation in summer 1842 would not tolerate delay. On the one side government measures, on policing, town government, control of poor relief, factory hours and education along with its detailed commissions of investigation following the Newport rising, were slowly but surely eroding the pre-existing base of working-class power locally. On the other, the depth of the industrial depression of 1841-42 demanded action. Unprecedented cuts in wages were being demanded and politically the employers were using the situation very skilfully to mobilise support for an alternative political project, the repeal of the corn laws, already detaching the shopkeepers in particular from their alignment to the Charter. Doing nothing – apart from collecting more signatures – would doom Chartism as a mass movement and in consequence also, as a result of government and local employer action, also see the end of a mobilised working class.

NCA leaders in most localities had loyally followed the policy of the NCA leadership after the rejection of the petition in May (partly at least because the alternative call for a political general strike was suppressed in the *Northern Star*) . Yet when it became clear in the course of the first week of August that the industrial heartland of South Lancashire had declared for a political strike action, the response was very quick. When the columns of marchers arrived, the reaction of workers was to support. A few local NCA leaders loyally stuck by O'Connor's line – seeing the dangers to the local bases of support built over the previous generation. But the workers, who left the mills and factories as the marchers arrived voted almost universally for strike action. Koditschek quotes a description of the march into Bradford:

> they came pouring down the wide road from Horton ... the great multitude were in the prime of life, full of excitement. As they marched they thundered out a good old tune, a stirring melody 'Men of England, ye are slaves, tho' ye rule the roaring waves.[10]

And, as the workers marched in, the carriages of the local millowners could be seen speeding down the road on the other side of town.

Malcolm Chase quotes an intercepted letter from a young Ashton worker dated 11 August: 'now is the time or never – lose this opportunity and we are lost, lost!! ... We have stopt'd every trade. Now's the time for Liberty. We want wages paid 1840 ... if they won't give it us Revolution in the consequence...'. The letter claims that the soldiers were ready to desert and shopkeepers in support.[11]

For Manchester, Jenkins describes the conduct of the marchers, two days before this, as they entered the city on 9 August. Soldiers were ordered to bar their way. The marchers were instructed by the strike leaders to march round them. With great courage they did so. The army commanders, at that stage with limited numbers, were fearful of repeating the mistakes of Peterloo. Discipline was maintained. The marchers continued – growing in number as each workplace emptied until they had effectively taken control of the city. As in some of our previous case studies, such as Clydeside and Belfast in 1919, many of the marchers were young, in their teens and twenties. Many were also women – from industries in which women, such as machine weaving, formed a majority of the workforce. But, possibly unlike Clydeside and Belfast, the young as well as the older workers were fully aware of the stakes. They came from a culture of disciplined resistance, of frequent arrests and underground organisation – much as the marchers in Apartheid South Africa or Derry in 1971.

August 1842: 'the terrible tide of thought and energy'

How, then, do we define this 'practical moment' ? The course of events, as we have seen, was determined in the last week of July and the first ten days of August. But this time action had been well prepared in two senses. Long-term the working population in these areas had developed, at least in many of its communities, a decades' old culture of defiant, intelligent underground organisation. Second, since the rejection of the 1842 Chartist petition in May there here had been, at local level, something like three months of preparatory debate and discussion.

Peter McDouall himself effectively supplied the answer to this question towards the end of 1842 when he wrote from exile in France to the Manchester Chartists (he was virtually the only major leader to escape):

> The question of having or not having a strike was already
> decided because the strike had taken place; the question of
> making or not making that strike political was also decided
> because the trades had decided, almost unanimously, to
> cease work for the Charter alone ... the question was whether
> Chartism should or should not retain its ascendancy in its
> natural territory.[12]

What, therefore, did he mean – 'retain its ascendancy in its natural territory'? Probably two things. One immediate. The other long-term. The long-term referred to the erosion that had been taking place through the 1830s of the local community base of working-class power. As already noted, the Whig reforms of the poor law (taking it out of the control of the vestries), of the police (equally) and of factory legislation. In most areas there had been resistance. Still in the early 40s poor law reform had not been enforced in a number of localities in Lancashire and Yorkshire. However, these areas were diminishing and so also was effective local resistance to the new county police. On top of this there was, as already noted, the more immediate challenge. In May-June, Chartism was seemingly immobilised, fruitlessly seeking, as McDouall and his colleagues would argue, new signatures for a failed petition. On the other hand, the Anti-Corn Law League, both at national level and in detail through local employers in each community, was calling for a common front against the Tory government and the landowners.

This was the challenge. Should Chartism retain its ascendancy in its 'natural territory' ? This is seemingly what William Moorhouse was referring to 11 August when addressing the workers at the factory village of Compstall in Derbyshire: 'they could get it but if they did not, they need never try again'.[13]

The arguments put at all these meetings were that, without working-class power in and over parliament, trade union power would be always be negated. In making the argument speakers almost always linked conquest of parliamentary power – through universal suffrage – to the ability to protect wages. The 'theme' of vulnerable, unprotected wages, and of starvation in the future, gave meaning to political action.

From the *Northern Star* for 20 August: Manchester block printers: winning the Charter was the 'only means to secure good government and a protection for their wages'; Heywood: 'all out not alone for wages but also for the means of protection for their labour'; Littleborough: 'all at a stand not alone for wages but for political justice; Glossop 'for a fair day's wage … and to obtain the People's Charter to protect such wages for the future'; Hyde: 'coming out for the Charter to get good wages and protect them for the future'.[14]

From the *Northern Star* 27 August: Middleton (South Lancashire): a show of hands was taken for the People's Charter and also all those who would wish to have their wages at the mercy of the manufacturers'; Holborn London 1,000 shoemakers: 'fight on wages nugatory: the inefficacy of trade unions unless backed by political power'. William Campbell (the original secretary of the NCA): 'Let the producers of wealth cease their labour and stand with their arms folded and contempt for those who oppress them. A people so acting would at once obtain their liberty'.

From the *Northern Star* 3 September 1842: Leith, Edinburgh: 'we consider class legislation as the primary cause of our existing distress'; Glasgow: the distressed state of the country … is wholly caused by class-based laws. Class legislation is the cause of our present national calamities'.

Wages were linked to political rights – and increasingly to the threat of more 'class legislation' that menaced the existing position of labour.

Was the response by Chartism's 'Northern' leaders, in terms of initiating the call for a general strike, foolhardy ? In scale the general strike of 1842 was far larger than any other in the nineteenth century – bigger by far than the political general strikes that did win extensions of the suffrage in Belgium and Sweden prior to 1914. It continued in its industrial heartland for up to five weeks well into September. It did so despite harsh repression and violence. Once reinforcements had arrived from the south, troops had been ordered to fire on unarmed assemblies of workers in Preston (12 August), Skipton, Halifax and Blackburn (15 August) and Burslem, Stoke (16 August). Many were injured and some killed. But the strike continued. There was little or no return to work. It was in this context on the 17 August that the NCA Executive issued its defiant declaration from its meeting in Manchester – the words written by Peter McDouall:

> Labour must no longer be the common prey of masters and
> rulers … labour, the real property of society, the sole origin
> of accumulated property, the first cause of national wealth
> … is not possessed of the same legal protection as is given to
> those lifeless effects which labour has created … we do now
> universally resolve never to resume labour until labour's
> grievances are destroyed …

> The blood of your brothers reddens the streets …Be firm, be
> courageous…What tyrant can then live above the terrible tide
> of thought and energy that is now flowing fast … The Trades,

> a noble and patriotic band, have taken the lead in declaring
> for the Charter… centuries may roll before such universal
> action may be displayed … we rely on your firmness …
> Officers of the Association are called upon to aid and assist…'.

The strike continued to grow. As we have noted, still two and three weeks later new areas were joining. In its heartland of Yorkshire and Lancashire and in the mines and iron furnaces of Scotland the strike continued well into September. Despite martial law, many industrial centres remained under the administrative control of the NCA. Strike committees, some called 'Committees of Public Safety' and others 'Operatives Committees', and composed of trade union delegates, issued licences for work essential to the working-class communities, for the transport and production of food and the enforcement of public order. Evidence of the operation of these committees was detailed by the Attorney General at the trial of the leaders in Spring 1843:

> I have ever considered the existence of these committees as
> one of the most formidable evidences to which the 'strike' as
> it is called, pervaded all classes of operatives.[15]

In most areas shopkeepers donated to food and financial support. Even in the big cities. attempts to mobilise Special Constables broke down. In Manchester the Chelsea Pensioners were paraded – but then broke ranks and fled.

It was this experience that convinced first Engels and then Marx that it had to be the working-class itself, in the mass, mobilised and organised, that would have the capacity to challenge capitalist state power and it alone, once possessed of this class knowledge, that would have the ability to create a new order.[16] For Marx and Engels this revolutionary process was not essentially about the use of force (necessary though this might sometimes be). It was about the mass social transformation, 'the tide of energy and thought', required for the development of a new collective identity and a new society.

The ruling-class response

The response in 1842-1843 was truly that of a 'ruling' class. It was ruthless and repressive. But it was also strategic: about how to maintain capitalist 'rule' into the future and how the form of this rule would have to be modified and transformed through, as Marx put it in *Capital*, a fundamental 'change of front and speech'.

In their private correspondence government ministers were clear about the scale of the challenge. On 26 August the Home Secretary reported to the Prime Minister that, when the Queen had commented on the disturbances being as bad as those of 1839 (which included an armed rising), he had replied 'more serious'. Although the north was well garrisoned, he assessed troop numbers entirely insufficient to meet the first wave of strikes in early August. 'Even if you had a standing army ten times greater... it would be impossible to provide troops for every town and village.' On 17 August the officer commanding Northern District General Sir William Warre was replaced. His failure to take sufficiently decisive action was blamed for the vacillation of local authorities. On 21 August Graham wrote to Lord Brougham that the 'mad insurrection of the working classes' had taken up all his time' and to Wellington on 24 August that in future 'great precaution and vigilance will still be required'. On 30 August Graham was still gravely concerned: 'the assailants are united; in the defence the greatest dissension prevails'.

The initial response was brutal. In the north-west alone there were 1,500 arrests. They were tried at Special Commissions by government appointed judges. Most of the prisoners, were young, a majority at the Chester assizes were aged 18 to 24. A quarter were sentenced to transportation and others imprisoned for periods of a year or more. The presiding Judge Lord Abinger lectured on the dangers of democracy for Britain:

> they wanted to carry the principle of the Charter. That is
> to say that the labouring classes who have no property are
> to make laws for those who have property ... a popular
> assembly devoted to democratic principles ... the first thing
> such an assembly would be to aim at the destruction of
> property.[17]

Across Britain the number of arrests probably well exceeded three thousand.

The ultimate fate of the leadership was different. By October the government had seized most members of the NCA's Executive and of supporting trade unions (in practice the leaders of a majority of the country's major unions). These 60 prisoners were charged variously with sedition and conspiracy. Preparatory correspondence discussed capital sentences to be handed down at a show trial in London.

However, this did not happen. The 60 leading trade unionists and Chartist officers were held till March 1843 and then tried in Lancaster. After eight days of deliberation and discussion it was announced that the charges had not been properly framed and the prisoners were released.

Instead, the trial was transformed into a public dialogue between the government's Attorney General Sir Frederick Pollock and the leading prisoners. The Attorney General admitted the scale of working-class hardship, acknowledged the good faith of trade unionists in seeking redress and, separately, of the legitimacy of the Chartist movement's call for parliamentary reform as long as pursued within constitutional channels.

The prisoners were invited to respond in similar terms. O'Connor for the NCA told the presiding judge Baron Rolfe:

> you have prescribed the exact limits by which agitation
> should be bound, and beyond these limits I will never stray;
> and I feel I may include the leaders of the Chartist party in
> this bond and covenant ...[18]

Pollock similarly addressed the trade union leaders. He was:

> proud of the talents of the defenders and of the effect of the
> education of the working classes ... it is perfectly true ... that
> without labour capital may be valueless. It is just as true that
> in an advanced state of civilisation labour would be quite as
> valueless if there were no capital to give employment ... these
> two great elements ought not to be placed in hostile array ...
> labour and capital ought to have one common protection and
> ought to be directed to the common end of all...[19]

For the leadership of the NCA this meant disavowing strategies of class mobilisation – above all, any attempt to use the extra-parliamentary pressure of organised labour to change the policies of constitutional government. Conversely, for the trade union leaders it meant restricting their activity – although within what were soon to be somewhat more liberalised legal limits – to those of collective bargaining by trade. The linkage between industrial and political action, the use of mobilised class power against the state power of capital, had to be repudiated.

This trial was, therefore, the first, but critical, stage in the 'change of front and speech' as described by Marx. This change of front and speech was, however, far more comprehensive than a simple restatement of constitutional protocols. To quote Marx again:

> however much the individual manufacturer might give rein
> to his old lust for gain, the spokesmen and political leaders of
> the manufacturing class ordered a change of front and speech
> towards the workpeople ... they promised, therefore, not only
> a double-sized loaf but the enactment of the Ten Hours Bill.[20]

These legislative moves followed intense internal discussion within Peel's Conservative government which, although publicly pledged to defend the interests of landed capital, also had strong links with manufacturing (Peel's family controlled one of the biggest combines in the cotton industry). In 1846, in speaking in support of the bill for the repeal of the Corn Laws, Peel's Home Secretary Sir James Graham prefaced his remarks with a reference to the events of 1842:

> We had, first of all, the painful and lamentable experience
> of 1842 itself—a year of the greatest distress, and, now that
> it is passed, I may say, of the utmost danger. What were
> the circumstances of 1842? Allow me just to glance at them.
> We had in this metropolis, at midnight, Chartist meetings
> assembled in Lincoln's Inn Fields. Almost for nearly three
> weeks there were assembled in all the environs of this
> metropolis, immense masses of people, greatly discontented,
> and acting in a spirit dangerous to the public peace. What
> was the condition of Lancashire, the seat of our great staple
> manufacture, depending for its prosperity on uninterrupted
> tranquillity and labour? Such was the madness of the people
> on that occasion, that a great combination existed to stop
> machinery, and to put an end to the means of employment
> on which they depended for their daily bread. What was
> the duty of the Government under these circumstances?
> It was my painful duty to consult with the Horse Guards
> almost daily as to the precautions that were necessary for the
> maintenance of the public peace; a large force of infantry and
> artillery was despatched to Manchester by railway; and for
> some time the troops were continually called on, in different
> parts of the manufacturing districts, to maintain public
> tranquillity. I can safely say that, for three months, the anxiety
> which I and my Colleagues experienced with reference to
> the public peace, was greater than we ever felt before with
> reference to public affairs. Those were days of high prices
> and scarcity, of low wages and diminished employment. I
> am certain, from what I have since observed, that turbulent
> disposition, that dangerous disposition, mainly arose from the
> want of adequate sustenance, in consequence of the high price
> of food and low wages.[21]

The correspondence between Peel and his Home Secretary and others in
summer-autumn 1842 reveals not just a fear of mass revolt but also an
awareness of the multiple contradictions of Britain's industrial economy. At
the end of October Peel wrote: 'the tendency of reduced prices ... sharpen the
wits of the master manufacturers and urge him to improve his machinery;
the downward effect on manual labour and the wages of manual labour,
first of this reduction in price and secondly by the attempt to countervail
it by improvement in machinery' inevitably result, he concluded, 'in rapid
rises in unemployment...These are things I am more worried about than
the price of pork.'[22] To another correspondent the same day he wrote again

noting the contradictions inherent in unbridled industrial growth. '[T]the condition of this country is a very alarming one' and then argued, in terms of ameliorative action, both for an income tax and a repeal of the corn laws.[23] The previous month his Home Secretary Graham commented:

> in every country where manufacturing machinery has been introduced, the power of production has outstripped the means of consumption.[24]

'The change of front and speech'

It is in this context that we have to understand the transformation of governmental policy over the years 1842 to 1847. It represented a fundamental shift and ushered in a new period of politico-economic development: a switch to the export of capital and 'informal' empire. 1842 saw the introduction of income tax and the abolition of the ban on the export of machinery – liberating the flow of Britain's advanced technology abroad. 1843 saw Lancashire cotton spinners and employers moving towards a level of mutual recognition in terms of union organisation within the law.[25] The 1844 Bank Act tightened controls over liquidity creation, which had fuelled anarchic investment in factories and railways, and thereby provided sterling with a more stable platform for external investment. The 1846 repeal of the Corn Laws not just cheapened food imports but also ushered in a new era of overseas investment in railways and the other infrastructure required for the full opening of the Americas for food production. Finally, in 1847 the Ten Hour Factory Act both restricted output and also answered one of the central strategic demands of the working-class radicals. And in terms of world influence, these moves also took place in the context of a radical expansion of Britain's formal and informal empire. In 1842-43 Peel was able to announce to parliament both the opening of Chinese ports to British trade (overwhelmingly of opium) and a radical extension of British military control over north-west India (India produced the opium).

As the East India Company administrator, J.S. Mill, put it in 1848 in his *Principles of Political Economy*:

> improvements in production and the emigration of capital are what we have chiefly to depend upon for increasing [the gross product and the demand for labour at home] ... It is only in the backward countries of the world that increased production is still an important object.[26]

He added:

> of the working men, at least in the more advanced countries
> of Europe it may be pronounced as certain that the patriarchal
> ... system of government is not one to which they will again
> be subject ... the prospect of the future depends on the degree
> to which they can be made rational beings.[27]

Already in 1843 Graham, as Home Secretary, was preparing a new scheme for the education for children in factories which, as he put it to the Bishop of Chester, may 'dispel the darkness of ignorance which overshadows the manufacturing districts and which portends a fearful storm'.[28] Large funds were also made available for the building of churches in industrial districts and for subdividing parishes.

Locally also these years witnessed the parallel responses of the big manufacturers. For Bradford, where, as we noted, the millowners mostly fled in face of the working-class mobilisation of 1842, Koditschek documents their efforts from the mid and later 1840s to create a new popular alliance around urban improvement and poverty relief (their leader W.E. Forster, later Bradford's MP, was the architect of the 1870 education act). Similarly in Oldham the mid and later 1840s saw the big employers in both textiles and textile engineering intervening to co-opt local leaders among the shopkeepers and petty bourgeoisie, as well as some trade union figures, to support employer-nominated candidates in local and national elections.

However, these moves were possible only because the local hegemony of working-class power had been broken. Thousands of key local leaders had been arrested. Many others had to relocate or emigrate. And probably more important still, the wider Chartist movement had been immobilised. The drive to unite political and industrial action, the political mobilisation of the trade union movement, had been officially renounced. In 1843-44, a period of trade recovery, had seen a revival of trade-union organisation – but in the main only for those able to use their market power as skilled or apprenticed workers to negotiate sectional deals. In the new circumstances the local culture of class unity – as well as working-class control of the local administrative structures – quickly fell away.

It was in this context that a new stratification began to crystallise typified by the emergence of what Marx and Engels called an 'aristocracy of labour' composed of the minority of workers able to take advantage of the new dispensations.[29] For those not so advantaged the crystallisation of new identities was further complicated by the arrival from 1845 of up to a million refugees from the Irish famine and the emergence (and in some areas the active employer deployment) of further division arising from anti-Irish racism. In Oldham we see a new cultural absorption of skilled engineers, especially those working in the textile engineering plants (now largely feeding export markets) within the orbit of a new populist liberalism. Conversely, less skilled workers in textiles tended to gravitate towards an equally populist Conservative Party deploying an aggressively 'localist' culture implicitly, and sometimes explicitly, posed against the growing population of Irish immigrants.[30]

The fears of McDouall and his colleagues were therefore borne out remarkably quickly – though only in the context of a profound shift of policy by the ruling class. For Marx and Engels, however, these events also demonstrated, critically for their understanding of revolutionary change within capitalism, the potentially profound effects of such class mobilisation, a transformation by which the working class en masse could become 'fitted to found society anew'.

NOTES

1   Address of the Chartist Executive, 17 August 1842 from Mick
     Jenkins, *The General Strike of 1842* (London 1980).
2   Karl Marx, *Capital* volume 1: *Collected Works* Volume 35 (Moscow
     1996) p. 286.
3   G.D.H. Cole, *Chartist Portraits* (London 1941); F.C. Mather, 'The
     General Strike of 1842', J. Porter (ed), *Provincial Labour History*
     (1972 Exeter 1972); Naomi and TDW Reid, "The 1842 Plug
     Plot", in Stockport', *International Review of Social History*, 1979/1;
     Malcolm Chase, *Chartism: A New History* (Manchester 2007);
     Robert Fyson. 'The Crisis of 1842: Chartism, the Colliers Strike
     and the Outbreak in the Potteries', in J. Epstein (ed), *The Chartist
     Experience* (London 1982), Peter Gurney, 'The Democratic Idiom:
     languages of democracy in the Chartist movement', *Journal of
     Modern History*, 2014, vol. 86/3; Theordore Koditschek, *Class Politics
     and Urban Industrial Society: Bradford 1750-1850* (Cambridge 1990);
     Paul Pickering, *Chartism and the Chartists in Manchester and Salford*
     (London 1999); Robert Sykes, 'Early Chartism and trade unionism in
     south-east Lancashire' in J. Epstein (ed), *The Chartist Experience.*
4   Anthony Smith, 'The Strike for the People's Charter in 1842', PhD
     London School of Economics, 2002, p. 33.
5   I. Prothero, 'William Benbow and the Concept of a General Strike',
     Past and Present, Volume 63, 1, May 1974; Malcolm Chase, 'From
     Millenium to Jubilee', *Past and Present*, No 129, November 1990.
6   Tom Scriven, *Popular Virtue: continuity, change and radical moral
     politics, 1820-70* (Manchester 2017); Gregory Varga, *An Underground
     History of Early Victorian Fiction: Chartism, radical print culture and the
     social problem novel* (Cambridge 2018), Matthew Roberts, *Chartism,
     Commemoration and the Cult of the Radical Hero* (London, 2020)
     and John Saunders, 'John Douthwaite and 'John Powlett': trade
     unionism and conflict in early 1830s Yorkshire, *Labour History Review*
     87/1, 2, probably 2022. This amplifies and carries forward earlier
     research by John Baxter, 'Early Chartism and Labour Class Struggle:
     South Yorkshire 1837-1840', *Essays in South Yorkshire History*, ed. S.
     Pollard and C. Holmes (Sheffield 1977) and, with Joseph Stanley, *The
     Road to Insurrection in the Industrial West Riding 1819-1820*, Borthwick
     Paper, 131 (York 2020).
7   N and T Reid, as cited, *IRSH*, 1979.
8   J. Foster, *Class Struggle and the Industrial Revolution*, p. 216.
9   The government commissioner, H S Tremenheere, appointed
     after the events of 1842 to assess working-class attitudes in the
     Lanarkshire coalfield, reported, as a measure of the effects of this
     cultural ignorance, that the miners were reading Plato's *Republic*,

a 'Communist' text: Report of the Commissioners of the Mining Districts, 1852, p. 41.

10   T. Koditschek, *Class Formation and Urban Industrial Society: Bradford 1750-1850* (Cambridge University Press, 1990) p. 345.
11   M. Chase, *Chartism: a new history* (Manchester 2007) p.215.
12   Paul Pickering, *Chartism and the Chartists in Manchester and Salford* (Macmillan 1999), pp. 69-70.
13   Anthony Smith, PhD, p. 33
14   All from *Northern Star* 20 August 1842: noting that the editorial policy of the paper remained hostile to the strike and also that any statements were in danger of being used by the government for purposes of legal prosecution.
15   Jenkins, op.cit., p 251 provides evidence of the widespread character of these committees; quotation from *The Trial of Feargus O'Connor and 58 others at Lancaster on a Trial of Sedition* (1843 no publisher) pp. 11, 178-9, 248-9.
16   Though clearly put in *The German Ideology* of 1845-46, this position was outlined most effectively in their rebuttal of Proudhon in *The Poverty of Philosophy* of 1847.
17   Jenkins, op.cit, pp. 226-227.
18   Jenkins, op. cit. p. 236.
19   Ibid.
20   Marx, *Capital* vol.1 Marx Engels, Collected *Works*, vol. 35 (Moscow 1996) p.286.
21   Sir James Graham, *Hansard*, Tuesday 10 February 1846.
22   Peel to Croker, 30 October 1842, C. S.Parker, ed., *Sir Robert Peel From His Private Papers* (Murray 1899) p. 531.
23   Peel to Arbuthnot 30 October 1842, Parker op. cit. p. 532.
24   Graham to Peel 1 September 1842 Parker, op. cit. p. 546.
25   Mick Jenkins, *The General Strike of 1842*, p. 255.
26   J S Mill, *Principles of Political Economy* (Toronto 1965) Vol II, p.758
27   Ibid, p. 755.
28   Graham Papers, Cambridge University Library: Graham to Bishop of Chester 19 January 1843, spool 33.
29   Since the 1980s historians have generally abandoned any analytical use of the concept of the 'labour aristocracy' as developed by Marx, Engels and later Lenin. They largely did so in deference to the claim by G. S. Jones that Marx never used the term 'aristocracy' of labour and, as a believer in the iron law of wages, Marx could never have accepted Engels's very mechanical conception that a stratum of workers could exist, as he and later Lenin claimed, that secured long-term privileges and higher wages (G.S. Jones, 'Some Notes on Karl Marx and the English Labour Movement', *History Workshop*, No. 18, 1984). Apparently, Jones had not noticed that Marx himself

used the term 'aristocracy of the working-class' in this way in *Capital* or that Marx detested the concept of an 'iron law of wages' as much as he detested its main proponent Lasalle: Marx, *Capital* Volume I p.660: *CW*, vol. 35 (Moscow 1996) for Marx's use of the term.

30   J Foster, *Class Struggle*, p.243.

THIS PAGE LEFT INTENTIONALLY BLANK

6

Conclusion

the education and organisation of the working and exploited
masses ... their liberation from egoism, sectionalism, from
the vices and weaknesses engendered by private property,
their transformation into a free union of free workers – all this
is only possible in the actual course of acute class struggles.
Lenin 1920

This study has sought to do three things. First, to show the continuing
analytical and political relevance of Marx and Engels's understanding
of revolutionary change. Second, to demonstrate the importance of
the Soviet theorists of language and social change in analysing how such
moments of revolutionary challenge occur. Third, to do so in terms of the
history of working people in Britain, the first country to fully develop
industrial capitalism – an imperialist state deriving a significant part of
its material and human resources from the politico-economic subjection
of other countries and particularly its neighbour, Ireland, upon whose
experience we also draw.

This conclusion will briefly return to the theoretical approach of Marx
and Engels and of its application by the Soviet theorists of language and
then consider its relevance to the key turning points identified in our five
case studies.

Theoretical approaches

Marx and Engels, as we noted at the outset, stressed both the relative suddenness and the socially transformative character of moments of revolutionary mobilisation. They did so in light of contemporary experience, particularly Britain in 1842, and of their underlying analysis of social change, of the processes of class mobilisation and, conversely, of alienation and reification.

In all previous class societies, they argued, the ruling class appropriation of the surplus, of all products of labour beyond the needs of subsistence, had, among other things, served to secure the resource required for economic and social development as well as their own class dominance. There was indeed therefore an 'alienation' of the products of labour. Under capitalism, however, the process for doing this was different and particularly far-reaching in terms of its social character and consequences. It involved not just the appropriation of what labour produced but the sale of labour power itself. In this form it represented a far more direct negation of what Marx described as humanity's 'species being'. By this he meant the cooperative, mutually supportive process by which knowledge is developed across generations, a process also seen in the development of every child. This process is one, as detailed in particular by Vygotsky, by which each child is nurtured and taught to use language socially and productively as a tool – and, by mutual reinforcement, to collectively draw on humanity's existing store of productive knowledge. Yet under capitalism it was this facility itself, the ability to labour creatively, that had to be sold and its use surrendered. It was 'labour power' itself that was alienated.

The social consequence, argued Marx, was a process of 'estrangement' or 'reification', the re-definition of social purpose in terms of consumption not production, of the 'things' that could be bought by the monetary proceeds of selling labour power ('re' being the Latin for 'thing'). In this way levels of consumption defined both social position and social purpose and cumulatively the identity of the individual – in large part by invidious comparison with others. It was therefore for this reason that Marx and Engels argued in 1846 that mass revolutionary mobilisation was required not just to overthrow capitalist rule but for the class doing so 'to rid itself of the muck of ages' in order to found society anew.

In the 1920s Soviet social psychologists, who had themselves lived through such a period of mass revolutionary transformation, sought to deepen the practical understanding of this process. In terms of the specific social role of language they saw it as having a twin function within and for capitalism. It served both its overall social purpose of enabling society's productive life and development but also of sustaining and defending an exploitative social order – by seemingly making this order's existence eternal and inevitable and at the same time, among those exploited, bonding and sealing communication within specific groups as defined by their life roles and consumption, filtering out invidious comparison.

For individuals, as Leontiev put it, these socially restricted meanings 'dig themselves into their connections with people forming the real circle of their contacts'. If they make a choice it is not between meanings 'but between colliding social positions'. At the same time, to quote Voloshinov:

> the ruling class serves to impart a supra-class, eternal
> character to the ideological sign, to extinguish the struggle
> between social value judgements ... the inner dialectic quality
> of the sign comes out fully in the open only in times ... of
> revolutionary changes.

And, as noted earlier, this exposure of the 'inner dialectic quality of the sign' is not a passive or automatic process. Social value judgements, any critiques of the existing order, have to be won by argument and discussion – by exploiting what Voloshinov called the dialectic of theme and meaning. By 'meaning' he meant the rough and generalised 'meanings' that people will have absorbed in order to understand their wider social environment and then, within this, their constant search for what a particular word might really 'mean', its theme, in a specific context. It would be by understanding how to transform this social context, to shift these points of reference, and doing so by linking what was familiar to something that was new and socially challenging (as Eisenstein sought to do in cinema with montage) that perceptions of meaning might be transformed.

However, this could not be done, or done easily, from 'outside'. It demanded a knowledge of, and effectively participation within, people's 'real circle of contacts'. Politically, in Soviet Russia in the 1920s, this would have been seen as a 'Bolshevik' style of work: that of a working class party, with socialist objectives, whose members were embedded within and authentically part of such 'real circles of contact'.

It is against this background that we have sought to analyse five instances where working people have, as a class, attempted to challenge, or at least combat, the existing capitalist order. In no case, as we have seen, did these challenges in Britain come near to overthrowing that order – though in some closer than others. In all, however, those responsible for defending the existing order saw it necessary to make concessions, to incorporate some systemic demands and to do so in a way that would socially isolate those they saw as responsible for the challenge. On this basis they reconfigured patterns of consumption, of social authority and social identity – but also usually in ways that would again, in time, ultimately come into conflict with the economic constraints of capitalism as a politico-economic system.

In what follows we will attempt to draw out the common features of these attempts, consider their more general implications for the understanding of capitalist social change and, within this, also consider the role of language –

noting that what people said, in debate and dialogue, formed a key aspect of the way in which Marx and Engels themselves wrote history and analysed social change.

Five case studies: common features and implications for social change

We started with the most recent episode: 1971 on Clydeside. For this period we could have chosen the miners' strike of January 1972. Or the incipient general strike of August 1972 that secured the release of the imprisoned dockers and marked the effective end of Edward Heath's Industrial Relations Act. All spoke to a heightened level of working class mobilisation.

But it was the take-over of the shipyards on the Clyde that came first and which represented the most fundamental challenge. It also marked the initial, and therefore most difficult, stage in the re-mobilisation of a mass shop stewards movement which had peaked early in 1969 – when it defeated Harold Wilson's *In Place of Strife* – and then ebbed. At that point parliamentary politics had taken over and it had been the Tories, not Labour, who won the subsequent general election. The language of government consequently changed and so did its tactics – even though the objective of Heath's Conservatives was largely the same as Labour: to demobilise the shop stewards movement, restore power to official trade union leaderships and use these leaders to control wages in a period of growing crisis of currencies, profit levels and global dollar control.

The conclusion of our review was, perhaps controversially, that the 1971-72 struggle on Clydeside reflected a higher level of working class consciousness than that represented by the general strike of January-February 1919.

How might this be so? Because, it was argued, it took the shop stewards struggles out of the workplace into the wider community and did so in a way that raised the question of the social control and purpose of production. Through the 1960s the struggles of shop stewards movement had been essentially defensive: to protect legal rights on the shopfloor (its central organisation was indeed called the Liaison Committee for the Defence of Trade Union Rights).The UCS went significantly further. It challenged the property rights of capital itself and, critically, in mobilising support across Britain around the right to work, posed the question of who controlled that work and made the struggle for the 'right to work' also about the right to work in a new way that was responsible to the wider community.

The Scottish context was important here in understanding how this transition was possible. It was at least in part because of the continuing strength of the Left. There remained at least a sprinkling of Communist councillors in local government from Inverness to Motherwell – allied usually with Labour Party Lefts – and this was important for the wider community and local government response. A similar Left alliance exercised a decisive strength in the trade union movement. Already in 1971-72 the Left was largely dominant in the STUC general council and among its officers. This made it possible to launch strategic challenges that went beyond the shop-stewards movement itself – as demonstrated by the STUC sponsored public enquiry of September 1971 and then at the Scottish Assembly of 1972.

At the same time the stewards' control of the yards enabled them to confront the government with strategic demands for a new form of democratic, but working class, control over the wider economy. The climax came at the 1972 Scottish Assembly with the call for a 'workers' parliament' in Scotland – although the question had already been posed by Alex Murray, Communist Party Scottish Secretary, in his speech during the second Scottish general strike in August 1971: 'if this system cannot provide it, let us have another…'

This explicit questioning of class power, and the wider impact of this across the trade union movement and the Labour Party, helped create the political context in which Tony Benn, himself closely involved with the UCS stewards, was able to take the policy initiatives that, with active backing from within the trade union movement, shifted the Labour Party as a whole strongly towards the Left – drafting Labour's programme for government as adopted in 1973, one that demanded an 'irreversible shift of wealth and power in favour of working people'.

No less relevant to this study, Jimmy Reid, when elected rector of Glasgow University, took the issue of 'alienation' out the realm of theory and posed it, practically and popularly, as a challenge to the way people lived within a society based on capitalist exploitation. It was this ideological challenge, linked to the immediate political challenge to social loyalties and identities represented by the work-in itself and the upsurge in working class militancy, that continued to exercise a significant impact on Scottish culture and politics through the 1970s.

The existence of recordings of the UCS Coordinating Committee and of yard meetings, makes it possible to understand in much more detail how, on a day to day basis, the shop stewards won the key arguments and managed to convince workers of the need to defy the government, to challenge the legal rights of property and also their own right-wing trade union leaders. These recordings enable us to see how the stewards framed their responses – using themes that resonated within workers' 'real circle of contacts', to transform 'meanings' as used by government and the press, and were able to do so because they were themselves part of, and understood, these circles of contact. The recordings also show the importance of timing. To be effective the stewards' responses had to have immediate, contemporary reference, in terms of what was being said that day in the press and on TV. This, in turn, reminds us of the 'time-bound' character of history. Success or failure depended on relevance to the 'immediate': to the stewards' ability to speak to what was being said within the 'practical moment', as Marx put it, and hence, on that basis, win the support of those who had the collective power to go on to make history.

What were the key triggers? In winning the original decisions to defy the government (and right-wing Confed leadership) it was the basic issue of solidarity, each yard supporting the others, and the wider fear of a return to the 1930s. But this was deepened with an appeal to workers' pride in their skill. Collectively they built the ships. It was the old owners who were 'not fit to run a bingo'. Later at the key turning point in September, when the whole force of the media was being turned against them, the stewards exploited the government's blunder in demanding adverse changes in terms and conditions for those in the 'saved' yards (visibly the result of demands from the owners of the private yards on the Lower Clyde). They linked this to the fear of the government 'coming back' later with further attacks on a weakened and isolated workforce that had betrayed the trust of their fellow workers and of 'the British working class'. The power of 'class solidarity' was made real. The price of class treachery equally so. From this moment the stewards had won – and the government knew it.

What are the questions that arise? Scotland's politics did change. Politically Scotland voted Labour in 1979, 1983, 1987 and 1992 when England voted Conservative. As Chik Collins has demonstrated Scotland's heartland working class communities continued to be seen, by both the Scottish Office and by Margaret Thatcher, as requiring special treatment. 'Urban development' programmes were launched largely designed to isolate and root out antagonistic 'class' leaderships as well as sideline councils that continued to reflect some form of democratic will – halting, for instance, water privatisation in Scotland. Yet more generally the wholesale re-engineering of British society, combining deindustrialisation with the privatisation of the public sphere, energy, communications and, above all probably, housing, did in Scotland, as elsewhere, do much to re-isolate and minimise the influence of the radical Left. As elsewhere also, trade union membership shrank by half, the old type of shop stewards movement largely vanished (its factory bases were closed), what remained of the labour movement retreated to limited defensive tactics and the Labour Party itself drifted to successively more reformist positions until in 2007 it was overtaken by a resurgent, but equally reformist, Scottish National Party.

Yet the great bulk of the Scottish population remained, as in England, dependent on selling their labour power and doing so, often, in increasingly difficult conditions outside manufacturing in the service sector. How did 'reified' identities recrystallise? How, moreover, did they do so in circumstances, where, for many sections of the population, the experience was one of visible defeat and loss, a loss heightened by the previous experience of a united and often victorious class challenge? This is a question that largely remains, in terms of detailed analysis, unanswered.[1] Some more general comments are made in the Appendix.

Our next case study was the Clydeside strike of January-February 1919.

In contrast to UCS in 1971 this was, at least initially, a more defensive struggle – to protect the advances secured by the shop stewards movement during the First World War and to do so in the knowledge that a very significant section of the working population was still gripped by the ideas of the old order. It was ultimately the mishandling of this challenge by the War Cabinet and particularly Churchill, resulting in the military occupation of Clydeside, that served to shift the political balance – with long-term consequences.

As we noted, Glasgow MP and Conservative leader, Bonar Law demonstrated an acute understanding of the underlying issues on the eve of the 1918 election – of how society 'is really built up of conventions'; that 'habits are formed… as strong as iron bands', that across much of Europe war 'has broken through the crust' but that in Britain 'people knew that whatever they could justly claim they would get by constitutional means' and that the Coalition's non-partisan inclusion of labour and trade union leaders, and its commitment to social reform, would ensure stability. Bonar Law well understood the strength (and political importance) of the 'reified' identities that still stratified the working population of his 'native city'.

This assessment was shared by John Maclean ('the majority' are not of our way of thinking) and Arthur McManus, one of principal leaders of the shop stewards movement on Clydeside. The immediate concern of the Strike Committee in the first week was to win the full allegiance of the majority of shipyard and engineering workers – specifically those who did not turn out for the strike on the first day, well over half, it seems. For this reason the materials issued by the strike committee never contained any mention of socialism or of the very acute struggles taking place elsewhere in Europe. Conversely it was the mainstream press (operating in very close cooperation with the government and employers) that sought to raise the bogy of revolution and link the strikers to events in Europe – stressing at the same time that all responsible trade union and Labour leaders opposed the strike.

This was not to claim, however, that those leading the strike did not have socialist objectives. Quite the contrary. As our narrative showed. all were active socialists and strongly influenced by the Russian revolution. All were also seasoned leaders of movements that had during the war repeatedly challenged the government. The stress laid by Gallacher and JR Campbell's on locality committees, 'Social Committees' as they called them in the pamphlet written later in 1919, drew on their wartime experience in the battles on rents, rationing and conscription. At the outset of the 40-hours strike Gallacher had been insistent that the establishment of 'locality' committees be included among the organisational objectives of the Joint Strike Committee and that they be responsible for the involvement of residents in local policing and ensuring the cooperation of shopkeepers.

After the military occupation the role of these committees, and their mobilisation of women in their thousands as pickets, would be of significant importance for the maintenance of the strike.

The 1919 Clydeside strike also evidences, through its *Strike Bulletin*, the key importance of immediate day by day responses. Its daily circulation of up to 20,000 enabled those directly involved at local level, on picket lines and at meetings, to answer the accusations of the mainstream press which was overseen editorially on a day to day basis by the local Employers' Executive and, less directly, by the government. Each issue of the *Bulletin* responded and did so in severely practical terms – using, very effectively as we saw, the dialectic of theme and meaning. To recap:

- Day 3 of the strike: its aim – to enable 'men and women coming back into civil life to get jobs with decent pay'
- Day 4: 'The government and employers don't want unemployment abolished ... Remember 1908 ... men, women and children went about the streets ragged and hungry ..'
- Day 7: 'Machine guns no remedy...
- Day 10: 'Terrorism fails'
- And on Day 17, the last day, finally, a more explicit discussion of class and class unity: 'the barriers of craft have gone... henceforth we fight as a class'

The outcome of the strike did lay the basis for further political transformation. While it did not itself directly question ownership or call for another social system and ended with the trial and imprisonment of the main leaders, it did see, in its final days, a major shift of government policy, Lloyd George's 'insurance against Bolshevism'. The resulting maintenance of government spending meant that relatively high levels of employment persisted through 1919 and early 1920 – in turn creating the material conditions for the unprecedentedly high levels of rank and file strike action through these months and the progressive loss of authority by right-wing trade union and Labour leaders. Without the resulting temporary transformation in the leadership of the TUC it is highly unlikely that the Councils of Action would have emerged in summer 1920. A direct causal line therefore runs between the two – including, it would seem, the concept, if not the name, of locality committees that brought together workplace collectivism with local communities and gave working class unity an immediately visible identity and force.

Perhaps surprisingly the parallel 1919 strike in Belfast was in some ways more 'political' than that on the Clyde. Its Bulletin was more ambitious and from the beginning its editors seem to have seen it as an educator on the nature of a class society – possibly because of the potentially far more dangerous and problematic circumstances in Belfast at the time.

Little more than a decade before, in 1907, Belfast had seen a dispute in its docks that brought its religiously divided communities together, witnessed the police wavering in their loyalty but then a sudden, brutal reimposition of sectarian division. Three years later Connolly arrived in Belfast to work as trade union organiser. He did so in what was then a far more naked, complex and challenging political environment than any in Britain. By 1914 the Unionist gentry and employers had openly armed themselves and (loyal) employees against a potentially Home Rule administration in Dublin and done so in legal defiance of the Westminster government. At the same time Dublin's workers were also challenging the Catholic bourgeoisie in the 1912-13 general strike and, to a limited degree, arming themselves against them with the creation of Connolly's Irish Citizen Army. In the North, war then brought both full employment and large-scale immigration to Belfast creating, for the first time, conditions for a strong movement towards unionisation among unskilled and semi-skilled workers – though in a period that also saw James Connolly leading his Citizens Army into the 1916 Dublin Rising.

This was the complex background to the Belfast general strike – itself taking place at the same time that Sinn Fein began to establish the basis of a rival government in Dublin.

Yet in terms of defining its class objectives its daily strike bulletin was far more 'class'-oriented than that in Scotland. Its anonymous feature writers provided daily lectures of (non-explicit) Marxist analysis. Already on the second day of the strike they wrote:

> even those workers who have not …understood the evolution
> of their historical struggle for a higher and better life perceive
> subconsciously that many of the most beautiful things of life
> have been withheld from them … now the worker is rising
> to a consciousness of his personal dignity. He refuses to be a
> "hand".

Underlying this was a clear understanding that a stress on the practical economic benefits of class unity was their key weapon against the traditional weapon of their opponents, that of religious division. This point was constantly underlined at public meetings. At the same time the Unionist elite appears to have been at a loss as to how to intervene. Bates, the practical leader of Ulster Unionism, would have been in and out of Belfast City Hall and the newspaper offices throughout the strike. His drafting of the call from the Grand Master exposes this defensiveness – as does his lamentations at the decline of the Ulster Unionist Labour Association and in particular the loss of the youth.

After the orderly termination of the strike – the employers did not dare to impose penalties – the situation worsened, for the Ulster Unionists, still further. The size and content of the May Day demonstration was so shocking that the *Telegraph*, the city's main mass circulation paper, refused even to report it. It was a portent of the equally shocking 1920 Belfast local election results seven months later. By then the Ulster Unionist high command was redrawing the prospective political boundaries of their proposed statelet specifically in light of the need, militarily if necessary, to cope with a hostile working class in Belfast. The pogrom of July 1920 was one outcome. Key targets were Protestant trade unionists in the shipyards, a thousand in named detail it seems, a massive number in terms of those considered active socialists – and enforced by an armed formation later compared by Lloyd George, approvingly or not, to Mussolini's Fascisti.

In this respect it is interesting to compare the outcome of 'Clydeside 1919' and 'Belfast 1919-1920'. Clydeside was in reality a strike wave that spread far beyond the Clyde, did produce at least a temporary transformation in the way in which the ruling class sought to rule, a reversion to the promised, but later abandoned, war-time plans for social welfare, housing, health and education. This change cost financially. More seriously, however, for Britain's rulers its consequences in terms of inflation and, even more, full employment directly cut across the government's wider economic goals of a quick return to a gold standard currency and meant that an integral objective of British imperialism had, at best, to be postponed. Those in government well knew and feared that the (at least temporary) maintenance of full employment would also have political consequences.

Belfast also saw change. But it was different in kind. Eighteen months after the general strike – and the subsequent electoral challenge – the nature of political control itself was modified. Sectarian rule was institutionalised through the long-term use of paramilitary force – as much to prevent further class mobilisation as to ghettoise and subdue Catholics.

Virtually simultaneously, across the water, plans for Councils of Action were being developed to challenge the government should it attempt to re-launch war against the Soviet republic in Russia.

The formation of the Councils of Action in August 1920 marked the climax of the post-war working class challenge. The scale of this challenge depended on both material and 'human' factors. Materially there was, as we saw, the continuingly high level of government expenditure. This combined full employment with very high inflation, 15 percent, and brought unprecedented levels of strike action, much of its unofficial, and a continued growth in union membership. Politically, within this rapidly growing trade union movement, there was a decisive shift to the Left. Those identified through their past actions as collaborating with employers and the Coalition government lost credibility and position. By June 1920 the Left had a majority within the TUC's executive and thereby also, because the trade unions still held a fully dominant position within its governing committee, the Labour Party. This 'Left' was almost by definition pro-Soviet.

Most of its members were identified with the Hands Off Russia committee and their wider influence was sustained by the *Daily Herald*, dominated by the Lansbury family, with a daily circulation exceeding 300,000. Most of its journalists were members of either the Guild Socialists, the British Socialist Party or the Left of the ILP.

However, none of this, as noted earlier, had been achieved without what Robert Williams described as tireless daily work by thousands of activists up and down the country – continuing the discussions and dialogues founded in the experience of the earlier challenge to government of January-February 1919 and the subsequent mobilisations in the mining communities and on the rails. The questions of pay, hours of work and the continuation of state control of mines and railways remained central. So also did those of empire and war, across the Middle East, in India and Russia itself where the British government maintained an active, if covert role, in the supply of armaments and military advisers.

As noted earlier, Britain's persistent military intervention in Russia, jointly with France, was not just, or possibly even primarily, motivated by dislike and fear of the new government's socialism. It was also about the settlement of war debts – the vast sums lent to Tsarist Russia and, in consequence, Britain's ability to repay the United States. Such a settlement was seen as crucial to Britain's ability to resecure the international banking and currency dominance which it enjoyed before 1914. The disastrous failure of the Polish military assault on Soviet Russia, financed and armed by Britain and France, brought this challenge to the fore. By the first week in August the threat of a major land war was immediate and 'Peace' was the word that mobilised the immense countrywide demonstrations.

But the slogan was not 'peace, bread and land'. It was just 'peace' – even though a peace with Soviet Russia did also carry a powerful ideological content. As we noted, particularly during what was probably the biggest weekend of popular mobilisation on 26 August, trade union leaders at the big London demonstration did not hesitate in calling for a 'dictatorship of working people' in Britain with George Lansbury claiming that the Russian people had done what British workers should have done long before.

But the limited slogan, Peace, but peace only, was also a weakness – though perhaps an inevitable one. Peace remained a real and mobilising issue through August and into September. Behind the scenes Lloyd George maintained discussions with Italy, and France also, about a new war alliance. But publicly the government backed away from any further discussion of war or visible support for it. The Poles did not move. Ultimately Wrangel was defeated and the Tsarist war debts remained unpaid.

By September-October an attempt to broaden the slogan was made. The Left sought to extend the agreed demands of the Councils to the defence of public ownership in Britain's biggest industry, coal. But by then economic conditions had changed. Unemployment was finally beginning to bite and, partly in consequence, the political balance within the TUC leadership was shifting to the right. Tom Mann no longer led the engineers and Robert Williams' still loose Federation of transport unions was in disarray. Attempts from South Wales and Tyneside to widen the remit of the Councils were blocked. The government itself waited another five months till unemployment had reached a massive 20 per cent of the working population.

The challenge posed by the Councils of Action was, nonetheless, a historic one. Across the first two and three weeks of August the government's freedom of action had been checked by the 'unconstitutional' mobilisation of a united labour movement. The government attempted to deny this at the time – and historians have since minimised the challenge. But the scale of the mobilisation is undeniable. So also is the socially challenging character of its form. Councils of Action united working people in across all major communities. And they did so to develop detailed plans to take over the functions of government under the authority of a united working class. The pages of the *Daily Herald* for the closing weeks of August 1920 reveal the intensity of this local movement. Virtually every town and village was holding mass meetings under the authority of the trade union and labour movement. Their object was to resist, and, if necessary supplant, the constitutional government.

In terms of longer-term impact on ruling class assumptions about how to govern in the new post-war circumstances August 1920 seems to have marked a key moment in the recognition that steps had to be taken to ensure that the TUC and Labour Party were themselves 'constitutionalised'-integrated into the structures of government in their own right and on their own terms. Reliance on openly compliant and corrupt leaders such as JH Thomas was no longer enough. Authentic trade union figures such as Bevin had to be brought onside as partners who remained leaders of a movement that was both independent, and seen to be based within the working class, but also ultimately loyal. In particular, the Labour Party had to become an integral part of the constitutional order. From this point Bonar Law and Baldwin saw the need to substitute Labour for the Liberal Party as the second party of government.

The 1926 General Strike was presented both as a postscript, but also a further stage, in this process.

It was a postscript because, while it maintained some elements of the earlier mobilisation, it was not organised with the intent of challenging state power or creating alternatives to it. Its leaders, the members of the TUC general council, were effectively forced into it by the government with the opposite intention – to finally discredit 'unconstitutional' action intended to apply external pressure on government. The government's own handling of the strike did not entirely succeed in doing this – but in the longer-run did create a wider political environment in which such an outcome became possible. It reflected the realisation, in government, that a pliant, reliable Labour Party could only be stabilised if the trade union movement itself was brought fully within the constitutional order, a necessary complement to the constitutionalisation of the Labour Party.

The strike's significance comes, as we saw, from the degree to which there remained within working class communities sufficient residual organisational and ideological capacity to challenge the government on its own terms, in some communities to recreate Councils of Action and in most to establish rudimentary organisational structures that were seen as usurping the powers of government. This residual capacity rested largely within the Communist Party (at the time individual members were still also Labour Party members), within sections of the Independent Labour Party (equally) and the Labour Party-Left as led by Lansbury. The Right, as directed by the TUC, sought to limit mobilisation, to exclude unemployed organisations and other 'Left' fronts from local strike committees while the Left sought to include them. In Glasgow the Left only won this battle in the last couple of days – and then sought to create locality committees across the city.

Overall the result was therefore patchy. But in a significant number of key areas, in mining communities, parts of London, the north east, South Wales, a progressive mobilisation of working class communities was taking place. The exercise of authority – as expressed in detailed administrative control over resources – did shift to the strikers.

It was this that the Treasury subsequently identified as the strike's most dangerous aspect. It was when government officers, civil or military, were compelled to negotiate on the strikers' terms. During the strike itself it was the knowledge that this process was taking place that most alarmed the leaders of the General Council. On the ground, in terms of activity by the police and special branch, it was also this that was the government's main concern. TUC's daily strike bulletin was not seen as an issue for police attention. What was targeted were the local cyclostyled newsletters produced by the Communist Party and its allies that challenged the arguments of TUC and instead sought to build working class control over local administration. This was where the great bulk of the arrests were concentrated. The government's focus on the seizure of this material, and of local printing equipment, again demonstrates the importance of the day to day control of the narrative of events and their interpretation in class terms. Written material was seen as almost as dangerous as people's voices in terms of contesting the government narrative.

So, to this extent, 1926 did see a culmination of the movement begun in 1920. In some of the mining areas of Fife workers militias were formed and council employees only re-employed after swearing new oaths of allegiance. But this was not typical. The strike itself was terminated in just nine days and was followed locally by detailed victimisation. At national level, despite some challenges, the right-wing then moved to secure more or less complete control over the trade union movement. This process was completed within eighteen months and, in doing so, re-defined the movement's objectives in terms of operating within, and not challenging, a system based on the private ownership of the means of production. Those in government like the Marquess of Salisbury, did see the need to incorporate labour in a new way. But the process remained incorporation and it was this that was the symbolic significance of the joint employer-trade union discussions headed by the industrialist Alfred Mond (along with Ernest Bevin) in 1928.

This sequence of struggles therefore brings out a number of key issues. The first is the importance of voices of challenge and argument in specific workplaces and communities, voices that were locally known and respected. And hence, for any nationally effective challenge, the need for many such voices in many workplaces. The second was therefore the need for coordination – for daily communication across these communities. The government feared this in 1920 with the massive circulation of the *Daily Herald*. In 1926, with that paper captured, the government's key targets were the locally produced cyclostyled daily news-sheets (informed by a network motorcycle despatch riders). The third development common to these years was the creation of local, community-based committees. These gave local form to the multiplicity – but also unity – of the working class, uniting all its elements in purposeful defence of its common class interests. These community-based committees were somewhat tentative in 1919 but by 1920 were seen as central (and equally so by the Left in 1926).

In 1842 all these features were also seen as critical. But 1842 was also in a way unique. It was important, first, because, as we saw, it directly influenced Marx and Engels and their theorisation of class mobilisation and demobilisation. Second, it was important historically as a key moment of change. It represented an organised political challenge to state power involving working class mobilisation at an all-Britain scale on explicitly class terms. In this it was the first – and it did so with sufficient effect to change the nature of class rule in Britain.

As a historical phenomenon its size, character and longer-term significance has remained largely hidden because of its apparently confused and incoherent origin and development. The work of Mick Jenkins and others has now helped us to see it for what it was and untangle the two simultaneous struggles that have confused historians. One was for control of the National Charter Association itself. The other, the real one in class terms, was mass mobilisation against the existing constitutional order.

The strike's success required, as we noted, the prior recapture of the NCA by those who had actually established it in 1840-41 and done so as a democratic centralist body based in the working class which by 1841-42 had affiliations of the main trade unions. This recapture became necessary after the take-over of the NCA executive by the older generation of

Chartist leaders released from prison in the winter of 1841-42. In spring 1842 O'Connor was determined to maintain constitutional methods and at the May executive successfully opposed any use of industrial action. In consequence the 'old' politics imposed by O'Connor had to be overcome by presenting the NCA's August executive with a fait accompli. The successful achievement of this objective is a striking measure of the real-life authority exercised by Chartism's 'class oriented' leaders and the degree to which this authority extended more or less across the entire country. It is also a measure of the very specific context in which they operated.

As we noted, Peter McDouall defined this context after the strike's failure. It was whether 'the Chartist movement should or should not retain its ascendancy in its natural territory' – or as one of those involved in organising the prior mobilisations before 16 August put it: 'lose this opportunity and we are lost'.

This 'loss' had two aspects. One was immediate and one long-term. Immediately the NCA had already suffered a historic defeat with the rejection of its three million signature petition. O'Connor could present no immediate objectives around which to regroup. At the same time the Anti-Corn Law League was offering immediate amelioration – effectively involving class collaboration – and was, in spring 1842, doing so in detail through local employers in Chartism's 'natural territory'. This was the immediate challenge.

However, the anticipation of loss also had a second and much more profound meaning. It was the threat posed to that collective culture of resistance that had for the past generation sustained working class communities and their control of at least some aspects of local infrastructure and hence their ability to use trade union power, illegally, on behalf of the working class community as a whole – the splendid 'thirty years struggle' later referred to by Marx in 1864. We have stressed the exceptional depth of this existing radical culture. This control in Chartism's 'natural territory' was by the early 1840s immediately threatened by Poor Law reform, the introduction of government-controlled police forces, local government reform (new town councils), the pro-employer systems of factory regulation (and schooling) and also continuing technological transformation then eroding the old-style skills. This was the issue. This was why it was 'now or never'. The response indicated the breadth of this understanding. The locally embodied Committees of Public Safety, specifically targeted by the government, symbolised this class unity.

The actions of the government and its advisers, in turn, demonstrated that they also realised that class relations had reached a decisive turning point. Their response was profound and sophisticated. It did indeed redefine relations – although at the cost of a major shift in the politico-economic assumptions of the ruling class and a fateful transition to an economy that was to become increasingly dependent on capital export, international banking and an expansion of formal empire.

Engels arrived in Manchester during the difficult aftermath of the strike. Its leaders and thousands of its bravest activists were in prison. Engels was nonetheless able to secure enough information to provide Marx with an example of how working people could indeed make history – and potentially remake society.

In conclusion: some unresolved issues of theory

What follows is not a conclusion in the normal sense. Rather than closing issues down, it seeks to identify what remains undefined and therefore demands further consideration and research.

The first and probably most difficult issue concerns the process of 'reification', the re-crystallisation of socially-aligned but also personal identities based on differential levels of material, cultural consumption, of life expectations and ethnic identity. In the decades after 1842 Marx and Engels argued that this is what had occurred in the industrial communities of Britain – with severely adverse consequences for class mobilisation.

What happened in the twentieth century? In the later 1920s and 1930s, particularly in Britain's south and east, new consumerist identities seem to have developed – while in the north and west responses appear to have been different but equally disabling (with the resurgence of sectarian conflict a significant part of it). The 1940s and 50s saw a new transformation. In terms of Britain's ruling class it was effectively a pre-emptive one within a dangerous and rapidly changing international context. As the chair of the Federation of British Industry Lord Courtauld put it in 1942 the alternative was now fundamental reform or 'complete socialist revolution'.[2]

The outcome was the 'managed economy' as designed by Keynes and Beveridge. For two decades sociologists and political scientists intensively examined how far relative full employment could safely crystallise new consumerist identities. Their surveys largely categorised people within the static classifications of Weberian sociology and omitted any living class dialectic – of how, very quickly in specific circumstances, class mobilisation could potentially take place.[3]

In Scotland, in the generation following the UCS, and through 20 years of de-industrialisation, new personal identities also emerged that were quite sharply differentiated. Initially, in the 1980s, aspirant professional and white collar workers celebrated the specially 'civic' and social democratic character of Scots as maintaining the British values of public service and social ownership abandoned in England – even though in origin won through the assertion of a new broad working-class identity during the struggles of the 1970s. Then, from the 2000s, this identity subtly merged into one that now expressed this 'civic' identity in 'Scottish' national terms – associated with the European Union and values of socially-responsible corporate enterprise. By contrast former industrial workers tended to react to their dispossession in quite different ways – in forms that are complex and still require proper definition. Among youth, and others, levels of drug use rose to internationally record levels – much as alcohol use did in the former Soviet Union after the dismantling of socialism.

These responses were very different – but served to insulate, temporarily at least, against any significant form of class mobilisation. How, therefore, have these processes evolved historically? What are their internal dynamics?

Vygotsky and Leontiev vouch for the significance of socio-linguistic processes in inhibiting, as well as facilitating, communication between those in different social groupings. Porshnev and the Frankfurt School Marxist Kurt Lewin (and his pupil Leon Festinger) identify one motive force as being what was later described as cognitive dissonance, the evasion of socially challenging comparisons. Lewin also stressed that such social groupings are not fixed and stable and he sought to develop an understanding of their internal dynamics in terms of a dialectic of 'in' and 'out' groups – orienting to, but also insulating from, wider social developments. One example might be found in immigrant Irish communities in later 19th century Britain where the power of religious compliance, mainly to exclude wider contact, was balanced against the influences deriving from political organisations such as the Fenian League and resulting 'external' associations. Complex, multiform individual identities certainly existed in the nineteenth century. Are they more complex today?

Conversely, what are the processes by which those directly challenging an exploitative social order are able to survive in a socially and politically 'active' way and, more than that, be able to identify and respond to those occasions when the system's own conflicts and contradictions leave it open to challenge?

As we have seen, these occasions are relatively rare. In any acute form they generally last only a few weeks or at most months. Often their duration is so short that they can, in terms of the historical record, be forgotten or dismissed. In fact, for all the cases we have examined, this is what has happened. 1842 became a minor episode in Chartism: 'the plug riots'. Clydeside in 1919 was reduced to another riot, this time in Glasgow's George Square. 1919 in Belfast is dismissed by most historians as a sectional grab for influence by Protestant workers. 1920 across Britain happened so quickly it could be written off as never happening – or, if it did, as safely under the control of right-wing labour leaders. Finally, 1971 has become little more than a misplaced attempt to save a doomed shipyard. The complex interlinkage with other struggles and, as in 1971-1972, their combined impact on government policy, is lost.

In general, therefore, history fails to 'see' the consequences of class mobilisation either for transformations in state policy or, longer-term, for the recrystallisation of social identities.

However, the impact was, as we have demonstrated, significant in all cases. In each it involved major shifts in strategy and resource allocation. And this is equally the case with the way in which these shifts in strategy served to tame these episodes of mass class mobilisation – and subsequently, therefore, how, in face of these governmental and State responses, new sectional identities crystallised.

Tackling these issues and clarifying the role of mobilised working class action, raises another, possibly more fundamental one: that is, how history is written and how the 'practical moment' is defined.

Marx laid great stress on the need to focus on the 'practical moment', understood as a specific 'conjuncture', the coming together 'dialectically' of the multi-fold contradictions of a class-based social system. In his writing of history, Marx's focus was always on the interactions of actual debate and within this on the material context of argument. This was not because the cleverness of argument itself determined outcomes – such outcomes arose from the wider material dialectic – but in deciphering this process itself: what material points of reference were, or were not, important in winning arguments and therefore in mobilising wider action by others, with triggering mass mobilisation and in some cases revolutionary action.

We have sought to follow this approach here. However, in doing so we have been faced with a wider problem: that all such processes are both very specific and very general. Winning an argument at a mass meeting in Ashton or Compstall on a certain day in early August 1842 was a key part of a wider mobilisation – but equally important would have been the debates elsewhere that were not won and the issue of why. To secure such wider understanding requires a history that is both far more comprehensive but also more finely textured than most of what is written today (and certainly more comprehensive than the largely impressionistic treatment attempted here).[4]

For Marx this issue of dialectical interconnection and context was a crucial one. And it is related to another. This is the role and continuing presence of actual people: of those who won the arguments that mobilised mass action – and how far, despite defeat and the collapse of any wider movement, they were able to carry forward the resulting lessons and develop a growing understanding of the nature of a class society. Conversely it has always been, as we have noted, a key concern of government to stop such transmission – immediately by physically removing such people, as happened in 1842, 1919, 1920 and 1926 but more fundamentally by transforming the political and social environment in ways that made their previous arguments irrelevant (as happened in all these cases and also after 1979).

This issue of how to maintain and co-ordinate such continuing detailed and intelligent presence within the working class was, of course a central preoccupation of Marx himself. It was why in 1846-47 he polemicised against Proudhon for his purely 'philosophical' approach in *The Poverty of Philosophy*. Proudhon's provision of an intellectual critique of property was, for Marx, beside the point. The response had to be organisational: a party embedded within the working class, linking actual people, and therefore able to develop action in detail across any particular nation. Coordination and communication were essential – and so also was historical memory, the ability to critically assess and sum up past experience, to develop theory.

Marx stressed this when drafting the founding documents of the First International in 1864. In its Inaugural Address he highlighted the new political and economic opportunities then opening up for the working class movement in Britain, France, Germany and Italy. At the same time as acknowledging the magnitude of defeat in the 1840s 'never before seemed the English working class so thoroughly reconciled to a position of political nullity', Marx then went on to stress what had been achieved by these struggles:

> After a thirty years' struggle, fought with most admirable perseverance, the English working class, improving a momentous split between the landlords and the money-lords, succeeded in carrying the Ten Hours Bill. The immense physical, moral and intellectual benefits hence accruing to the factory operatives … are now acknowledged … Most of the continental governments have had to accept the English Factory Act … But beside its practical import, there was something else to exalt the marvellous success of the working men's measure … it was the first time that in broad daylight the political economy of the middle class succumbed to the political economy of the working class…[5]

There needed to be, therefore, an organisation that could carry forward this 'real knowledge' of past working class struggle, of both successes and failures, and do so actively by winning, in the new circumstances, the necessary arguments for social system change inside labour's collective organisations, the bodies that could mobilise people as a whole..

A generation later, this was also the essence of Lenin's critique of Bernstein and others within the Second International in seeking to secure parliamentary office within existing capitalist states and not organised to challenge their capitalist character. For this to happen the essential component was, for Lenin, that working people organise themselves in specific workplaces and communities and be in a position to win, in detail, the arguments needed to trigger mass action. Only this could overcome the processes of 'reification' and thereby found society anew (as he put it in 1920).

It should also remind us of the key difference between capitalism and socialism. Capital's ability to exploit depends – as Marx put it and has recently been re-emphasised – on a 'mute compulsion': the creation of the material conditions by which the capitalist market for labour extracts the surplus automatically and without apparent external intervention or need for justification.[6] By contrast, socialism as a social system depends on that silence having been broken. It requires voices, many, many voices, exposing how the engine of exploitation works and how to end it. Without that, Marx argued, and without the continuing class mobilisation needed to sustain it in the longer-run, society cannot be founded anew.

NOTES

1 Alasdair Gray's dystopian novel *Lanark* published in 1981 paints a surreal but strikingly familiar picture. It details a submerging Glasgow whose people slowly lose their identities and 'disappear' – reappearing transformed in Cumbernauld New Town. Irvine Welsh's *Trainspotting* published in 1993 does the same, but more literally in terms of drug use, for the Lothians (by 2021 drug deaths in Scotland were four times the European average). The parallel electoral rise of the SNP temporarily offered a non-class identity of considerable plasticity – ranging from the liberal credentials of aspirant professionals to a raw chauvinism sometimes claiming descent from Red Clydeside.

2 Angus Calder, *People's War* (Jonathan Cape 1969) pp. 293-4: Courtauld was also father-in-law of the Conservative reformer R.A. Butler.

3 John Goldthorpe, one of the most perceptive of these analysts, whose massive fieldwork on British car workers was conducted in the early 1960s, had to write up and publish his results in the transformed circumstances of the late 1960s. Much of his introduction is given over to a long and somewhat inconclusive engagement with Marx and concepts of alienation and reification: John Goldthorpe and others, *The Affluent Worker in the Class Structure* (Cambridge 1969) Chapter 1.

4 An attempt was made to do so on a comparative basis, looking at three English towns in the earlier 19th century, but the treatment of debate and language was never sufficiently detailed to track such key moments: J. Foster, *Class Struggle and the Industrial Revolution*, 1974.

5 Karl Marx, 'Inaugural Address of the Working Men's International Association', 28 September 1864, Marx Engels, *Collected Works*, Volume 20, pp. 10-11 (Moscow, 1985).

6 S. Mau, *Mute Compulsion: a Marxist theory of the economic power of capital* (Verso 2023).

THIS PAGE LEFT INTENTIONALLY BLANK

Appendix

Language and class mobilisation: the wider context of the debate

In the mid-1970s Charles Woolfson published his pioneering article on 'Culture, Language and the Human Personality' in *Marxism Today* along with a parallel paper in the *Working Papers of the Institute for Cultural Studies*.[1] The key arguments subsequently appeared in book form in 1982 as *The Labour Theory of Culture*.

In it Woolfson took Engels' short and unfinished essay, published as 'The Part Played by Labour in the Transition from Ape to Man', and sought to substantiate its main thesis on the links between purposive instrumental labour and the development of language.[2] Woolfson used the research then available on the origins of the human species and did so in the theoretical context of the work of the Soviet school of socio-linguistics developed by Lev Vygotsky in the 1920s and 30s and post-war by Vygotsky's collaborators, Alexander Luria and Alexei Leontiev. Their thesis, which also utilised Engels, was that humanity's specific linguistic abilities were developed through purposive collective labour – a process that was, for each generation, also repeated through the rearing of each child through mutual, shared learning and purposive activity. For that reason also, in any class society, where the products of labour are alienated and where the processes of class control and exploitation are socially justified, language will normally be a key tool for domination and control. However, it can also, on occasion, be opened to its opposite: social resistance to such class oppression. As we have seen,

Woolfson subsequently used this approach, focusing on how these reified meanings could be penetrated and exposed, to explain how, in the process of mass debates in circumstances of sharp class struggle, the shop stewards in Upper Clyde Shipyards were able to transform understandings and thereby mobilise mass support.

In the 1970s this approach gained some wider acknowledgement among those studying processes of social change. But it did so only temporarily. These years were marked by three developments which implicitly or explicitly rejected key aspects of a dialectical approach – developments all the more powerful because they appeared to come from the ideological Left.

The first was the rise of Western Marxism. The second, related but much broader in its academic impact, was the cultural or linguistic 'turn', adopting structuralist models which largely denied the relevance of class mobilisation. The third was the actual transfer of aspects of the Soviet school of Vygotsky for academic and practical use in the West – but in ways that hid or denied its revolutionary (and dialectical) essence.

The first of these developments, that of Western Marxism, took a diversity of forms. But its common feature was its rejection of Marx's dialectics, of his materialist transformation of Hegel, and instead the adoption of what Lenin would have described as 'neo-Kantian' procedures. These gave imperative precedence, in the analysis of society, to the prior 'idealist' definition of concepts. Examples would be definitions that sought to stipulate what might or might not, constitute 'class' or 'social formations' – rather than understanding their development within a historical process that constantly transformed such meanings. Processes such as alienation and reification, because they were inherently historical and contingent, were excluded both by Althusser's structuralism and by those using neo-Weberian models. More politically the hallmark of this Western Marxism was its belief that advance could be secured by winning an 'ideological hegemony' and that this demanded 'broad' alliances, broader than the narrow economistic preoccupations of the working class. In this context the kind of mass revolutionary class mobilisation, seen as so important by both Marx and Lenin, was abandoned. And so also, therefore, were those moments when, as defined by Vygotsky and Leontiev, mass transformations of understanding, the active dialectic of 'theme' and 'meaning', became possible. Correspondingly, the working class, often now defined in Weberian terms of manual labour, and therefore fast declining in size, was no longer seen as having a determining role. Moments of revolutionary transformation, as described by Marx and Lenin, became delusionary phantoms.

The wider cultural or linguistic 'turn' followed. This also had its roots in French academic structuralism. Some trends claimed a Marxist pedigree. Most not. Its central inspiration came from Foucault's evocation of long-term structures of linguistic meaning that overdetermined all individual expressions. Though later somewhat modified, this interlinked with, and sustained, the Annales school's re-engineering of historical writing: the concept of the 'Longue Duree', of 'long' and 'short' centuries determined by such over-riding structures of thought and sensibility.

In Britain these ideas were picked up, in a variety of forms, by historians such as Stedman Jones, Patrick Joyce and James Vernon to argue that a 'radical' sensibility, originating among enlightenment thinkers of the later 18th century, formed the continuing basis of populist politics, language and thought through the first half of the nineteenth century – merging later with populist Gladstonian liberalism – as the 'true' characterisation of British radicalism.[3] Somewhat later, these arguments were further extended, among others, by Eugenio Biagini and Alastair Reid.[4] They argued that the formation of the Labour Party as a 'class' party in the 1880s and 90s represented a tragic mistake, by dividing this broad majoritarian radical consensus. The creation in the 1990s of New Labour was portrayed as a return to this wider non-class consensus of 'British' radicalism. The earlier periodisation of Britain's working class movement, in large measure developed by Engels, Theodore Rothstein and taken forward by G D H Cole, no longer held.

It was in this wider academic context, in 1985, that the American psychologist James Wertsch published his *Vygotsky and the Social Formation of the Mind*. Although a number of the works by the Vygotsky school had been published in English in the 1970s, Wertsch's intervention represented the first major academic assessment that sought to relate the Vygotskian school to developments in 'Western' social analysis. It was followed in 1991 by his *Voices of the Mind: A socio-cultural approach to mediate action*. Together the two books introduced Vygotsky's work to Western audiences in significant depth. In doing so, however, Wertsch changed it. The dialectical assumptions of Vygotsky's work were minimised, its Marxist pedigree questioned and in particular its stress on moments of revolutionary mobilisation for transformations of consciousness omitted. Again the validity of a Marxist interpretation was questioned.

In combination, these developments significantly restricted any wider practical application of the pioneering work by Woolfson or of its further development in the 1980s and 90s, principally by Chik Collins.[5]

There were, however, later in the 1980s and 1990s, a number of counter currents. The first was the publication in 1991 of David Bakhurst's *Consciousness and Revolution in Soviet Philosophy: from the Bolsheviks to Evald Ilyenkov*. This reinstated the dialectical materialist core of the tradition that led from Lenin's *Empirio-Criticism* (and previously from Engels's *Transition*) to the Vygotsky school and in the 1960s to the work of Ilyenkov on materialist dialectics. It restored the stress laid by Engels and Marx on the material context of revolutionary mobilisation and its consequences for thought and language.

There was also a reaction by a number of historians against the attempts to eliminate any trace of active class mobilisation, and any consequent transformations of language and consciousness, from the understanding of working class history in Britain, particularly in the 1830s and 40s. Reference has already been made in the closing chapter to the recovery of the traditions of literary and artistic defiance within working class communities in Britain's industrial districts. However, mention should also be made of Richard Price's polemic against 'post-modernism as theory and history' published in 1997, to Paul Pickering's detailed recovery, in class terms, of the organised trade union base of Manchester Chartism (1999), to Marc Steinberg's *Fighting Words* (also 1999), the late Malcolm Chase's re-assessment of the strike of 1842 in 2000 and again in 2007, to Benjamin Scarborough's 'Revisiting the Linguistic Turn' and his use of Quentin Skinner's dialectic of context and meaning (2010) and, finally, among others, Peter Gurney's 2014 critique of the 'rhetoric of popular radicalism' and the attempts to use it to supplant the language of working class power, as expressed in the 1840s in the demand for democracy.[6]

More generally, there has also been a wider return towards the significance of class identity. Probably the fullest and most thoughtful was that provided by John Kirk which is concisely presented in his 'Marking the Moral Boundaries of Class'. It is important also because its limitations reveal what has yet to be retrieved.[7]

Kirk draws on Andrew Sayer's understanding of Bourdieu's habitus supplemented by the moral dialogics of Voloshinov/Bakhtin (as Kirk puts it) and Raymond Williams' 'structures of feeling'. His central theme is to stress the integrity of the lived worlds of working people and of the struggle to make moral sense of the contradictions of an exploited existence. He takes from Bourdieu the individual's will to patch together material and cultural resources as a 'habitus' of personal justification and legitimacy, then from Voloshinov/Bakhtin the internal dialogics by which this is secured and finally from Williams the 'structures of feeling' by which it is, internally or externally, expressed. Kirk's main empirical source of such understanding is drawn from working-class autobiographies.

However, there remains a significant gap between this approach and that initiated by Bakhurst, drawing on Ilyenkov and the Vygotsky school, in the 1990s or that originally developed by Woolfson in the 1970s and then Collins in the 1980s. Both Kirk and Bourdieu focus on the individual – not the social dynamics (or class dialectics) of the individual-in-society. Bourdieu makes this particularly clear in the following passage:

> another effect of the scholastic illusion is seen when people
> describe resistance to domination in the language of
> consciousness – as does the whole Marxist tradition and
> also the feminist theorists who, giving way to habits of

thought, expect political liberation to come from the 'raising of consciousness' – ignoring the extraordinary inertia which results from the inscription of social structures in bodies, for lack of a dispositional theory of practices. While making things explicit can help, only a thorough going process of counter-training, involving repeated exercises, can, like an athlete's training, durably transform habitus.[8]

Bourdieu presents us with the image of an individual somehow struggling as an individual in a 'process of counter-training' to transform 'habitus'. What the Vygotsky school sought to show is that people don't live like that. They may, and often do, live within multiple social alignments. And these social alignments do tend to be typified by a material, cultural habitus that is sometimes of 'extraordinary inertia' and, yes, language is a key part of this. Yet this is not the end of the matter. Language is multi-accented. Capitalism is not stable. Arguments about the nature of exploitation persist. And even if, as Volosinov argues, those who make these arguments only get a mass hearing in moments of crisis, these moments of wider mobilisation are the ones in which history 'changes', sometimes with revolutionary effect, sometimes as described here in terms of a reordering of social relations and of shifts in ruling class strategy.[9]

This objection equally applies to Kirk's use of Wertsch. Kirk describes individuals. He sensitively decodes attempts to make sense of a contradictory social reality. But the assumptions of his approach remain within a sanitised, non-dialectical version of the Soviet school. By contrast, both Vygotsky and Volosinov themselves saw the multi-accentual quality of the sign, of the dialectic of sense and meaning only becoming active in periods of class mobilisation. As Volosinov put it: 'this inner dialectic quality of the sign comes out fully in the open only in times of social crises or revolutionary changes'. And this, they stress, is a collective, not individual, process. It is in these circumstances that 'theme' can be used to tear away at, and expose, the reified character, as Leontiev put it, of group-defined meanings.

All these approaches, of Wertsch's version of the Soviet school, of Bourdieu, of post-Weberian structuralism, omit the active dialectic of language which itself can only be understood within the evolving contradictions of capitalism as a whole.

These are also the points made in critique by Anna Stetstenko, writing in the tradition of Leontiev, who over recent years has been the most prominent among those intent on recovering the dialectical engagement of the Vygotsky/Luria school in the West. Activity theory should be about how people can collectively exploit the contradictions of capitalism. Her most recent paper is entitled 'Making Vygotsky and Activity Theory Dangerous Again'.[10] Similarly Chik Collins and Peter Jones have sought defend the original thrust of the Voloshinov-Bahktin and Vygotsky schools:

understanding how capitalism's dynamic contradictions can be made explicit, spoken and contested.[11]

It is for this reason that this study has chosen five episodes which saw, to a greater or lesser extent, such crises making it possible to expose and actively exploit the 'inner dialectic quality of the sign' and to do so in order to mobilise working class opposition. In all cases, as we have tried to show, the resulting mobilisations were of sufficient scale to transform the tactics and strategy of governments and ruling class assumptions about how to maintain capitalist state power.

The final episode, that of 1842, is particularly important not just because of its scale – and its manifest impact on government policy – but because of the way in which it influenced Marx and Engels. It made concrete their understanding of the mass, transformative character of the revolutionary process, of how working people became – in the mass – ready to found society anew. The general strike of 1842, despite all its limitations and its catastrophic end, demonstrated this potential and did so at a key point in the development of what became historical materialism and of the understanding of the active role of people and in particular, within capitalism, of the creative role of a mobilised working class in making that history.[12]

NOTES

1 C. Woolfson, Working Papers in *Contemporary Cultural Studies* No.9 (Birmingham 1976); *Marxism Today*, Vol.21, 8,1977.
2 See in particular the edition introduced by Igor Andreyev, *Engels's 'The Part Played by Labour in the transition from Ape to Man'* (Moscow 1985) which refers to Boris Porshnev's *The Beginnings of Human History* (Moscow 1974) and to the work of A.N. Leontiev.
3 Patrick Joyce, *Democratic Subjects: the self and the social in nineteenth century England* (Cambridge 1994); James Vernon, Politics and People 1815-1867 (Cambridge 1993).
4 Eugenio Biagini and Alistair Reid, *Currents of Radicalism: popular radicalism, organised labour and party politics* (Cambridge 1991).
5 Chik Collins, 'The pragmatics of emancipation: a critical review of the work of Michael Huspek, *Journal of Pragmatics*, 1996 Vol. 25; *Language, Ideology and Social Consciousness: Developing a Sociohistorical Approach* (Ashgate, 1999).
6 Richard Price, 'Post-modernism as theory and history' in John Belcham and Neville Kirk (eds.) *Languages of Labour* (Ashgate 1997); Paul Pickering, *Chartists and Chartism in Manchester and Salford* (Macmillan 1999), Marc Steinberg, *Fighting Words: working cass formation, collective action and discourse* (Cornell 1999), Malcolm Chase, *Early trade Unionism: Fraternity, Skill and the Politics of Labour* (Ashgate, 2000) and *Chartism: a new history* (Manchester 2007); Benjamin Scarborough, 'Rethinking Chartism': revisiting the linguistic turn on the failure of Chartism, PhD thesis, Maryland, 2010; Peter Gurney, 'The democratic idiom: languages of democracy in the Chartist movement', *Journal of Modern History*, vol. 86/3, 2014.
7 John Kirk, 'Marking the Moral Boundaries of Class', *Sociological Research Online*, Volume 11, issue 1, 2006.
8 P. Bourdieu. *Pascalian Meditations*. Translated by R. Nice. (Stanford University Press, Stanford, Calif., 2000),172. I owe this quote to Gavin Brewis.
9 Jack Saunders, 'The British motor industry 1945-1977: how workplace cultures shaped workplace militancy', University College, London, PhD thesis, 2015, does, however, make interesting use of Bourdieu in examining the transformation of workplace cultures over these three decades.
10 Anna Stetsenko and Igor Arievitch, 'The self in Cultural-Historical Activity Theory: reclaiming the unity of the social and individual dimensions of social development', *Theory and Psychology*, 14 (4), 2004; A Stetsenko and I. Arievitch, 'The Vygotskian Collective Project of Social Transformation: history, politics and practice in knowledge production', *Critical Psychology* 2005; A. Stetsenko,

'Making Vygotsky and AT Dangerous Again', in A Levant, *Handbook on Activity Theory* (Columbia University Press 2023).

11   Chik Collins, 'Language and Discourse', *Theory and Struggle*, 2015; P.E. Jones and C Collins, 'Activity Theory meets austerity – or does it?, *Theory and Struggle*, 2016.

12   Eric Rahim, *A Promethean Vision: The Formation of Karl Marx's Worldview* (Praxis Press 2020) provides an important guide to the critical formative stages in the development of Marx's thought. I am personally indebted to him for this understanding.

About the author

John Foster was born in 1940, he studied at Cambridge and subsequently lectured at Cambridge, Strathclyde and Paisley/UWS. He published *Class Struggle and the Industrial Revolution* in 1974 followed by a series of monographs, jointly written with Charles Woolfson, on the 1971-2 Upper Clyde Shipbuilders dispute, the occupation of the Scottish Caterpillar plant in 1986 and the oil workers occupations of 1991-92. He has written widely on the national question in Britain and most recently contributed to the six-volume history of the TGWU/Unite. He was on the editorial board of *Marxism Today* 1967-85, was editor of *Our History* 1969-1985 and has been on the editorial board of Marx Memorial Library's *Theory and Struggle* since 2015.

ESSENTIAL READING ON CHINA

China, after its revolution, has achieved the greatest improvement in life of the largest proportion of humanity of any country in history. In *China's Great Road*, John Ross explains how China achieved this step forward. His unequivocal conclusion is that socialism is responsible for this advance. *China's Great Road* analyses Chinese reality and argues socialists worldwide can learn from China.

Carlos Martinez argues in *The East is Still Red* that the decisive role of the Communist Party of China and its commitment to building 'socialism with Chinese characteristics' needs to be more widely understood especially in the West.

https://redletterspp.com/collections/china

OTHER PRAXIS PRESS TITLES

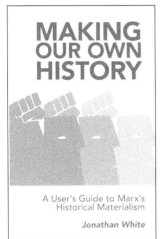

MAKING OUR OWN HISTORY by Jonathan White
A brilliant introduction to the Marxist approach to understanding and participating in social change.

MARX200
Leading scholars and activists from different countries – including Cuba, India and the UK – show that Marx's ideas continue to provide us with the analysis we need to understand our world today.

A PROMETHEAN VISION by Eric Rahim
"This small book is a very useful account of how Marx came to develop his materialist conception of history." Michael Löwy, *New Politics*

LINE OF MARCH by Max Adereth
A new edition of Max Adereth's historical analysis of British communism, focusing on the development of the party's various programmes. First published 1994.

1000 DAYS OF REVOLUTION
A fascinating account of the Allende Presidency, the dilemmas of peaceful and armed struggles for socialism, the role of US imperialism and domestic right-wing forces, and a self critical evaluation of the role of Chilean communists.

HARDBOILED ACTIVIST by Ken Fuller
A critical review of the work and politics of writer Dashiell Hammett, crime fiction legend, communist and staunch opponent of McCarthyism.

For more details, contact praxispress@me.com

ORDER online at www.redletterspp.com